The College History Series

BRADFORD COLLEGE

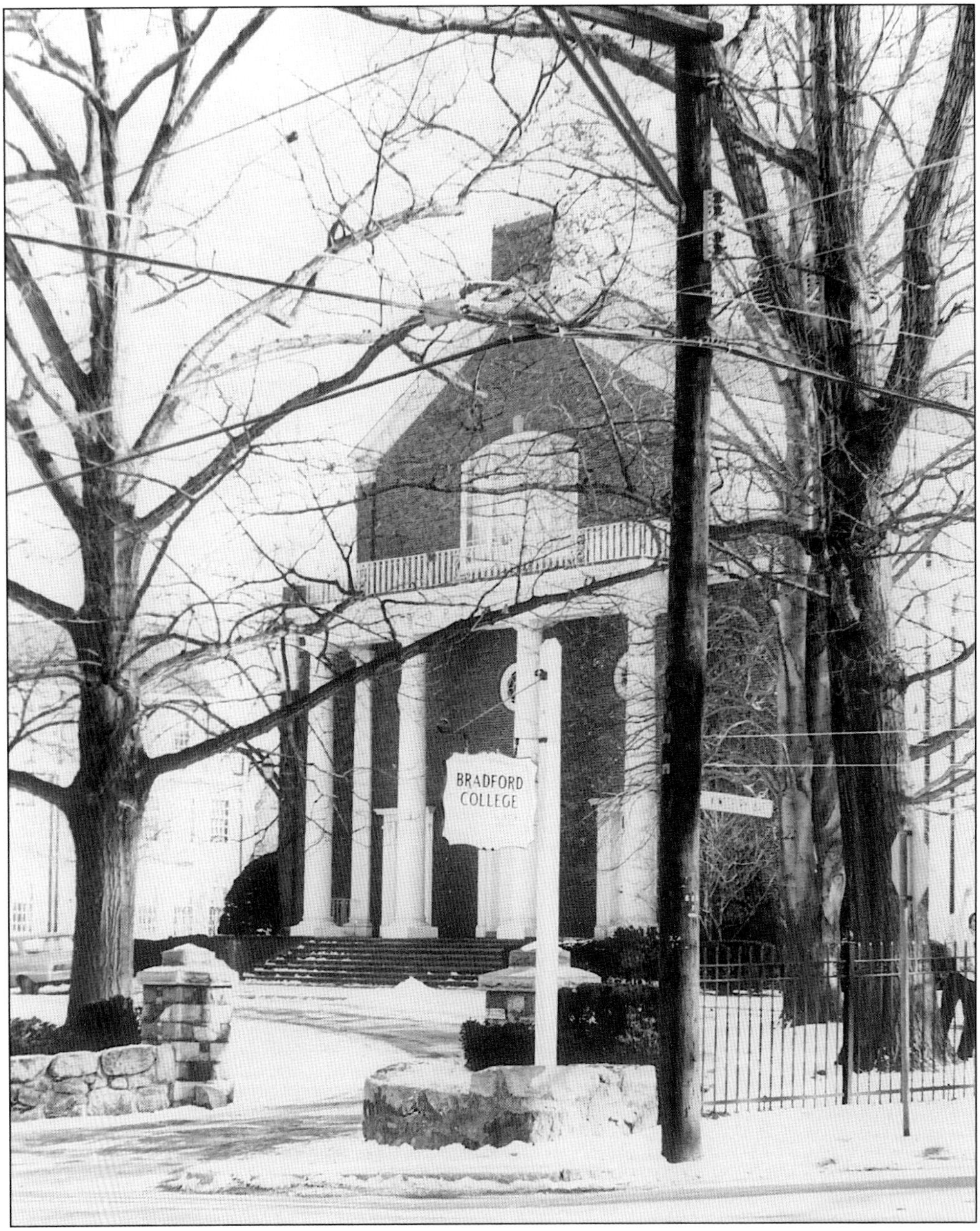

Bradford College, 1803–2000. Built between 1939 and 1940, Denworth Hall sits on the corner of South Main Street and Kingsbury Avenue in the Bradford section of Haverhill, Massachusetts. A few yards away, on the opposite corner of Kingsbury Avenue, is the site of the first Bradford Academy building. For 60 years, Denworth's red brick exterior and classical style, so evocative of New England and its centuries-old academic tradition, has welcomed one and all to Bradford College.

The College History Series

BRADFORD COLLEGE

DR. PATRICIA TRAINOR O'MALLEY

ARCADIA PUBLISHING

ISBN 978-0-7385-0409-4

Published by Arcadia Publishing
Charleston, South Carolina

Printed in the United States of America

Library of Congress Catalog Card Number: 00-101192

For all general information contact Arcadia Publishing at:
Telephone 843-853-2070
Fax 843-853-0044
E-Mail sales@arcadiapublishing.com
For customer service and orders:
Toll-Free 1-888-313-2665

Visit us on the Internet at www.arcadiapublishing.com

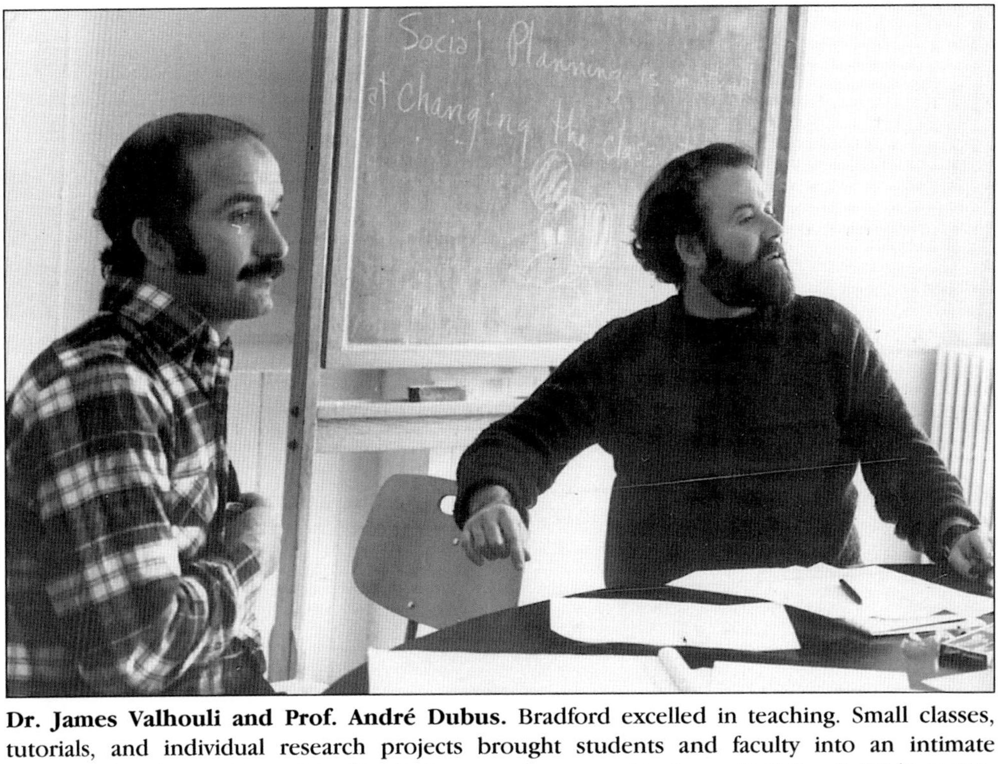

Dr. James Valhouli and Prof. André Dubus. Bradford excelled in teaching. Small classes, tutorials, and individual research projects brought students and faculty into an intimate intellectual exchange. Two of Bradford's finest teachers were Dr. James N. Valhouli (1941–1995), left, and Prof. André Dubus II (1936–1999). This photograph was taken in the mid-1970s.

Contents

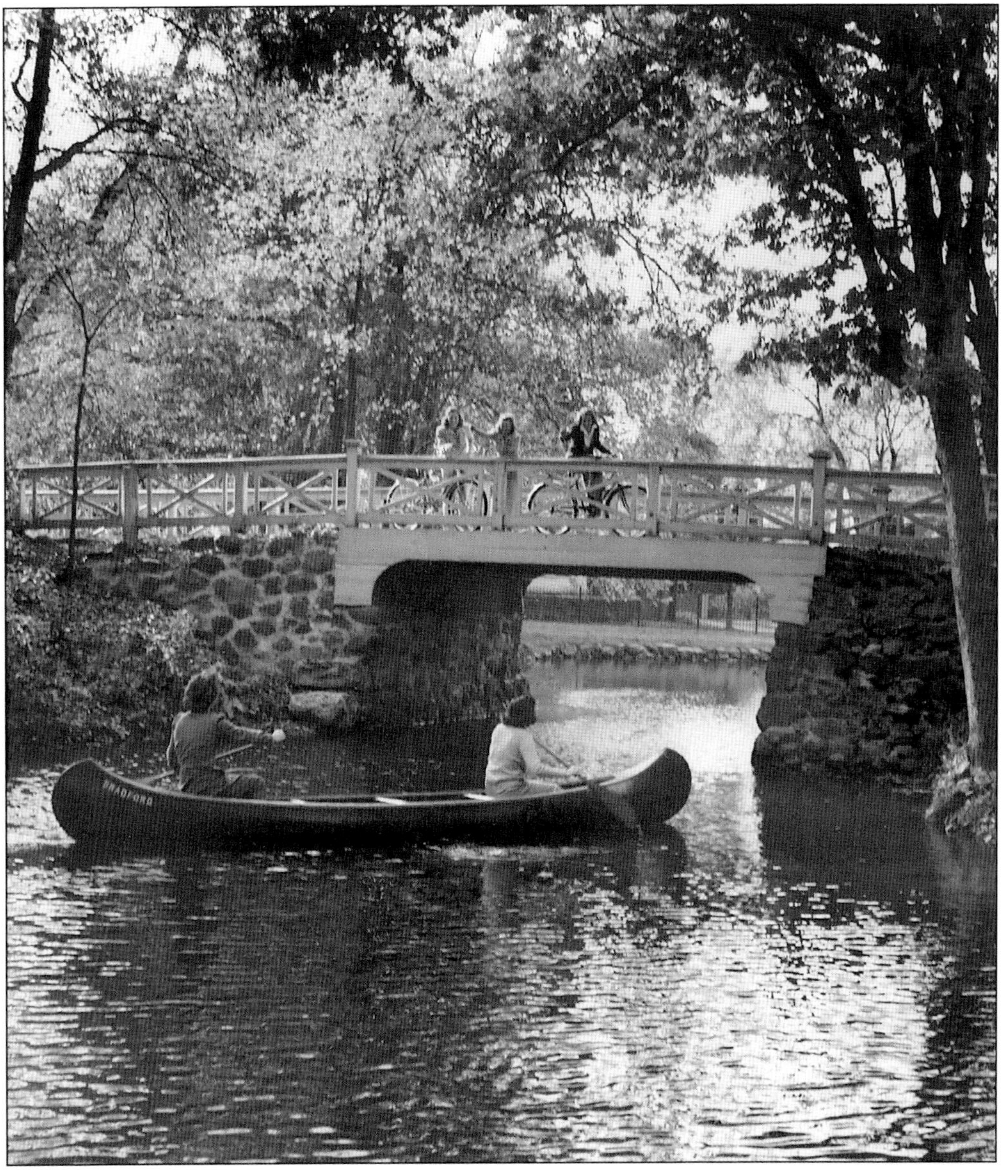

The Bridge and Tupelo Pond. Tupelo Pond, located in the center of Bradford's campus, added beauty and serenity to the grounds. The lovely wooden bridge once led to the picnic grove. From the 1960s on, it was the link between the front campus and the Tupelo, Cluster, and Town House residences.

Introduction

Sometimes all that is left are clichés. Cliché: all good things must end. Cliché: you don't know what you had until you don't have it any more. Cliché: nothing is permanent. It is hard to be creative, to go beyond the clichés, when all that had seemed solid and unchanging falls away and disappears so quickly. Cliché: that's life!

The announcement came on Tuesday, November 23,1999—two days before Thanksgiving—that the Class of 2000 would be the last to graduate from Bradford College. Fiscal responsibility had won out over sentiment. The school would close after 197 years, three years short of its bicentennial.

Each person connected to Bradford met the sad news in his or her own way: shock, sadness, anger, confusion, or concern. Students, faculty, staff, alumni, neighbors—all fell back on clichés. "It's so hard to believe!" "It can't be true." "What went wrong?" "It's like a death in the family." Clichés comfort by their familiarity. However, eventually each person affected by the closing of Bradford must deal with it in a private and personal way.

This book of photographs is my way of dealing with the loss of Bradford College. I have produced five previous photographic histories, including one on the old town of Bradford, which included a number of photographs of Bradford Academy. I had already discussed with President Jean Scott the possibility of a new history of Bradford for the bicentennial in 2003. Cliché: the best laid plans of mice and men . . .

So I have moved the timetable up by three years and have had to sacrifice the comfort of doing the research leisurely and thoroughly. This is a rush production, two months from initial proposal to delivery to the publisher. The best photograph was not always available, but what was selected was the best of what the archives offered, and the Bradfordiana archives had much to offer. I have chosen to begin this book with the presidency of Dr. Katharine Denworth, when Bradford became a junior college. Jean Pond's *Bradford: A New England School* covered the years before that more than adequately. I have assigned one chapter per decade, which permits about forty pictures for every ten years.

I cannot guarantee that the pictorial story is complete, but I hope that it is accurate and succeeds in its purpose of tugging at the strands of memory that tie us all to Bradford. Bradford College has provided my professional identification for 25 years. I was invited by Jack Armstrong and Downing Bowler to come and teach one class in 1975. With a brand new Ph.D. in hand, I jumped at the chance. I never left. However, my family roots at Bradford go back even further—to the beginning of the 20th century—not as students or faculty, but as waitresses, laundresses, and grounds keepers. That connection has helped to remind me on many occasions that the Bradford "family" is not just teachers and students but so many others in offices and kitchens and "below stairs" who have also put in their time and their labor to make this place memorable.

Bradford as an educational institution is no more; but it once was, and through photographs and history and personal memory it will continue to be.

Dr. Patricia Trainor O'Malley
Professor of History, Bradford College
1975–2000

To the thousands of students, faculty, administrators, staff, benefactors, and friends who have loved Bradford—Academy, Junior College, and College. But especially to Kathy, Terry, Patsy, Tina, Tom, Frank, David, Colin, Eunice, Wendy, Joy, Jonathan, Christi, Veronica, Takashi, Boun, Sara, Garry, Ericka, Leslie, Linda, Pat, Chris, Helen, Pam, and Jamie.
You made teaching a joy!
And to Judy, Ann, Arthur, and Jan.
You made Bradford a joy!

One

The Thirties

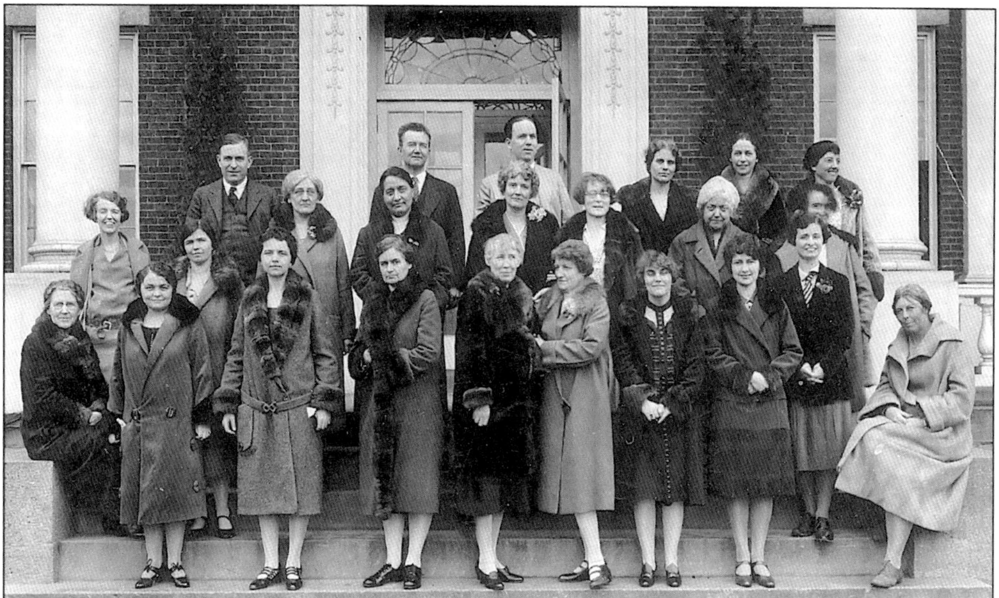

Faculty with President Denworth. When this photograph was taken in 1928, Bradford was still an academy for high school girls and postgraduates. Dr. Katharine Denworth, third from the left in the front row, came to Bradford in 1927 with a D.Ed. from Columbia. Faculty who can be identified include the three men: Albert Dangerfield, Frederick Johnson, and David McCloskey. In the second row are Dr. Edith Beck and Bertha Clough, third and fourth from the left, and Florence Eisenhardt Dangerfield, right.

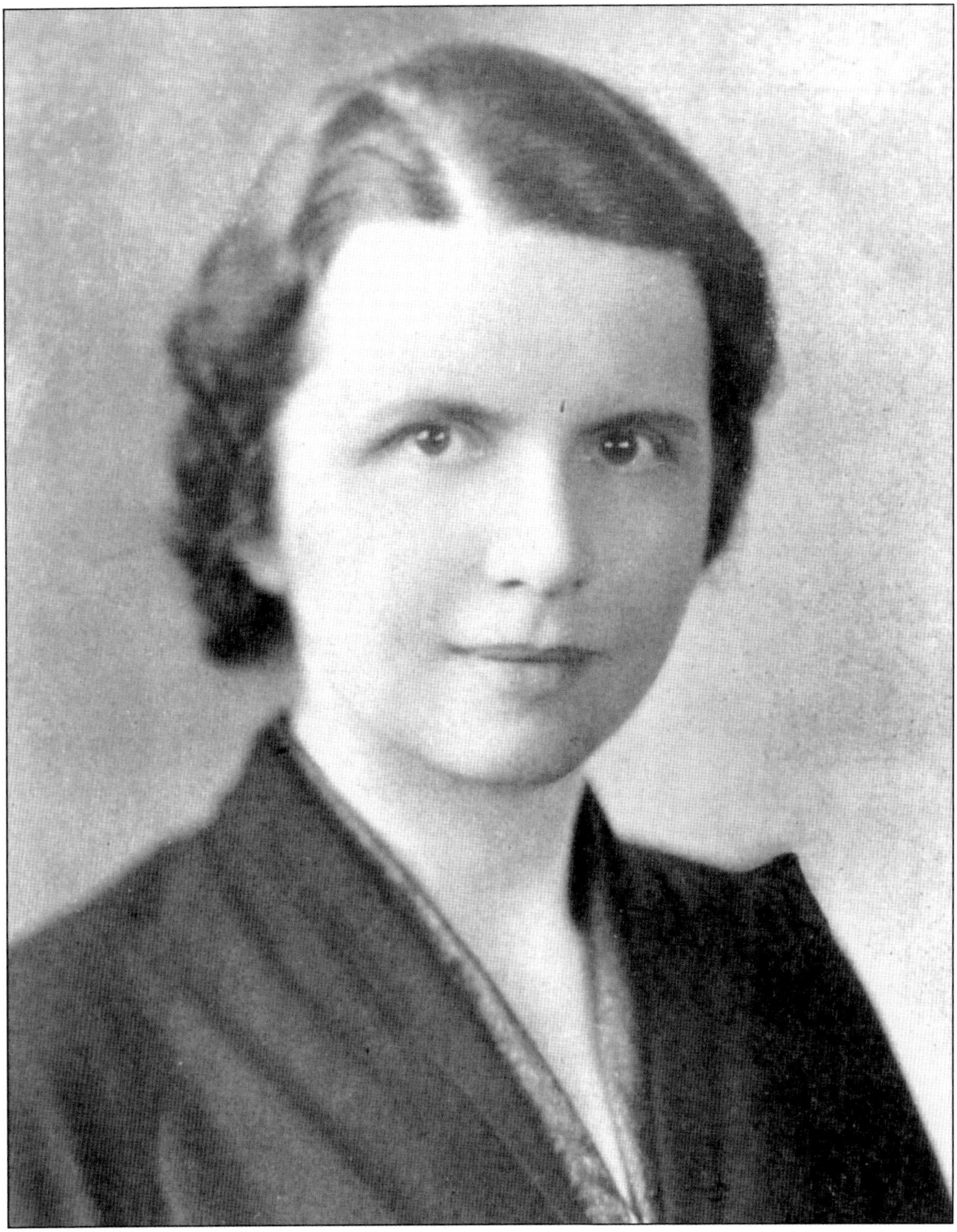

Dr. Katharine Denworth. Denworth led Bradford from 1927 to 1939. She was a graduate of Swarthmore and had a doctorate from Columbia, the first head of Bradford to hold that degree. She was also the first to hold the title "President." During her administration, Bradford became a junior college and the preparatory program was discontinued. The curriculum was revised to focus on a liberal arts preparation toward a bachelor's degree, or for a concentration in art, music, speech, or home economics. The tradition of no vocational courses continued. There was a liberalizing of privileges during the Denworth era, but a stiffening of etiquette, with evening dress mandatory at the president's parties for faculty and students, evening lectures, concerts, and dances.

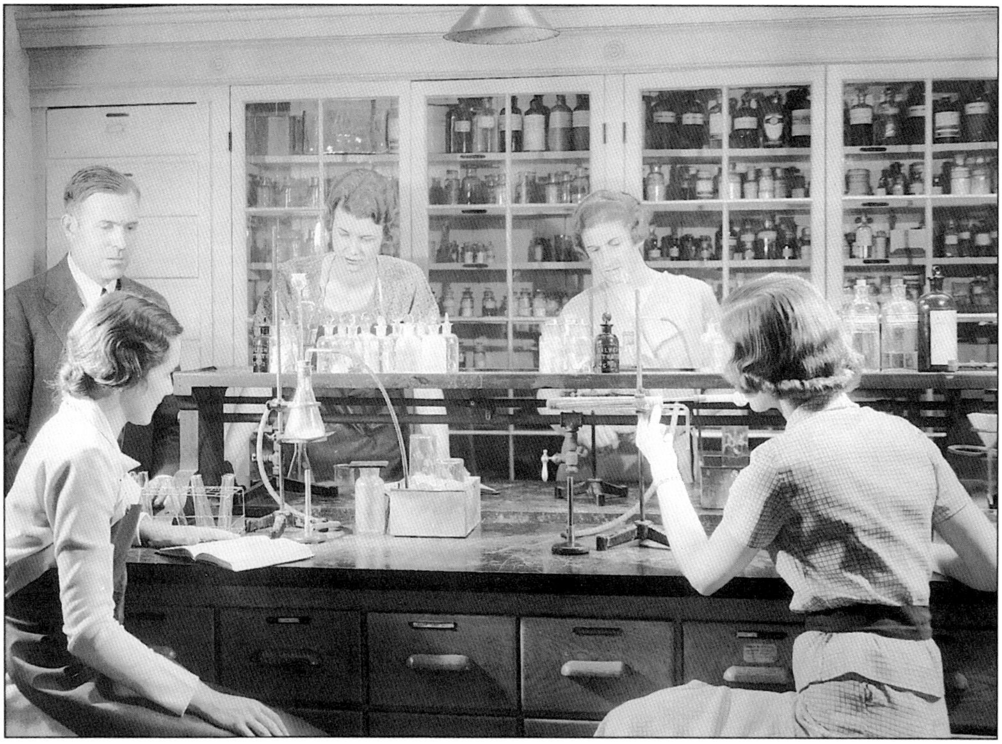

The Chemistry Laboratory. Until 1939, all classes were held in Academy Hall. This is the chemistry lab, which was located on the third floor West. Prof. Albert Dangerfield, shown, was at Bradford for 30 years, from 1922 to 1952. He had a bachelor's degree from Cornell, had done graduate study at Harvard and the University of California, and was a field geologist before his Bradford days.

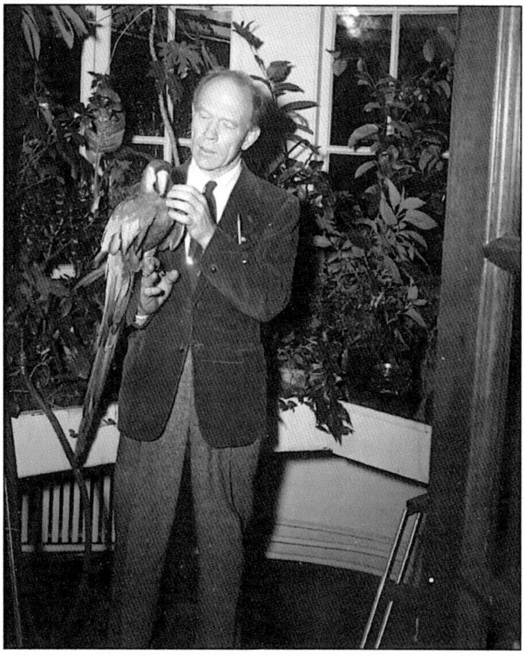

Dr. Wolfgang Pauli. Pauli taught biology at Bradford from 1931 to 1956. A native of the Caroline Islands in the South Pacific, he earned his degree from the University of Wurzburg, Germany. His wife, Margarete, who also had a Ph.D., assisted him in his class and laboratory. Pauli died at the home he had built in Orvieto, Italy, in 1987.

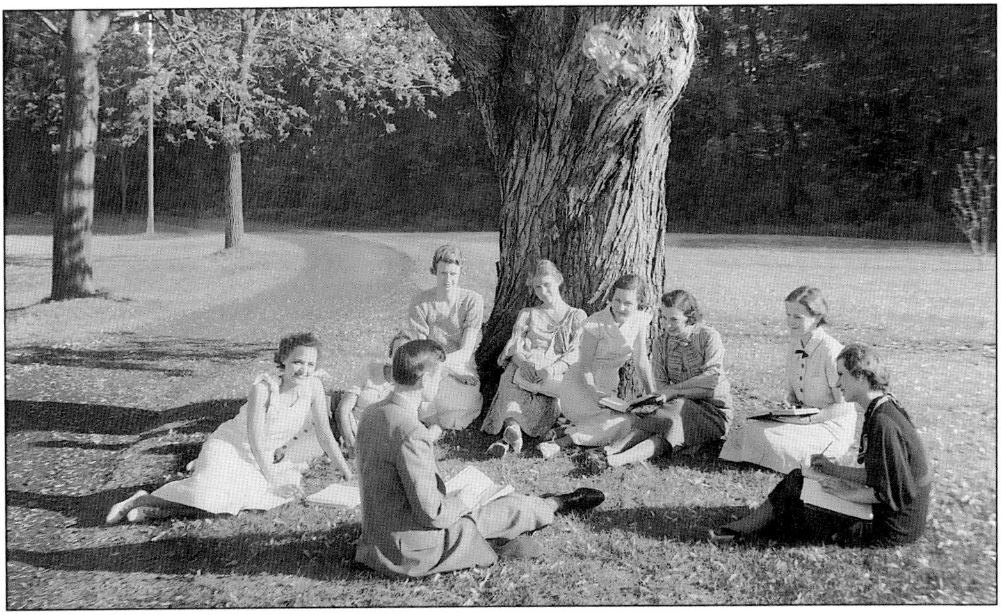

Class 'Al Fresco.' For decades, warm weather had brought classes out of doors. This photograph dates from the mid-1930s. The professor resembles Dr. Dale Mitchell of the English faculty. The class is seated under a large tree near Coats House Infirmary.

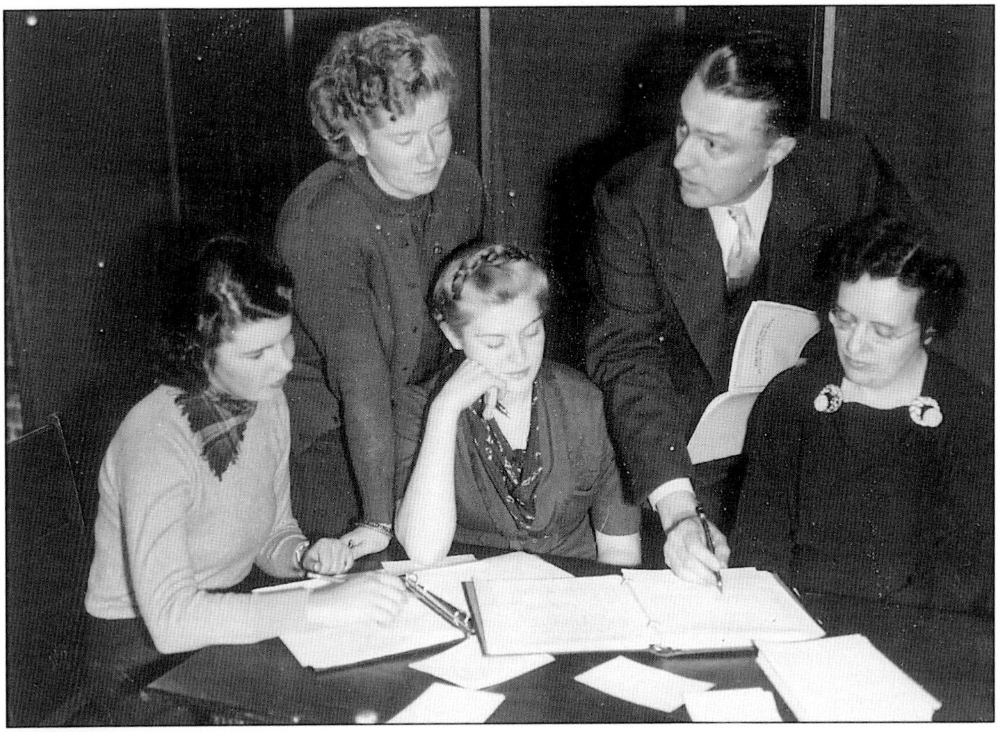

Registration, 1936. Seen here, from left to right, are as follows: (front row) Elizabeth Ann Fuller '37, Carolyn Pegg '38, and Dr. Eunice Acheson Pugh (1935–39), who was an early director of guidance, a Denworth innovation; (back row) Grace McLellan '38 and Dr. Earl F. Roberts (1934–38), assistant to the president and registrar.

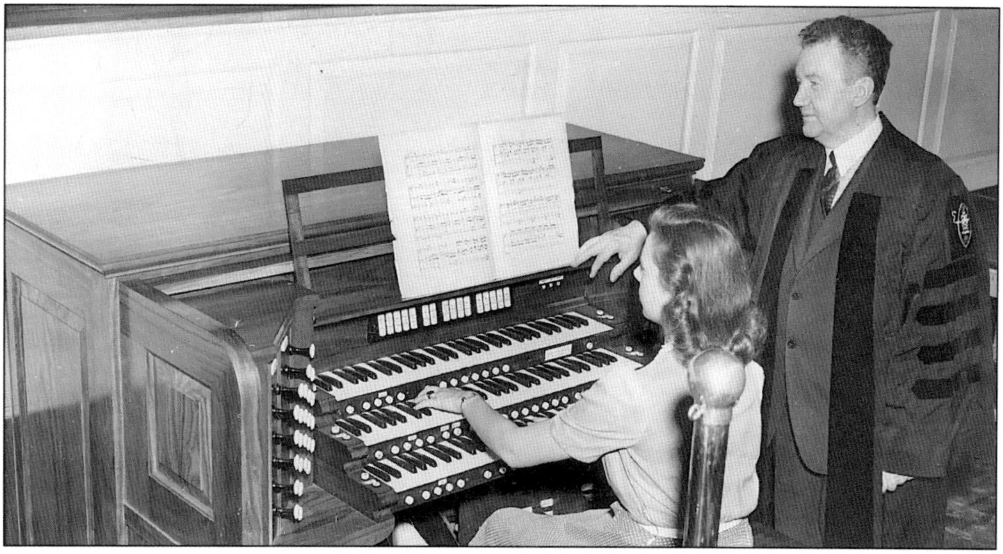

Prof. Frederick Johnson. Johnson, right, served Bradford for 33 years, from 1913 to 1946. He had a bachelor's degree from Harvard and was a Fellow of the American Guild of Organists. During his long term, he served under four heads of the school. The Commencement Prize in Music is named for him. Johnson left to teach at Boston University. He died suddenly on Palm Sunday in 1949. He is shown in this photograph with Lucy Ann Spaulding '40 at the Cornelia Warren Memorial Organ in the newly opened Denworth Hall. Warren, a trustee, had bequeathed $5,000 to Bradford for the organ.

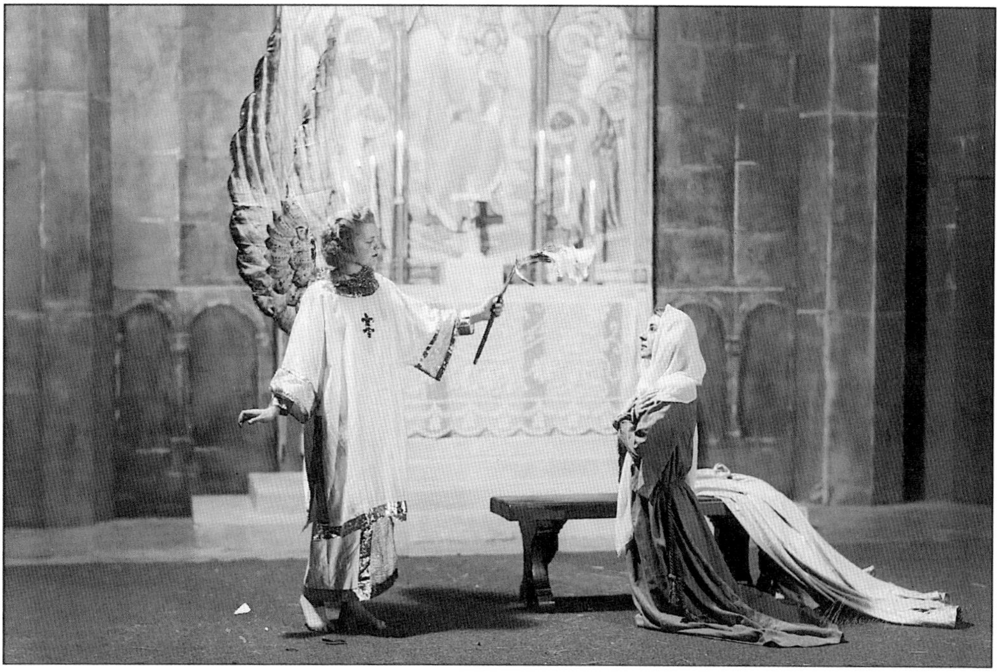

Scene from the Annual Christmas Pageant. The pageant was instituted by President Denworth in 1935 and carried on until 1948. The faculty planned the program, wrote the script, painted the sets, and made the costumes. Mothers of students were invited to the first pageant and thus began Mothers' Day, which became an annual event that continued long after the pageant ended.

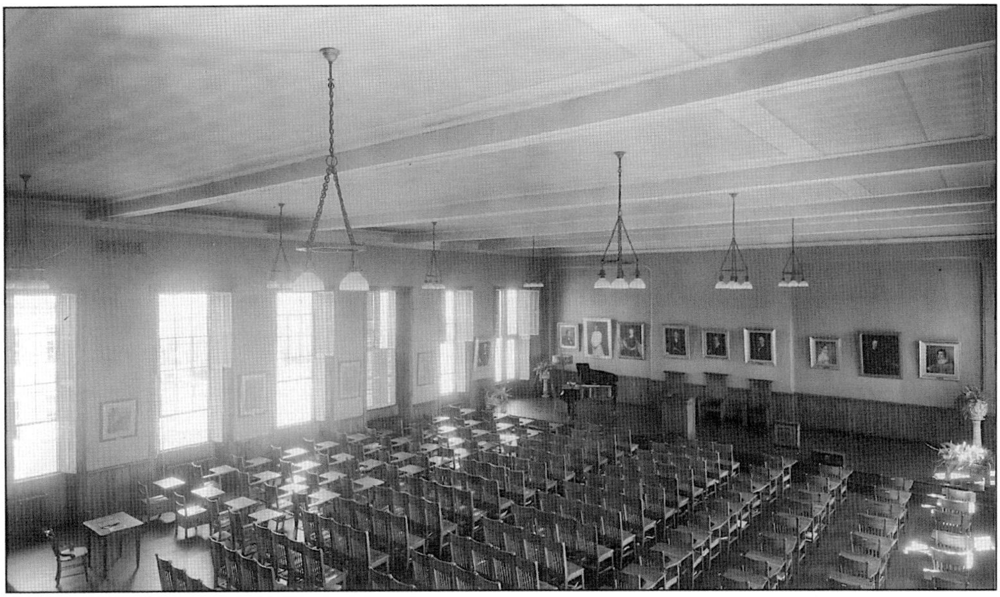

The Assembly Hall. This two-story space in the center of Academy Hall has had a number of lives. It served as a study hall, classroom/lecture space, and a chapel before becoming the library in 1939. The portraits, meant to inspire the students, were primarily of trustees, benefactors, and a few of the earlier principals of the school.

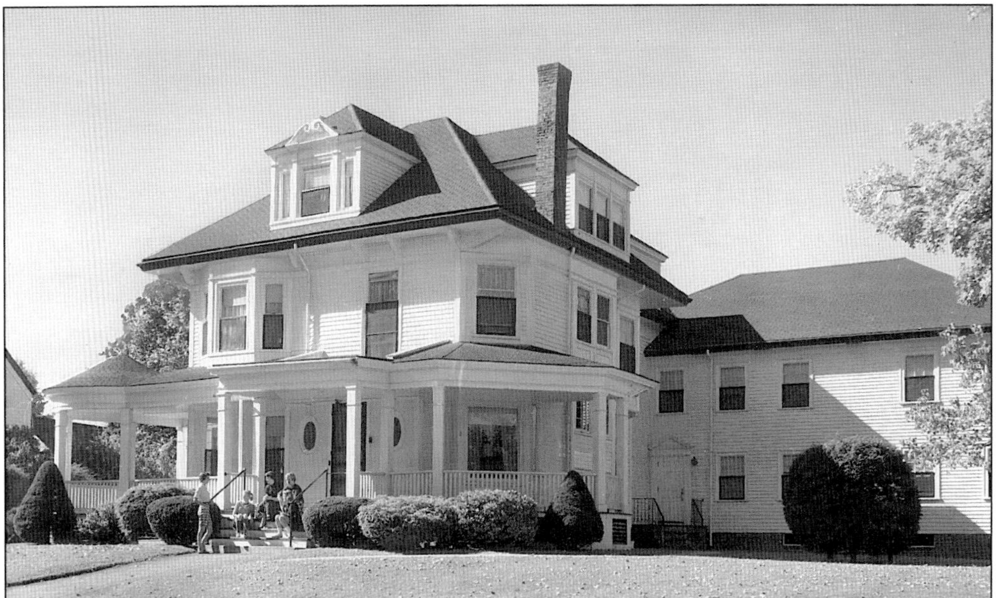

Greenleaf House. Originally, four students were assigned to each three-room suite in Academy Hall. When Principal Laura Knott decreed that the spaces be limited to two girls per suite, additional space for residents was found by renting rooms in nearby houses. Greenleaf House, on Kingsbury Avenue, was acquired as a permanent addition to the campus in 1933 because of a sudden increase in applicants. It was first used for faculty who had been living in Academy Hall. Greenleaf became a senior house in 1936. It is shown here with its 1950s addition, an 8-room wing for 16 students.

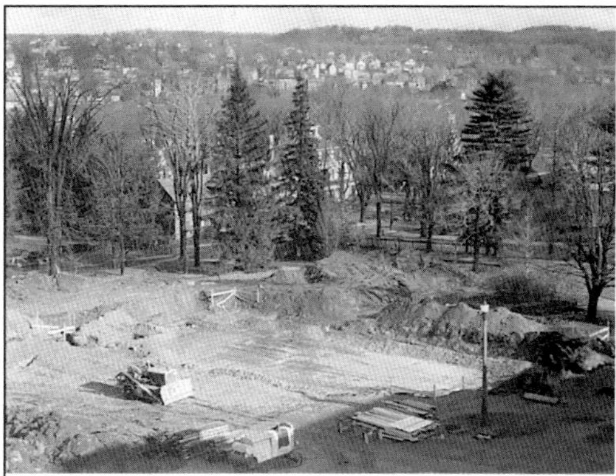 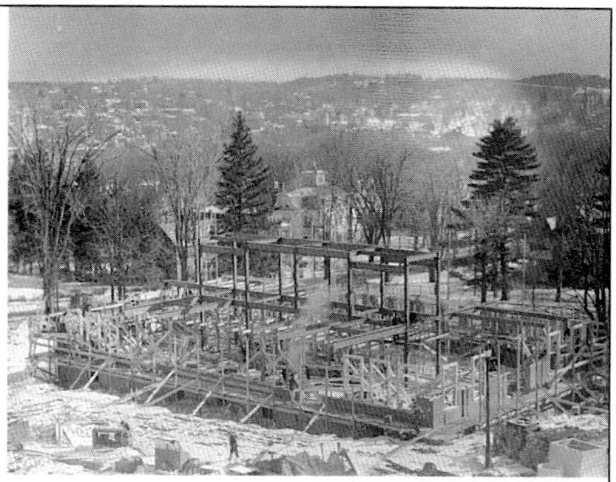

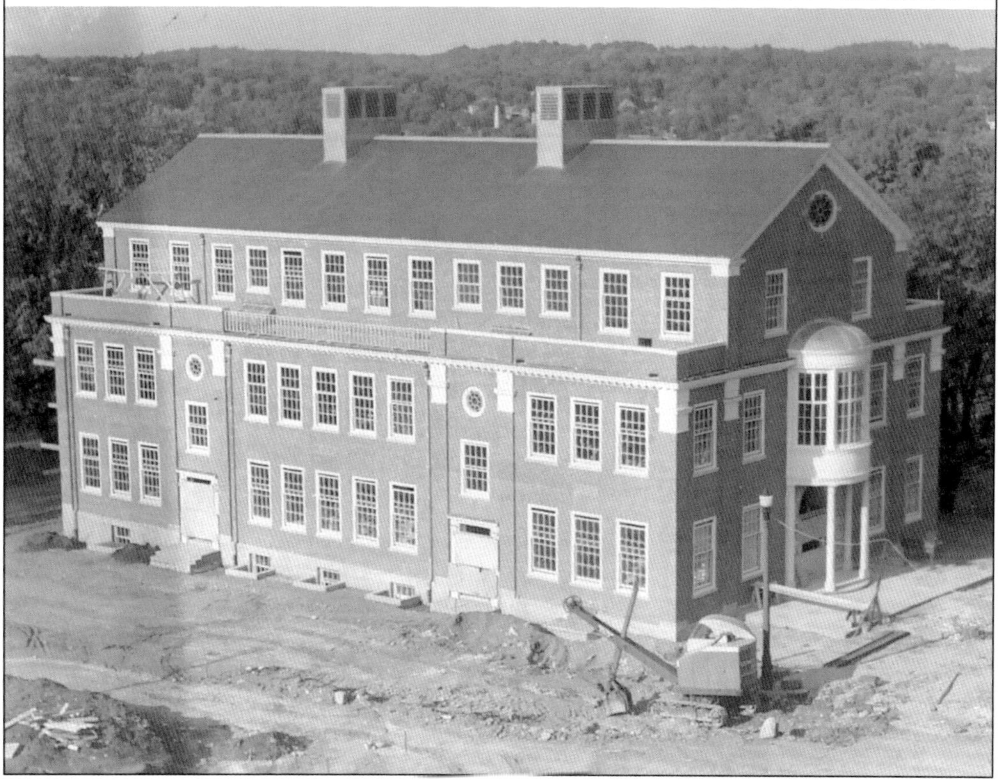

Hasseltine Hall Construction, 1939. For 70 years, Academy Hall had served as a residence, a schoolroom, a dining room, and offices. By 1938, there was no more room for students and the classrooms were outmoded. Despite the Depression, Dr. Denworth had paid off all debt and saved enough funds for new buildings. The first plan called for a single building at the rear of the campus. Dissatisfied, the architect, Edwin S. Dodge, proposed a new plan: two harmonious buildings in front of Academy Hall. Alumnae were outraged at the loss of the great front lawn, but the plan was approved. Hasseltine Hall, named for Principal Abby Hasseltine, was erected between November 1938 and the opening of school in September 1939. It housed classrooms and laboratories. Denworth Hall, the companion building, was opened the following spring.

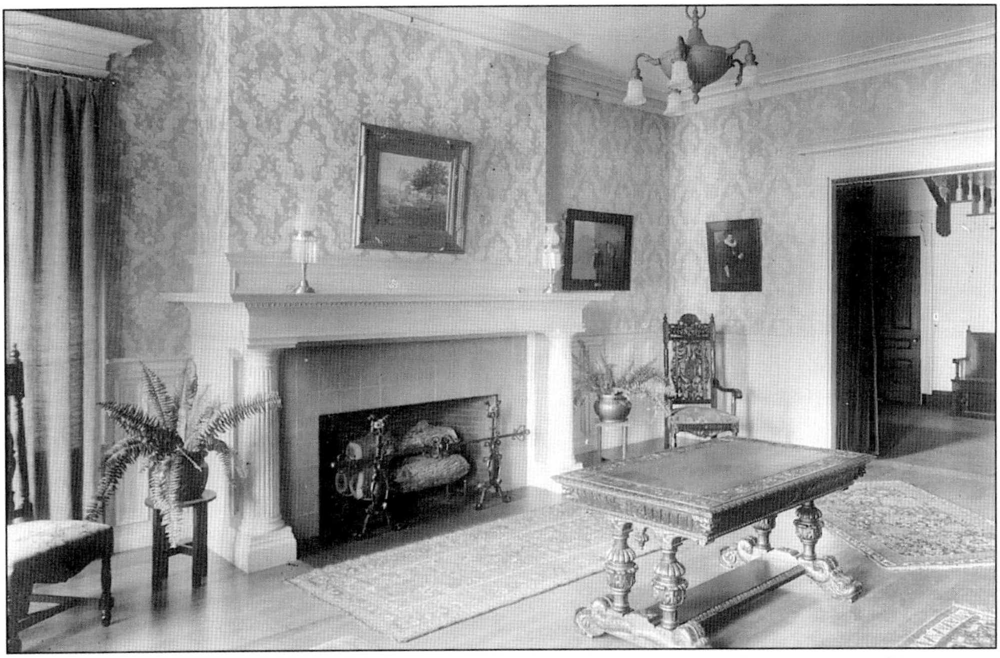

The 1890s Front Parlor. The front parlor was Bradford's face to the visiting public. Here, guests waited for students (no visitors were allowed above stairs). The parlor's previously plain appearance had been changed thanks to a class gift in the 1890s. The redecoration included this heavy mantle and elaborate Elizabethan furniture.

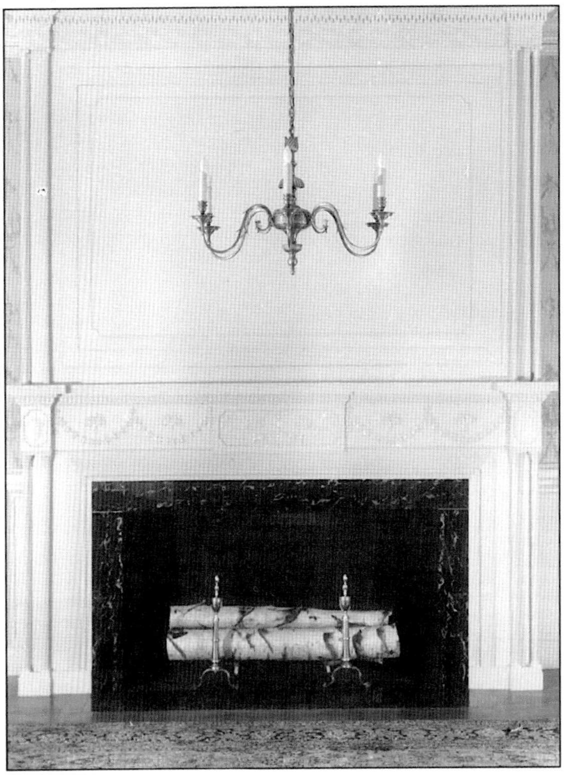

The 1930s Front Parlor. The Reception Room was transformed in 1932 when this Federal-style fireplace mantle was put up. It is a replica of one originally in the Eagle House hotel in Haverhill, and now in the Haverhill Room at the Metropolitan Museum of Art in New York City. The earlier furnishings were replaced with Duncan Phyfe furniture, complementary to the mantle.

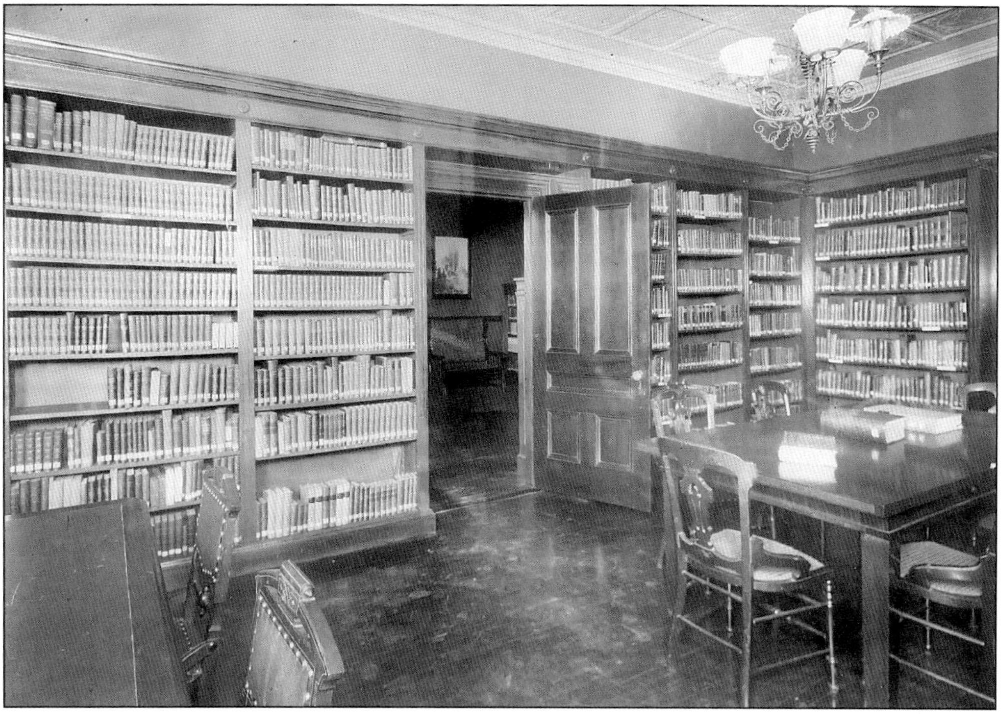

The Library, Academy Hall. The first library in Academy Hall occupied three rooms on the third floor. They were the center rooms of the main floor, opposite the doors to the Assembly Hall. Later, students knew the Assembly Hall as the Dance Studio.

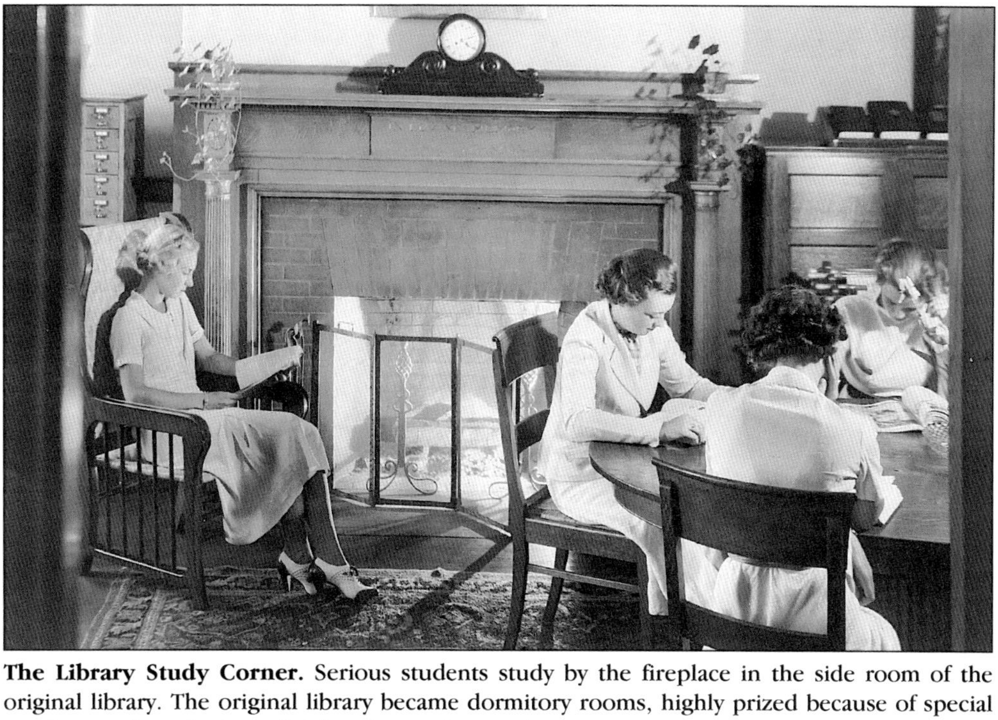

The Library Study Corner. Serious students study by the fireplace in the side room of the original library. The original library became dormitory rooms, highly prized because of special touches, such as the beautiful fireplace and mantel.

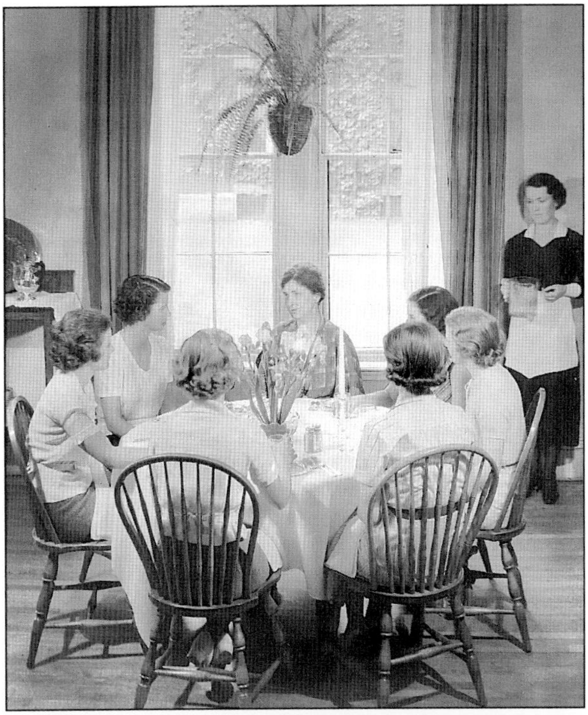

Housemothers and Waitresses. Residential life at Bradford through the 1930s reflected an ideal of gracious living. In the formal dining room with its round tables and Windsor chairs—a gift of the Class of 1932—students sat with faculty and housemothers and were served their meals. Waitress Mary Trainor, right, was originally from Prince Edward Island, Canada; she was one of six sisters who served at Bradford.

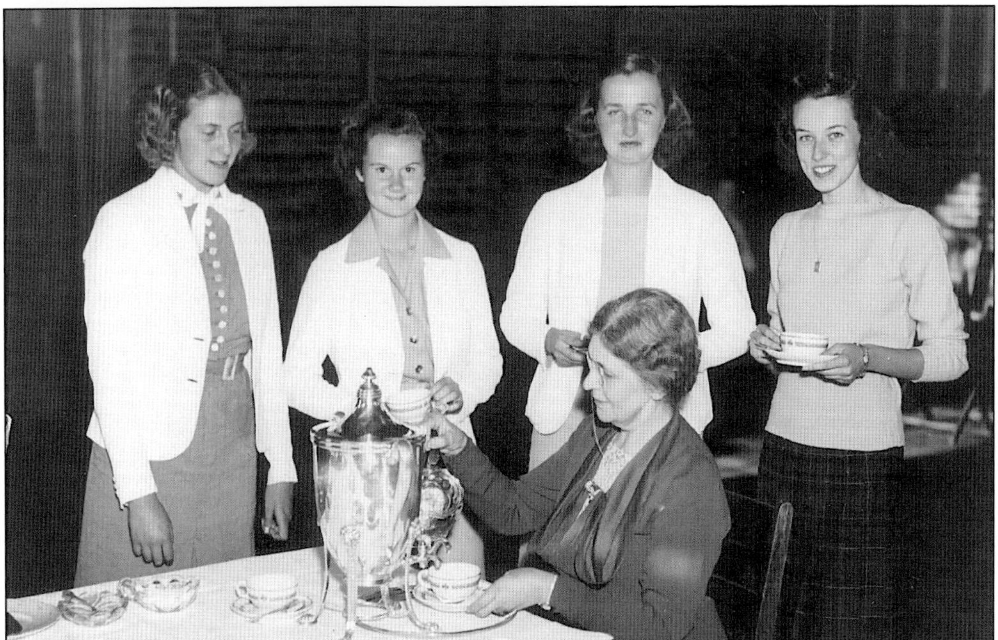

"Mother" Knowlton. Inez Knowlton served as housemother for Academy Hall from 1917 to 1940 and dean of residence for all students. Her affectionate title of "Mother" attests to her success in making her girls comfortable. Here, near the end of her tenure, she pours tea for Ann Hemingway '38, Jane Wheaton '38, Constance Nixon '38, and Allene Stover '38. She died in 1971 at the age of 97.

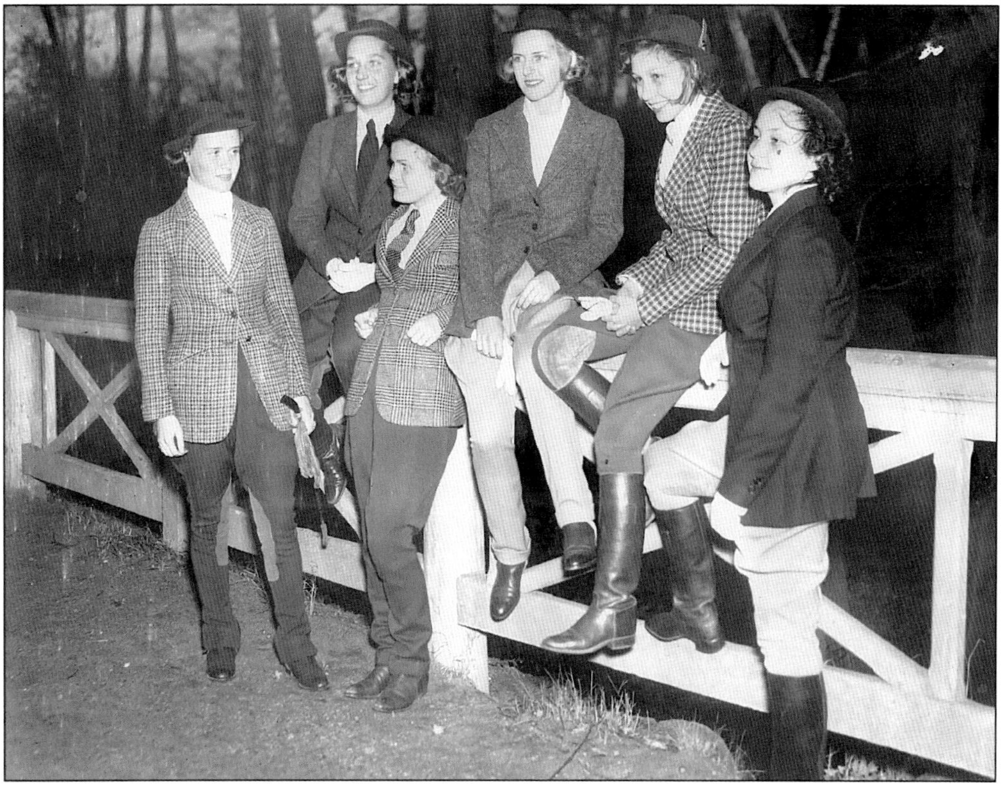

A Gathering of Equestrians. Horseback riding was an option for Bradford students until the 1990s. This photograph, taken on Tupelo Bridge in November 1937, shows, from left to right, Betty Ham, Sanna Klaveness, Ellen Dickens, Phyliss Albrecht, Ann Spence, and Dodie Rainalter.

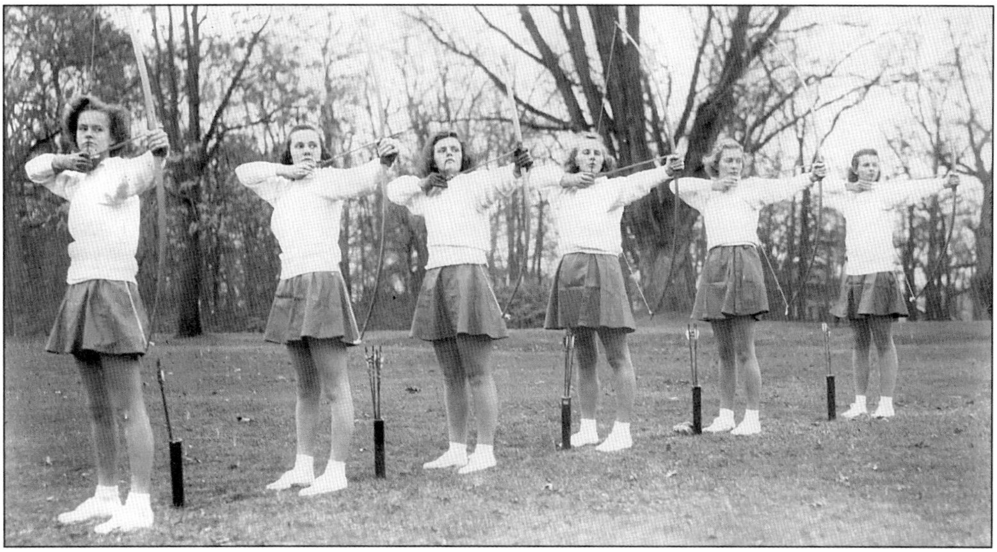

Archers. Archery was also available to students until the 1990s. This photograph, taken in November 1937, shows archers on the athletic field adjacent to Coats House, where the extended parking lot now exists. Seen here, from left to right, are Sue Haskins, Virginia Egolf, Rosamond Scott, Frances Dyckman, Betty Jones, and Lenore Macdonald.

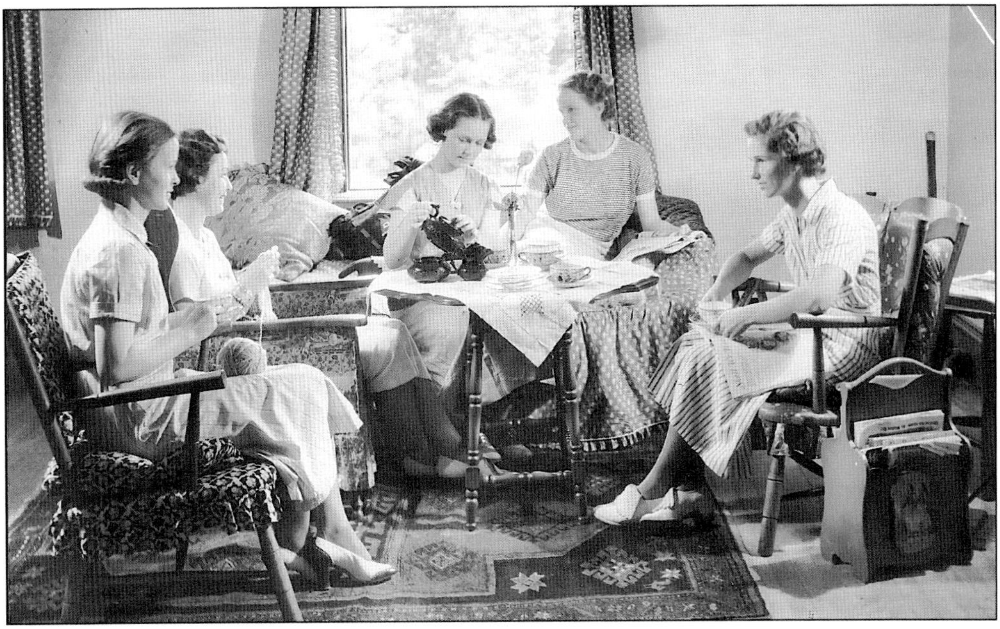

Teatime in a Dorm Room. In 1934, all of the bedrooms in Academy Hall were provided with new, Colonial-style furniture to replace the "hodge-podge of washstands, marble-topped bureaus, iron beds, and mission chairs," as an earlier historian described it. This docile, well-mannered group of young ladies, with their knitting and tea service, may have been posing for a photographer, but it is most likely that they are representative of their classmates in their decorum.

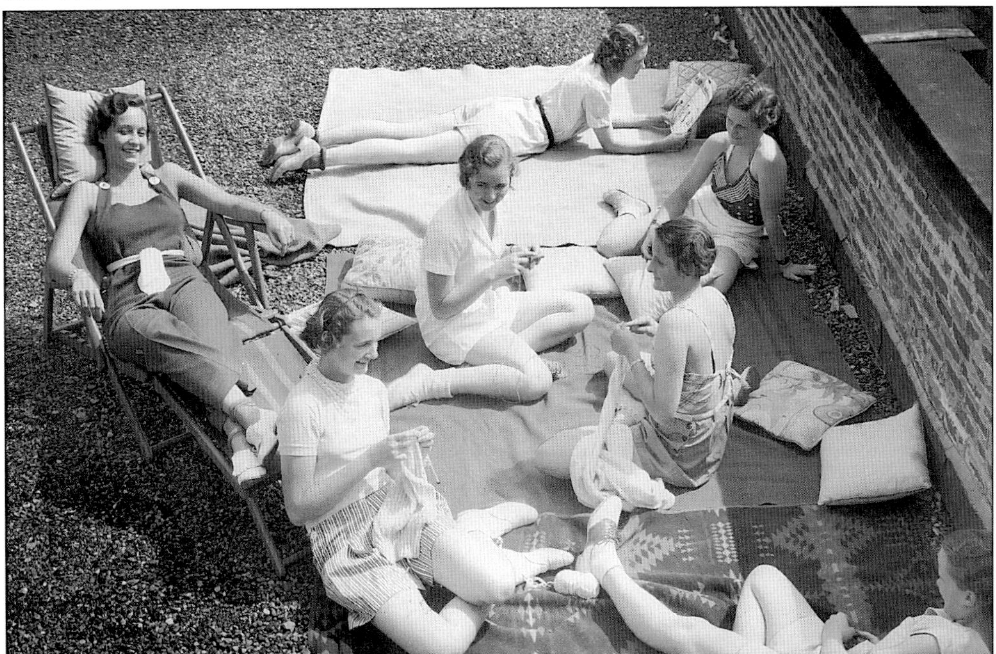

Up on the Roof. Sunbathers relax on the gravel of the roof of Academy Hall in the late 1930s. This spot was a favorite escape for many decades until insurance concerns forbade it.

Two

The Forties

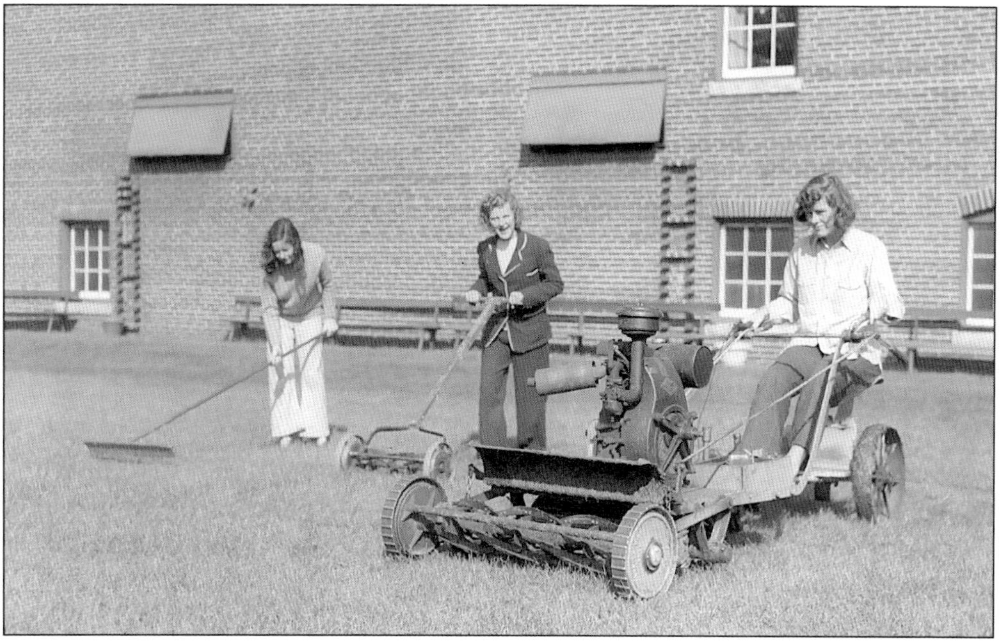

The Dorothy Bell Era Begins. Dorothy Bell became the president of Bradford College in 1940. Her tenure lasted until 1967 and in that time, she led Bradford to international renown. First, however, she had to get the college through World War II. When the wartime draft took away most of the buildings-and-grounds crew, students took over some of the yard work. This photograph was taken in September 1942 and shows Mary Pitcher with a rake, Eleanor Cady with the push mower, and Rosamond Sabine driving the power mower.

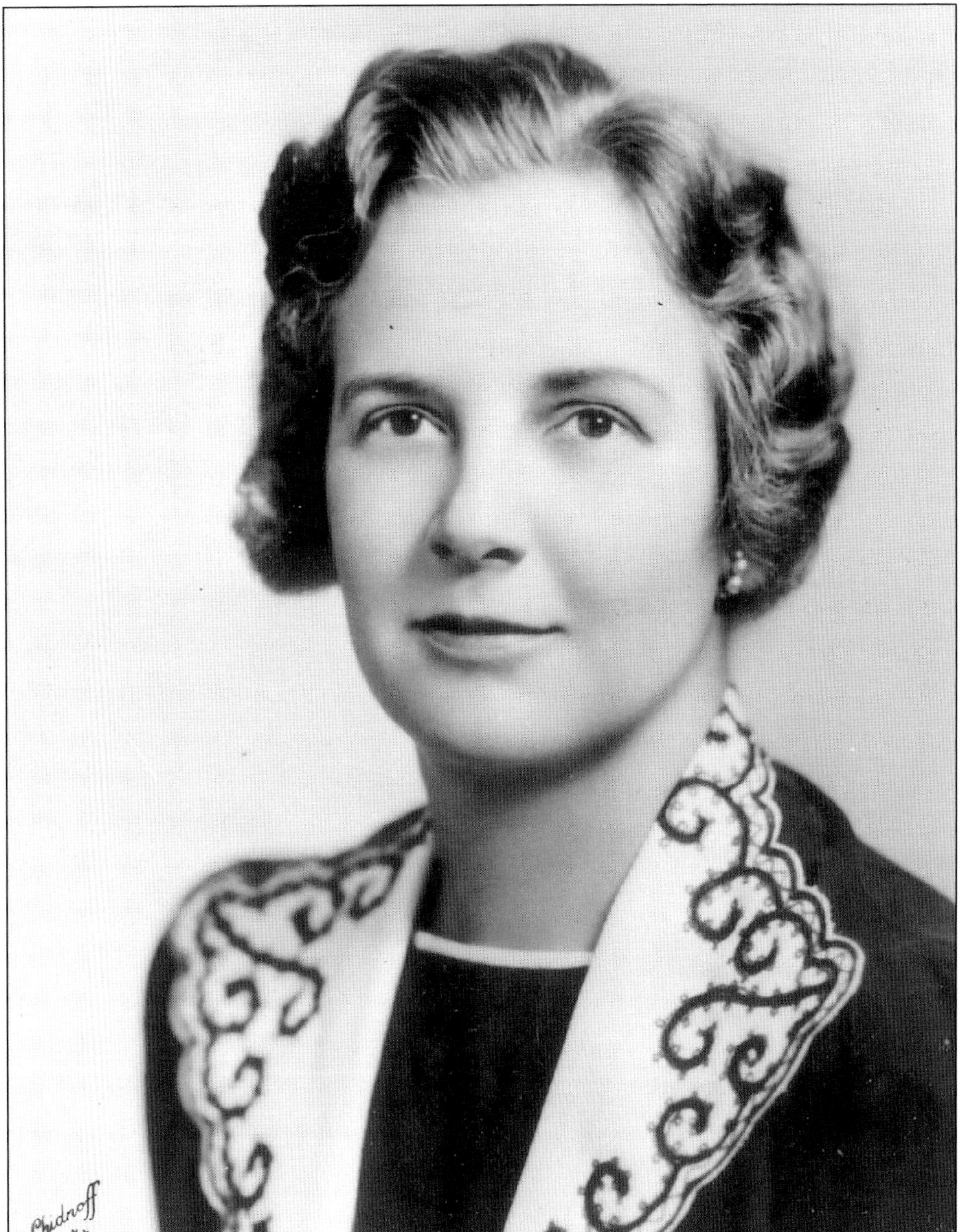

Pres. Dorothy M. Bell. Katharine Denworth resigned the presidency of Bradford Junior College to return to her previous faculty position in Pennsylvania. Dr. Dale Mitchell served as interim president until the trustees selected an instructor in the classics from Oberlin College to be the next president. Dorothy M. Bell had a M.A. in classics from Smith College and a solid reputation as a scholar. Her 27-year tenure as president was second only to that of the legendary Abby Hasseltine. Building on the foundation laid by Denworth, Bell brought Bradford Junior College to national attention as one of America's most prestigious two-year schools for women.

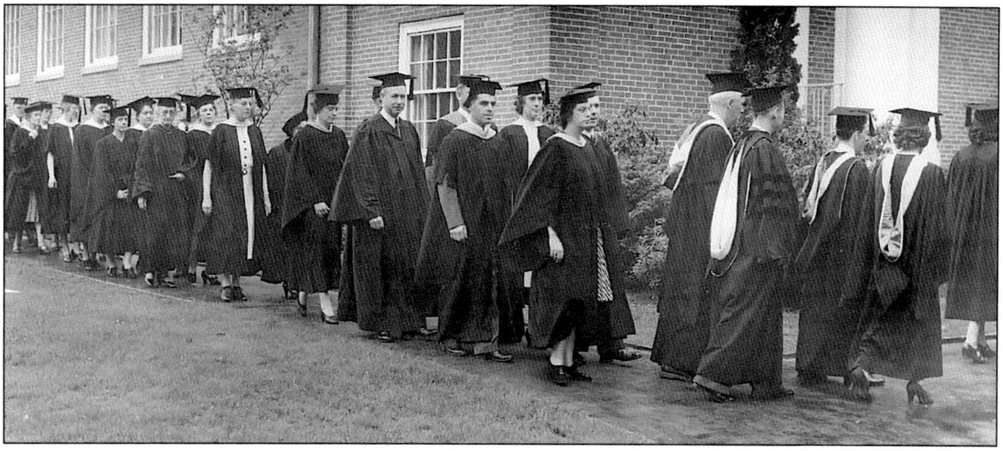

Faculty Procession, Commencement 1940. The faculty that President Bell inherited proceeds into the newly opened Denworth Hall for the 1940 Commencement. By tradition, the professors line up according to the year they began teaching at Bradford with the newest at the beginning and the senior members at the end of the procession. In the 1939 to 1940 school year, there were 19 full-time and 6 part-time faculty members, 13 female and 12 male, for about 250 students. Six of the faculty held doctorate degrees.

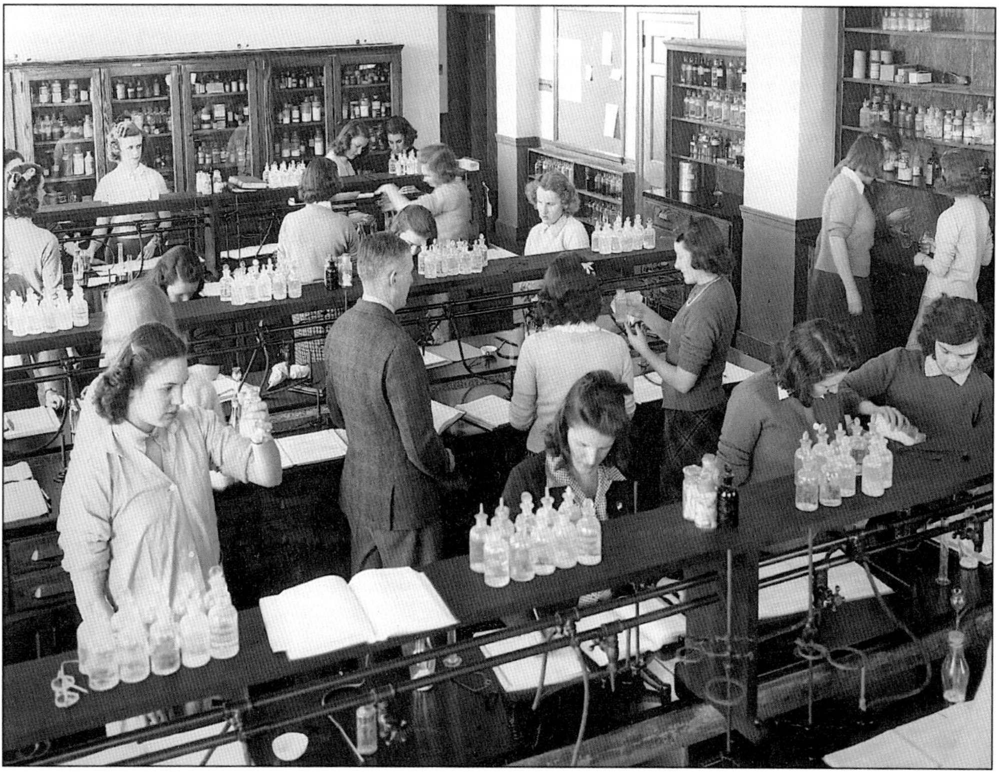

The New Chemistry Laboratory. Hasseltine Hall opened in 1939. Its first floor contained 11 classrooms; its second floor, two classrooms and three laboratories, for chemistry, physics and biology; its third floor, a classroom, laboratories for foods and clothing, and a practice dining room, which served as a reminder of the importance of home economics in the curriculum. Prof. Albert Dangerfield, center, is shown with students in the chemistry lab.

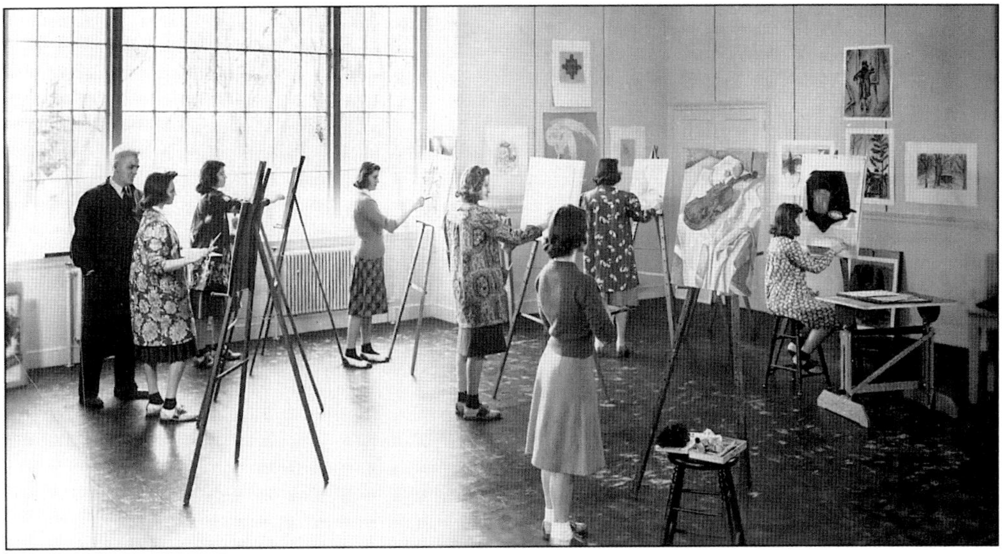

The New Art Studio. Art classes had long been a Bradford curriculum staple (they were once a requirement). Before Denworth Hall was built, the art studio was located in the west wing of Academy Hall in the third-floor rooms that have skylights. With the opening of Denworth, the large room on the third floor with its north-facing window became the mecca for budding artists. The art professor from 1939 to 1953 was Robert Wade, a painter with a national reputation but no college degree, a sign of President Bell's openness to talent, with or without academic credentials.

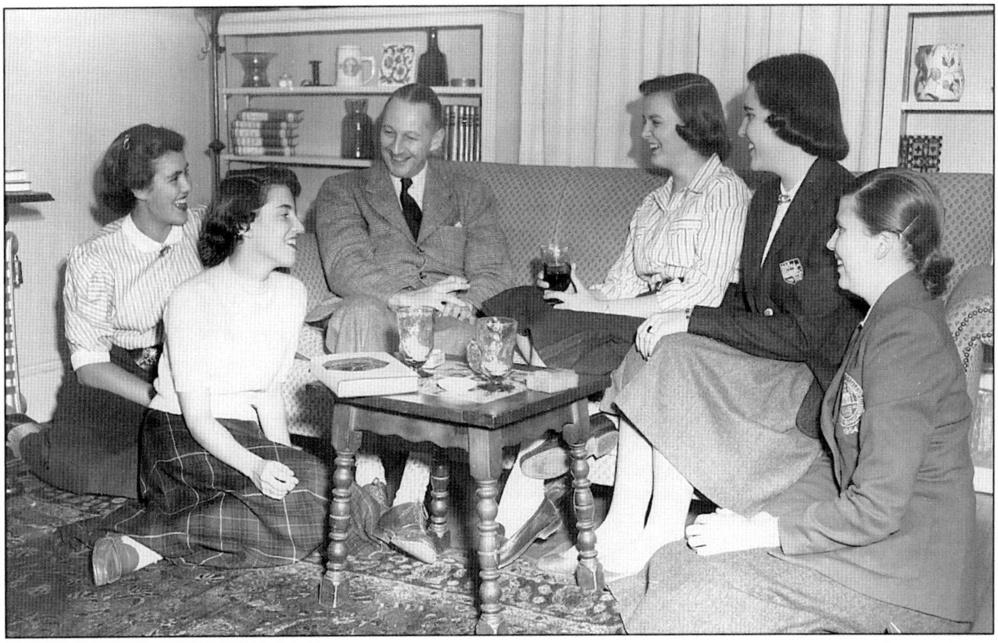

Dr. Edmond McAdoo Gagey. Gagey shares a laugh with students from the Class of 1954. He arrived at Bradford in 1939, as did Robert Wade, during the interim between presidents. All three of Gagey's degrees were from Columbia University. He inspired in two generations of students a love of literature and the English language. Gagey also served as adviser to the yearbook, *The Annals*. He retired in 1969 and was given emeritus status. He died in 1989.

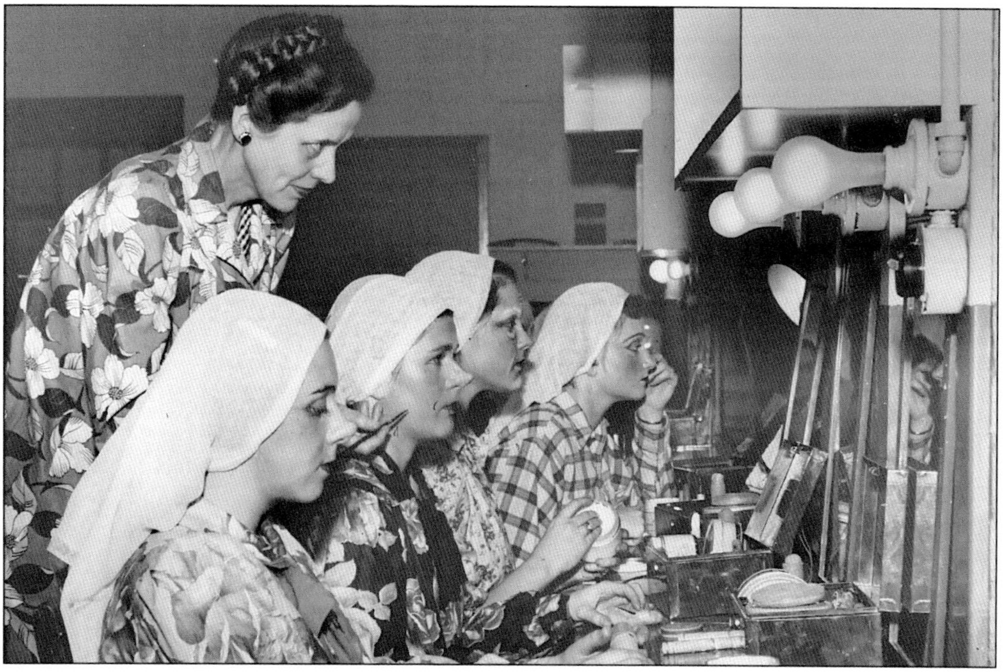

Professor Mors, Speech and Theater. Theresa Mors, left, came to Bradford in 1942 with a B.E. from the University School of Music at Nebraska. She continued on the faculty until 1970. With her in this photograph are four students in a theatrical makeup class in Denworth Hall during the 1944–45 academic year, from left to right, Dorothy Crance, Carlotta Schuster, Doucie Snyder, and Patricia Congdon. The annual prize in theater is named for Professor Mors.

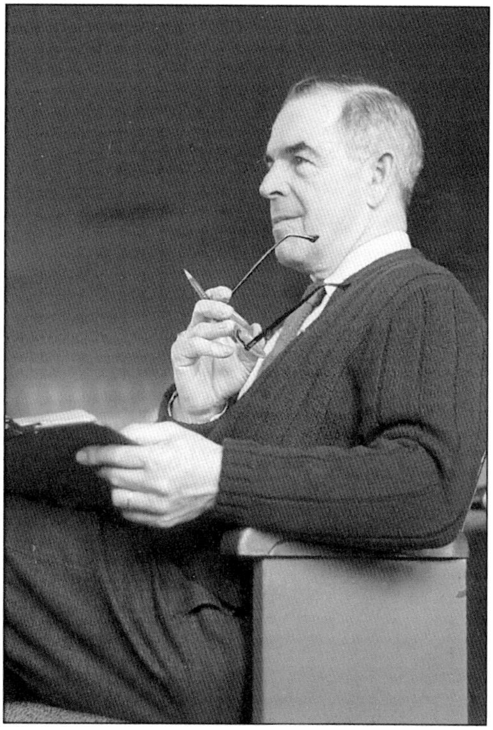

Professor Batchelder, Director of Speech and Drama. C. Wesley Batchelder was appointed to the Bradford faculty in 1937 by Dr. Denworth. He had a B.L. from Emerson, a B.S. from West Texas State Teachers, and an Ed.M. from Boston University. He gave long and faithful service to the college and was the star performer in the annual faculty show. He was given emeritus status when he retired in 1969. He died in 1985.

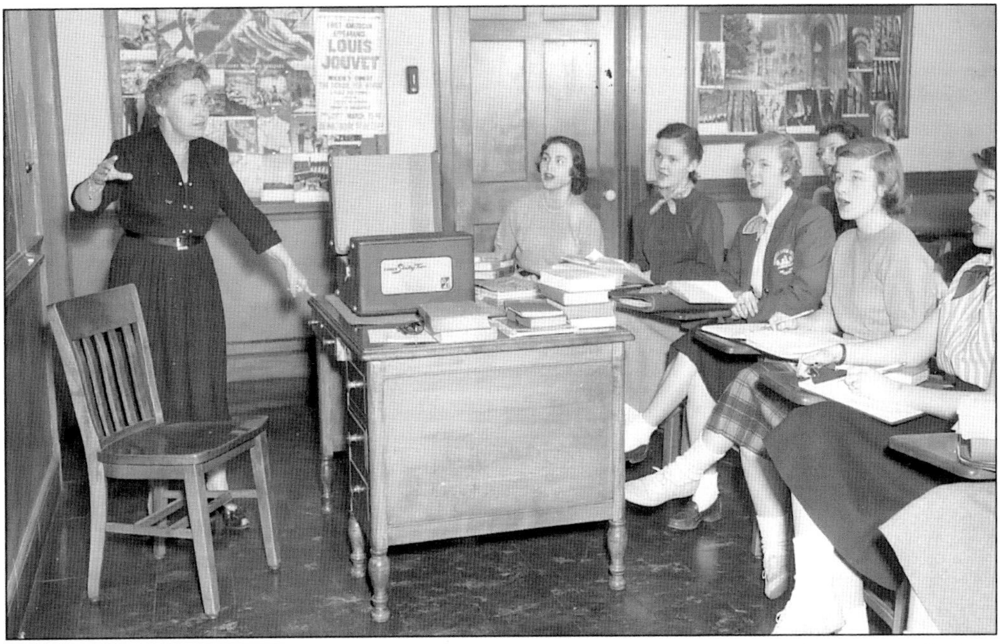

Mlle. Mathilde Boutron-Damazy, French. Mathilde Boutron-Damazy came from Paris. She had studied at the Sorbonne and also at Wellesley. Professor Boutron-Damazy joined the Bradford faculty in 1929 and taught language and literature courses and advised the Romance Languages Club. She retired after 25 years at the school in 1954.

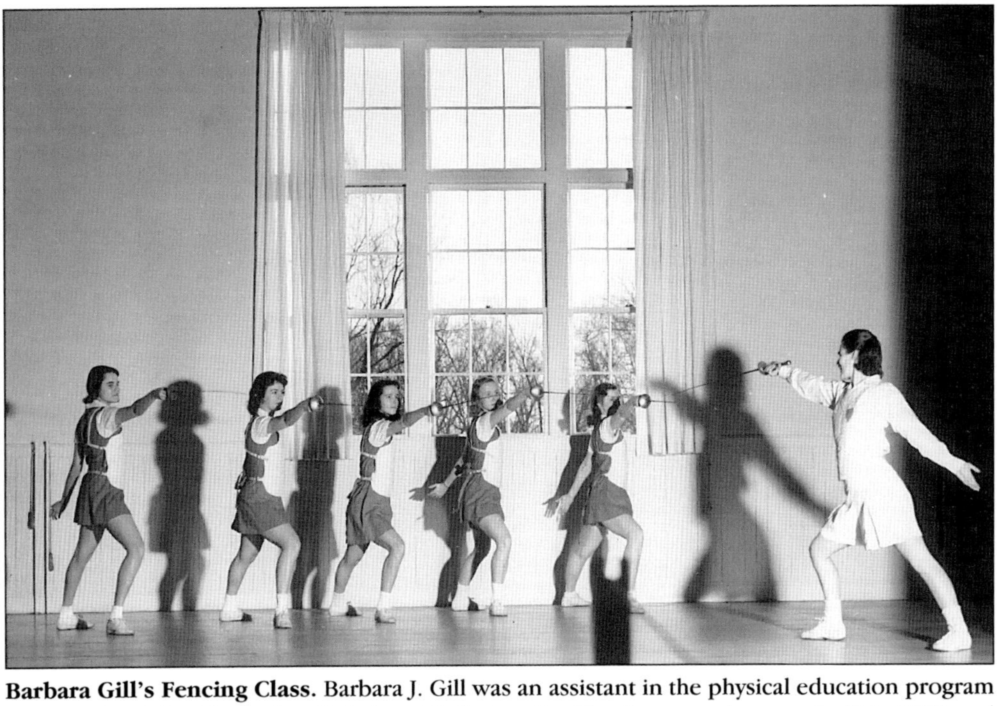

Barbara Gill's Fencing Class. Barbara J. Gill was an assistant in the physical education program in the early 1940s. She had an M.S. from Wellesley. Bradford's gymnasium was built in 1903 and was extended in 1920 with a stage and a swimming pool. In the 1940s, President Bell had this large window added to the stage area to brighten what had been a drab space.

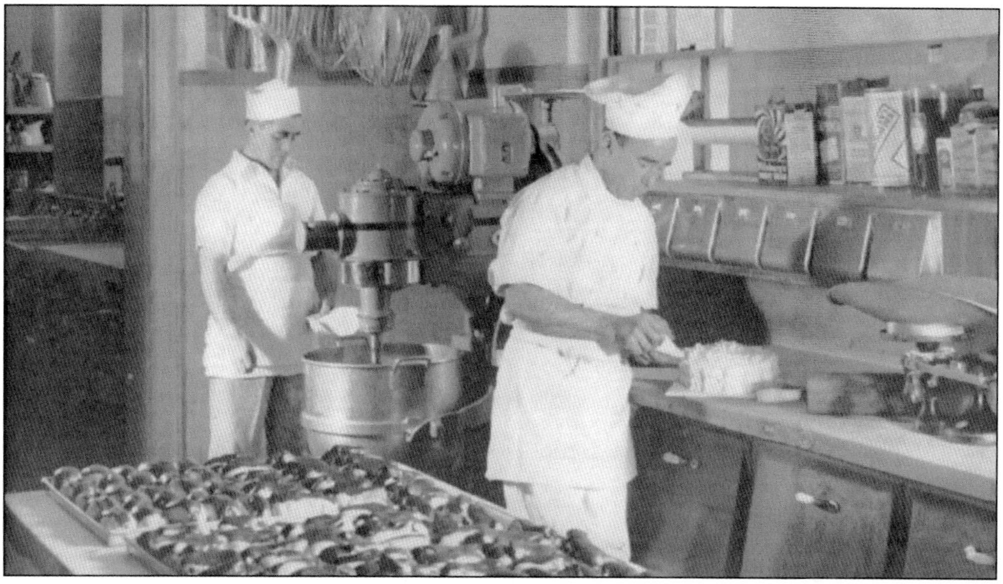

Bradford's Bakers. Faculty, staff, and students came and went with regularity, but two men in the kitchen seemed to be at Bradford permanently. Bernard Bradshaw, on the left at the bread machine, and Ralph Carrington, decorating the cake, both began to work for Bradford in the 1930s. Except for a tour of military service in World War II by Bradshaw, they continued on baking their breads, muffins, biscuits, cakes, and pies for decades. This photograph first appeared in the 1941 *Annals.*

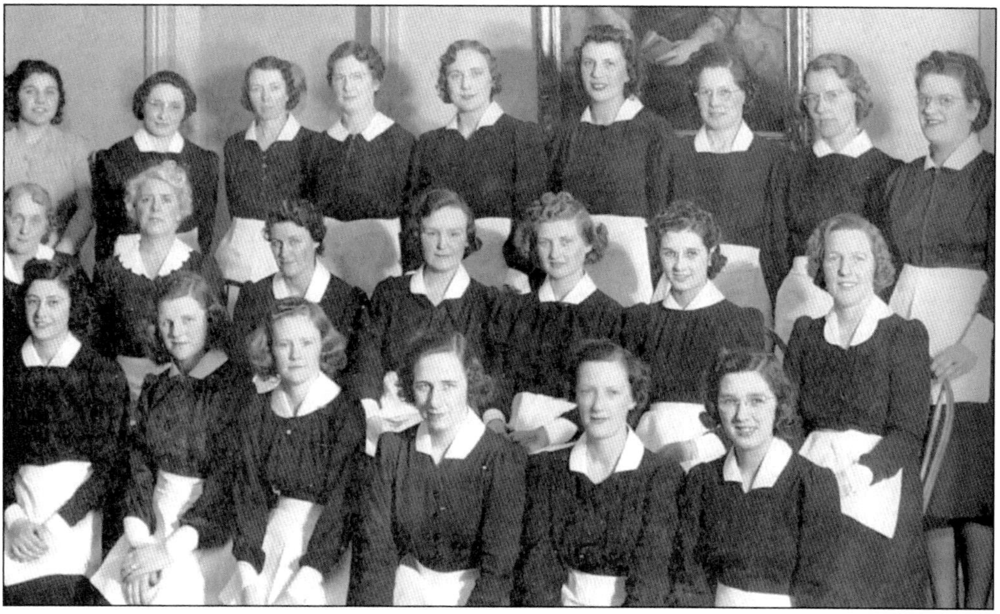

The Dining Room Staff, 1941. Uniformed waitresses at each of the three meals a day were a fact of residential life at Bradford for decades. Not until the 1940s were students expected to take their turns at serving each other, but the waitresses continued as part of the staff until the dining room shifted over to cafeteria-style service. Seated in the middle of the second row is Elizabeth Trainor Keefe, who came from Canada in 1919 and served the students and faculty at Bradford for more than 40 years.

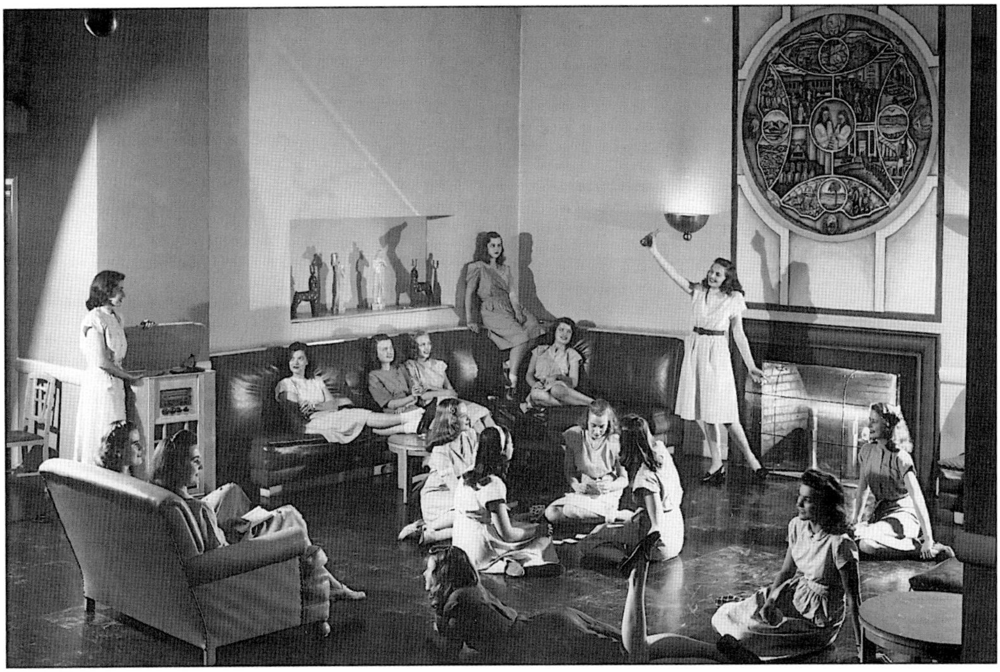

The Recreation Room. Dr. Denworth insisted that the new auditorium building contain a space where students could relax. Thus, it came to pass that a recreation room was put into the lower level of Denworth Hall. The room was opened to the students in February 1940 at the faculty party for seniors. This event occurred weeks before the rest of the building opened. At about the same time, the celebrated tunnels connecting Academy, Hasseltine, and Denworth Halls came into use. The mural over the fireplace was painted by student Muriel Tether '42 and demonstrates various aspects of life at Bradford

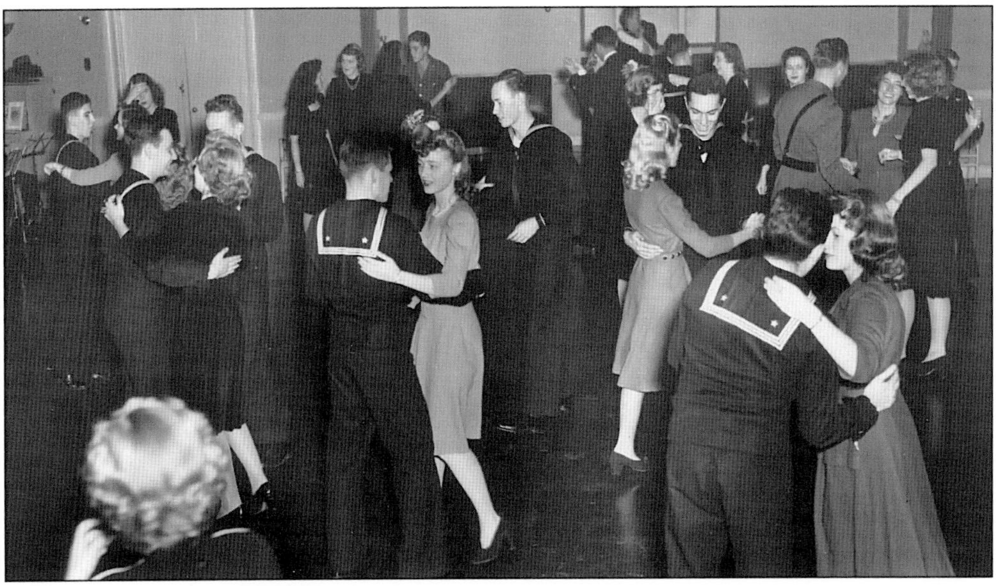

A Dance for Visiting Military. The "Rec Room" served a wide variety of purposes, but none more patriotic than the dances held there during World War II for soldiers and sailors at nearby military bases. In the 1980s, the room was transformed into a Little Theater with a thrust stage.

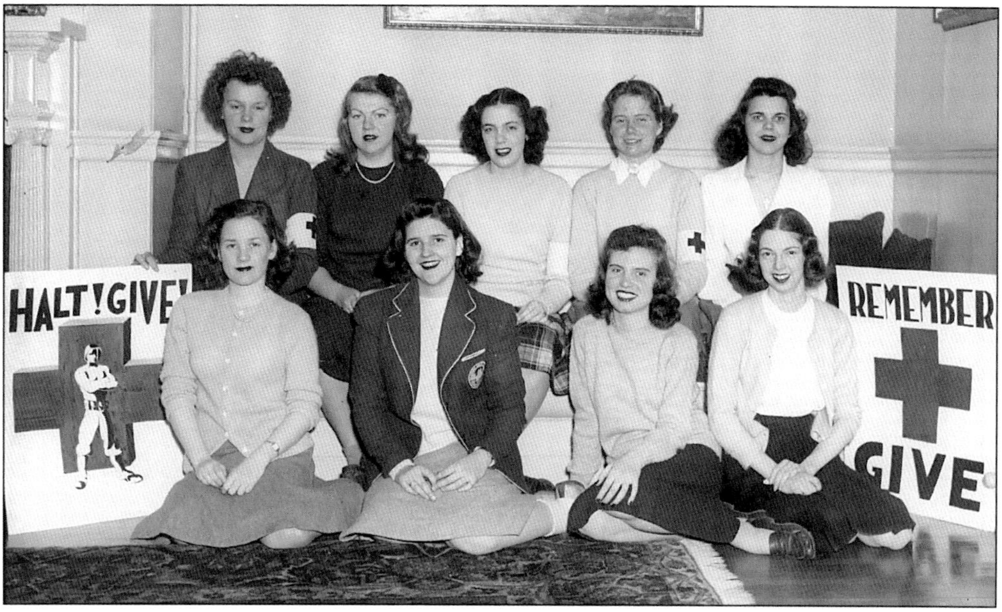

A World War II Red Cross Drive. Bradford girls did their part for the war effort in many ways. In March 1944, they sponsored this Red Cross blood drive in the second-floor living room. Seen here, from left to right, are the following: (front row) Ethel Isenberg ex '45, Bartow Lammert '45, Kathryn Rogers '44, and Nancy Golding '44; (back row) Virginia Peirce '44; Margaret Sim '44; Ann Elder '45, co-chair; Jean Hemingway '44, chair; and Barbara Driscoll '45.

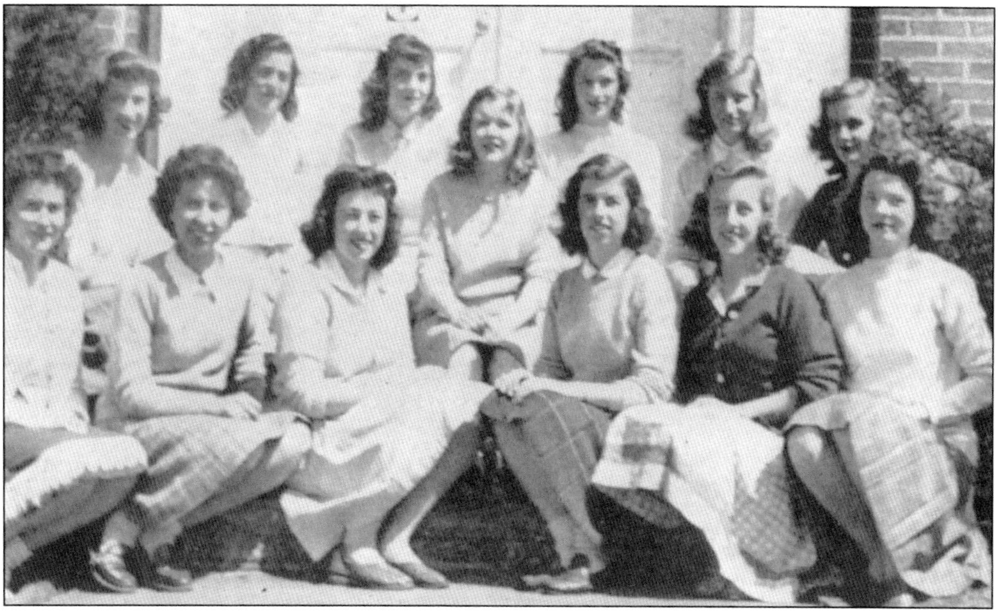

The Original Tabooz. Bradford's a cappella group was formed in 1943 to perform at the annual Freshman Show. The Tabooz survived until the 1970s and was revived by Prof. Mark Peterson in the late 1990s. Pictured, from left to right, are the following: (front row) Jean Gannett '44, Ann Williams '44, Sally Sherman '44, Phyliss Darling '44, Emily Reynolds '44, and Marylin Kissick '45; (back row) Clare Kittredge '45, Dorothy Simons '45, Ann Elder '45, leader Sally Pitcher '44, Barbara Chickering '45, Kay Hyde '45, and Polly Petersen '44.

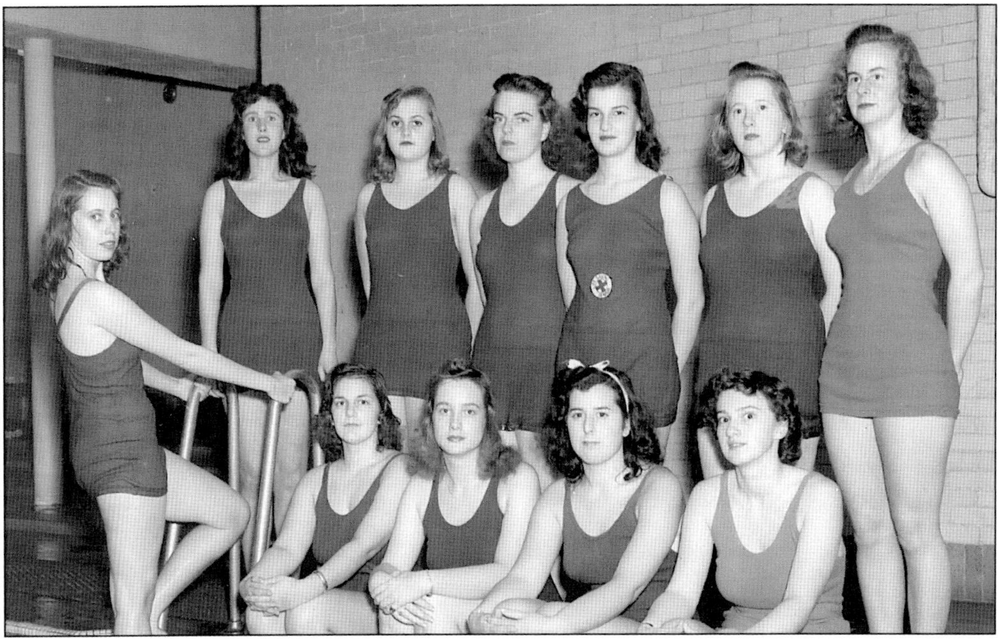

Everyone in the Pool! Bradford added a swimming pool to its gymnasium in 1920 and for many years, it served not only for recreational swimming but also for lifesaving classes, synchronized swimming, and even intramural inner tube water polo. In 1994, after Bradford had signed on with Cedardale, a local health and fitness club, the pool was covered over and the post office and print shop placed atop it. Swimmers at the pool in December 1941, from left to right, are as follows: (front row) Ann Seabury, Nanette Currie, Betty Fisher, Dorothy Arnold, and Muriel Tether, who designed the Rec Room mural; (back row) Elizabeth S. Ryan, Elizabeth Van Stone, Nancy Behre, Deborah Hazelton, Helen Truxal, and V'Onay Gilbert.

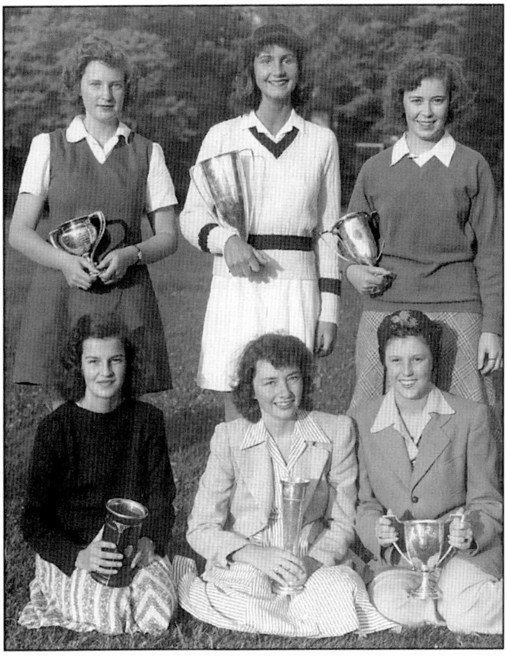

Award Winners in Athletics, 1942. Bradford did not make a serious commitment to physical education until the principalship of Laura Knott (1901–1918). The first trophy, in tennis, was awarded in 1909. By the 1940s, athletics was serious business and the annual trophies were highly contested. The winners in 1941 were, from right to left, as follows: (front row) Debbie Hazelton, swimming; Helen Keenan, dance; and Betty Anne Cooke, field hockey; (back row) Virginia Cornwell, basketball; Sally Smith, general excellence in athletics; and Dorothy Roddy, archery. The silver cups in dance and general excellence continued to be awarded up to the year 2000.

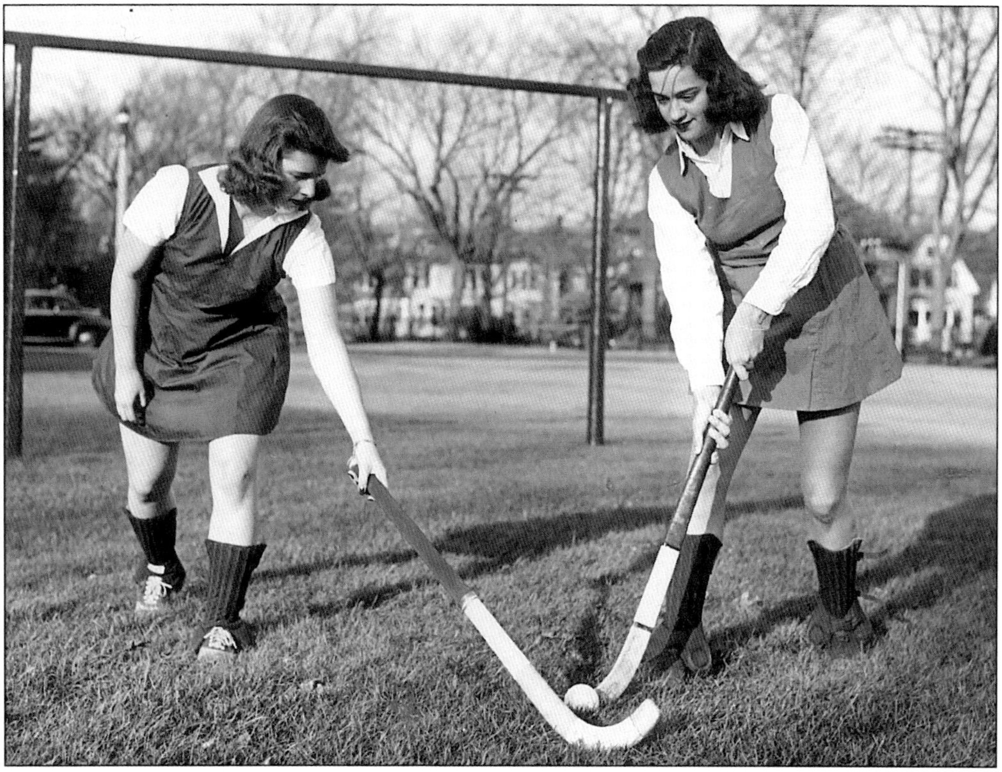

Field Hockey All-Stars. Marjorie Bouvé introduced field hockey to Bradford girls in 1903. The first playing field was a small cleared space in the chestnut grove that stood between the gymnasium and Kingsbury Avenue. The sport grew rapidly. In 1942, Joan Standing, left, and Dorothy Simons were chosen for the College Hockey Team of the Boston Area.

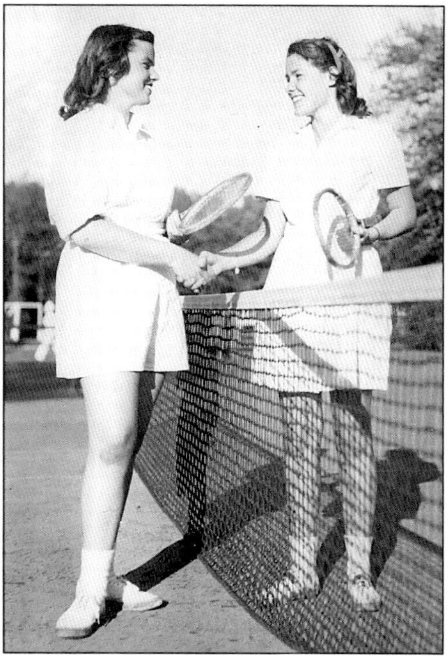

The Tennis Finalists, 1947. The chestnut grove beside the gymnasium eventually became the tennis courts. Each May, during Field Day, the tennis matches were some of the most hotly contested of the competitions. The seniors provided the two finalists in 1947: Ellen Simonds, the winner, and Mildred "Sis" Metzler, runner-up. Both girls were all-around athletes who were also on the tennis, hockey, basketball, badminton, and ski teams. Simonds additionally was on the baseball team.

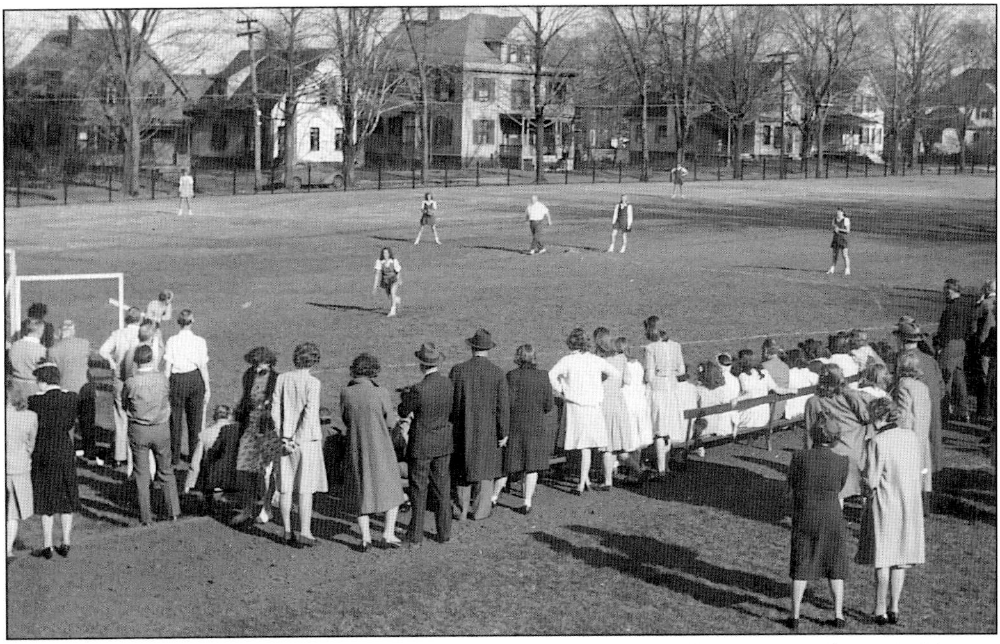

The Father's Day Softball Game. Father's Day was inaugurated in 1937 and was held on a Spring Saturday. The afternoon was always reserved for a softball game between fathers and daughters. This photograph was taken during the 1944 Fathers' Day and shows the athletic field between the gym and South Park Street. The area became a parking lot in the 1990s.

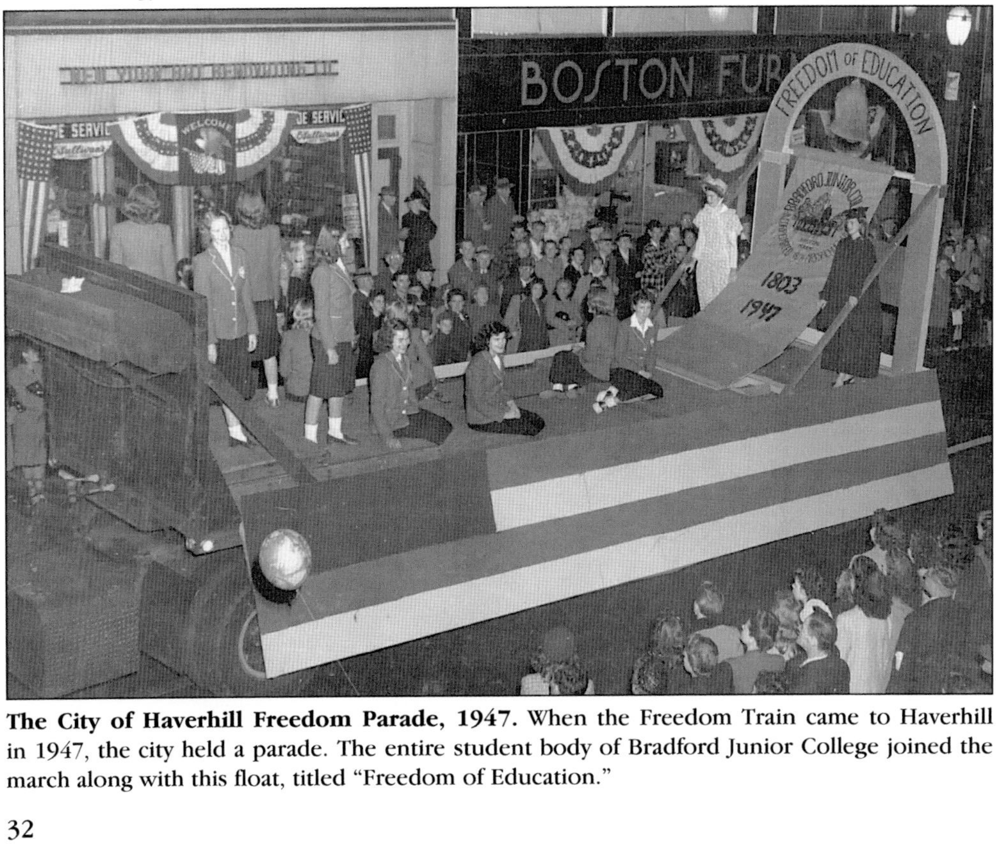

The City of Haverhill Freedom Parade, 1947. When the Freedom Train came to Haverhill in 1947, the city held a parade. The entire student body of Bradford Junior College joined the march along with this float, titled "Freedom of Education."

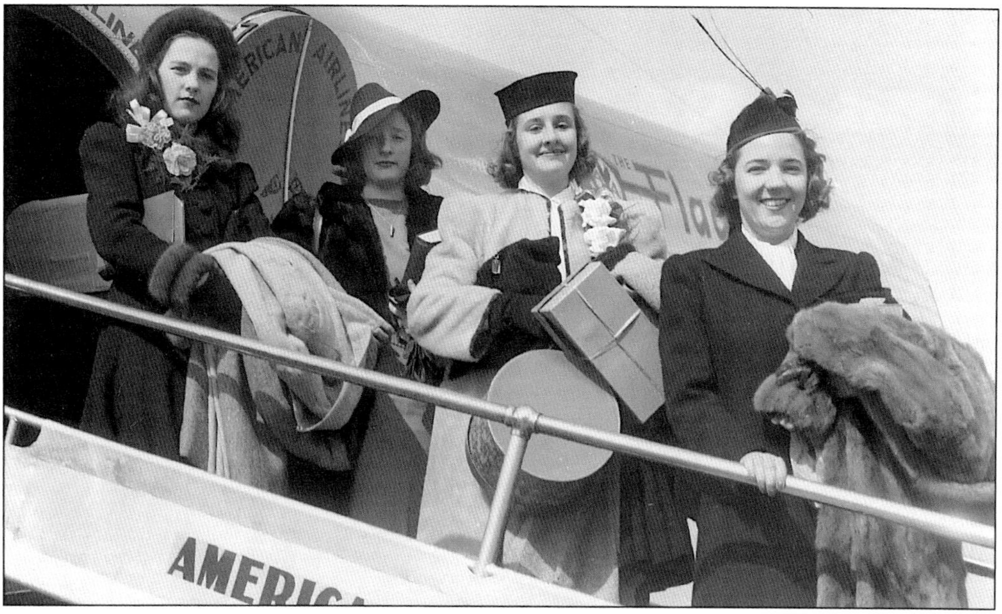

Easter Break. Four Bradford Junior College girls prepare to board an American Airlines plane at Logan Airport at the start of their ten-day Easter break. All are properly dressed with hats, gloves, heels, and hose. They present a far different picture from the 1990s vacationing students. Seen here, from left to right, are Lois Friedman '41, Patricia Barker '40, Jane T. Guptil, and Betty Woodruff '41.

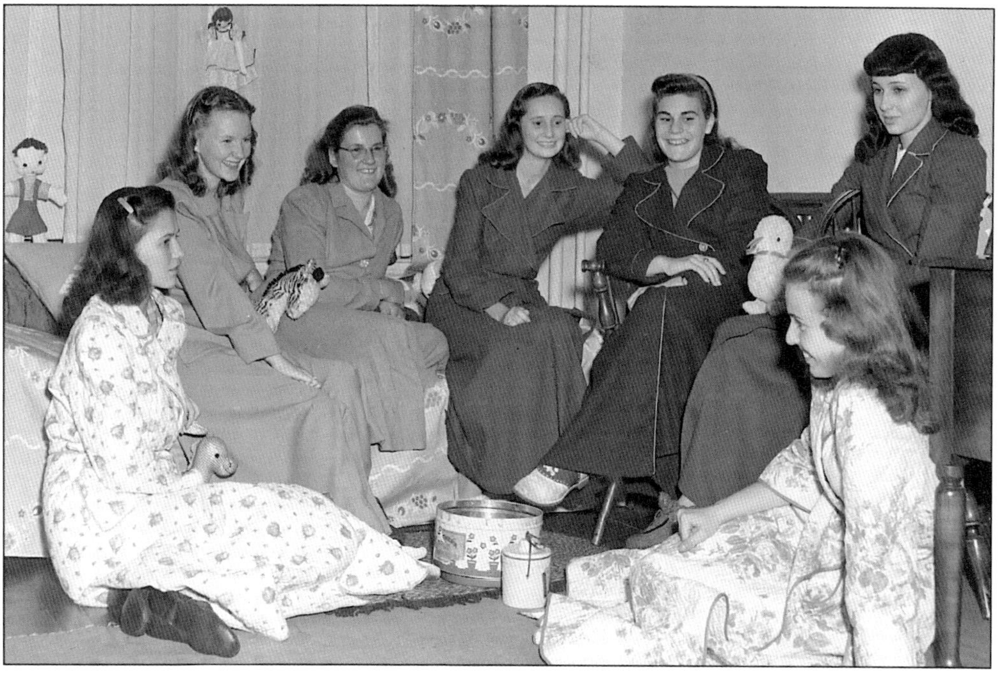

A Late-Night Snack in Academy Hall. This photograph was taken in 1947, but it is a familiar scene with which students from many decades can associate. Pictured, from left to right, are Priscilla Ripley, Mary Crowe, Camilla Webber, Nancy Mikesell, Margaret Thomas, Shirley Foynes, and Dorothy Anne Curtiss.

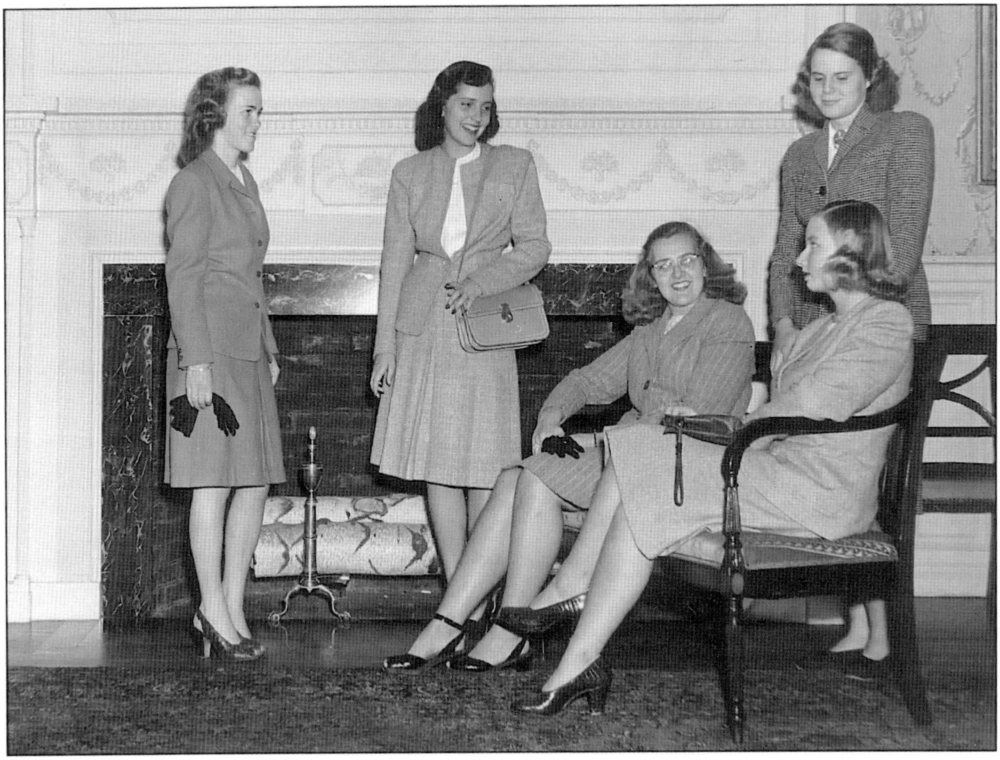

A Family Tradition. Generations of a family made their way to Bradford. Each year, the public relations office took note of all the daughters, granddaughters, sisters, and nieces in that year's group of freshmen. In the front parlor, from left to right, are Elizabeth Hendee, Nancy Sanders, Elizabeth Jenney, Patsy Hemingway, and Mary Altmaier—all freshmen in the Class of 1947 who were daughters of graduates.

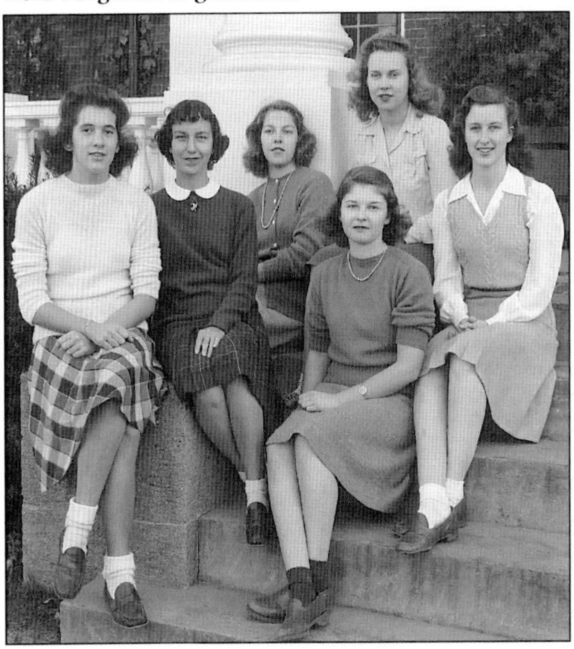

Boston Area Students. Students from Greater Boston pose in front of Academy Hall for a publicity shot. They are, from left to right, Anne Favinger '42, Jane Blish '43, Aileen Chadwick '42, Louise Stevens '43, Kathryn Cummin' 43, and Ruth Kingman '42.

Prof. A. Elizabeth Weber, Physical Education. Betty Weber joined the faculty in 1944 and by the time she retired in 1978, was the most senior of Bradford professors. Weber had a B.S. in education from Tufts and an M.Ed. from Massachusetts State College at Salem. She was appointed head of the Physical Education Department in 1949, which made her responsible for all classes in physical education and all athletic teams. The department also included the dance program. At her retirement, Weber was granted emeritus status and became the first faculty member to be awarded the Dorothy Bell Medallion. In this 1965 photograph, she leads a class in a lacrosse lesson.

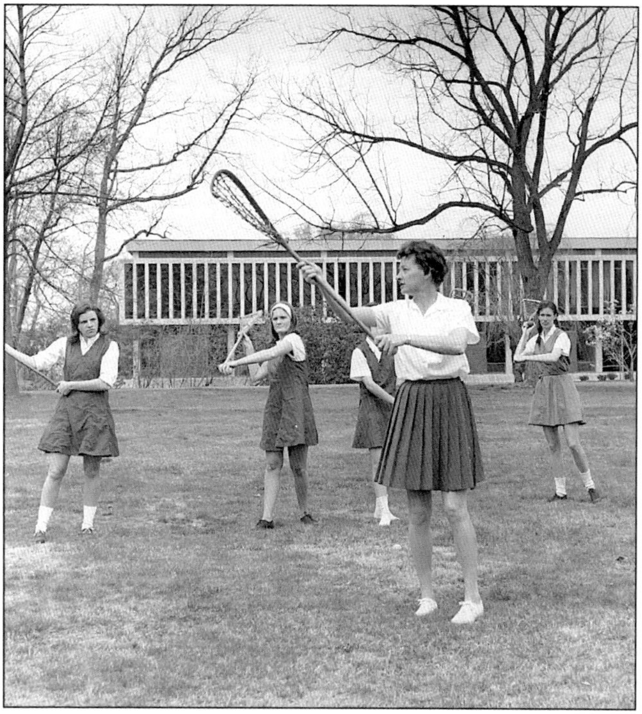

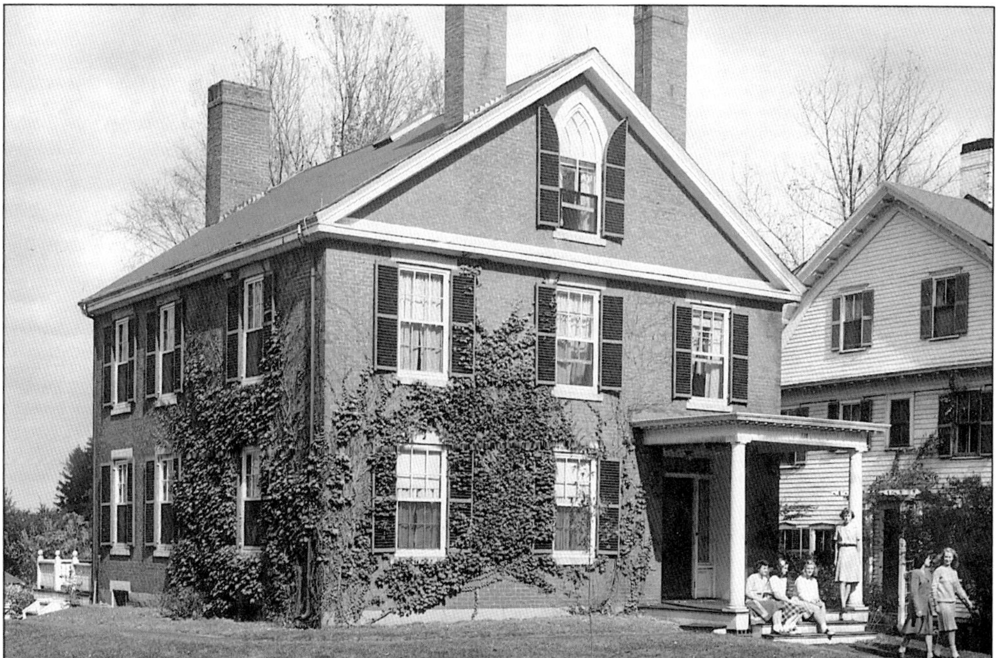

Hatch House, South Main Street. Mary Hatch, Class of 1877, lived in her family home, an 1820s Greek Revival house, at the corner of South Main and South Prospect Streets. After retiring from teaching in the Bradford public schools, Mary served as alumnae secretary at Bradford. The college acquired her house in 1939, after her death. Hatch House opened as a freshman house in 1940 and continued to be used until the Tupelo dormitories were built in the 1960s.

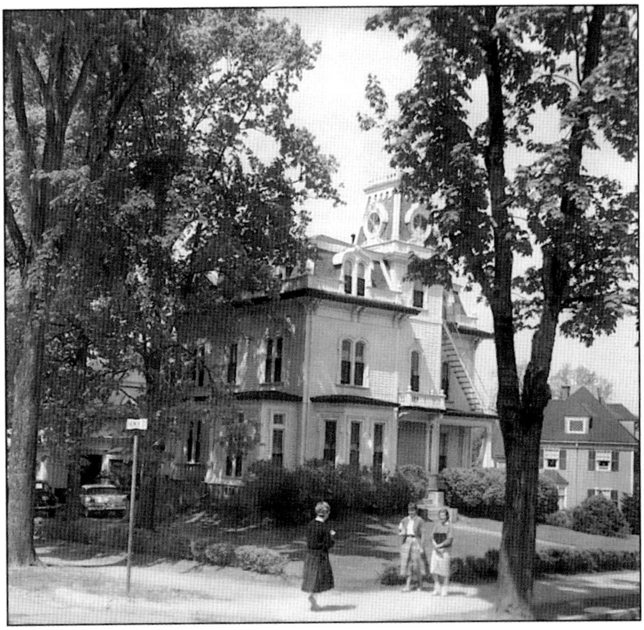

The Johnson House (Albert Laburton Kimball Home). Between 1920 and 1924, Principal Marion Coats tried an experimental "Junior Bradford" as a feeder school for the academy. The Kimball House, at the corner of South Main and Chadwick Streets, was acquired for this purpose. The experiment was short-lived and the house was turned, first, into faculty housing and, later, into rooms for the school domestics. In 1945, the house became a dormitory for college freshmen and was renamed Johnson House in honor of 19th-century principals Abby and Annie Johnson.

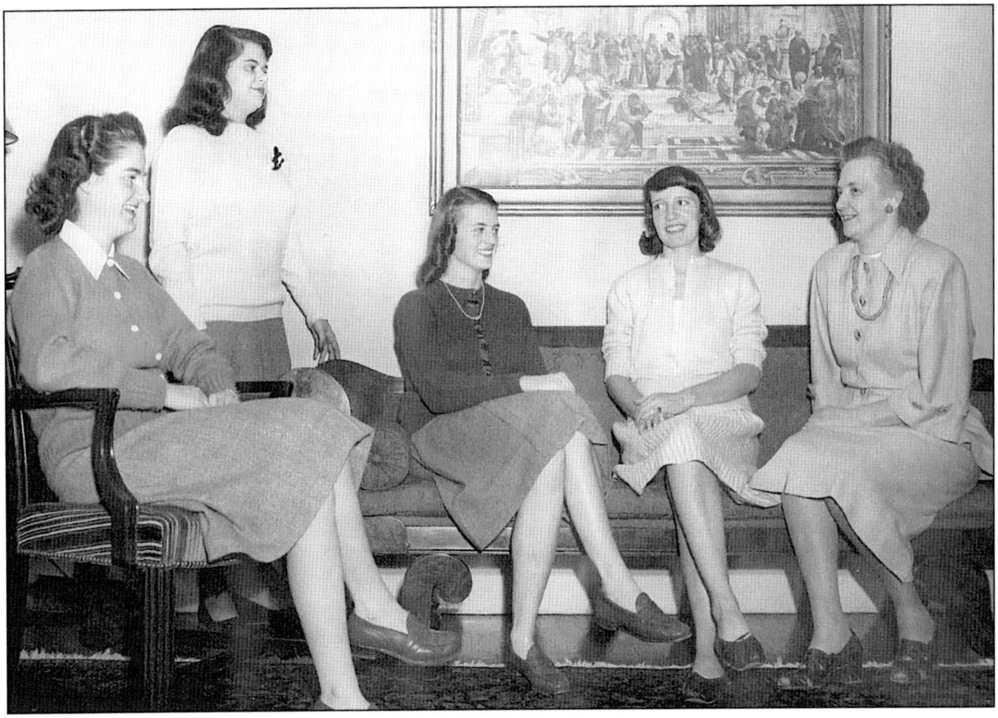

President Bell and Students. Dorothy Bell, right, entertains some students, whose hair and clothing styles suggest that the photograph was taken in the mid-1940s. When the east wing was added to Academy Hall in the 1890s, a suite of rooms was set aside as living quarters for the head of the school. Except for Dr. Denworth, who kept rooms in the west wing accessible by a spiral staircase from her office, all principals and presidents used the east-wing suite until a house was provided. The president's office was in the west wing, in an area that had originally been used as a limited gymnasium.

Three

THE FIFTIES

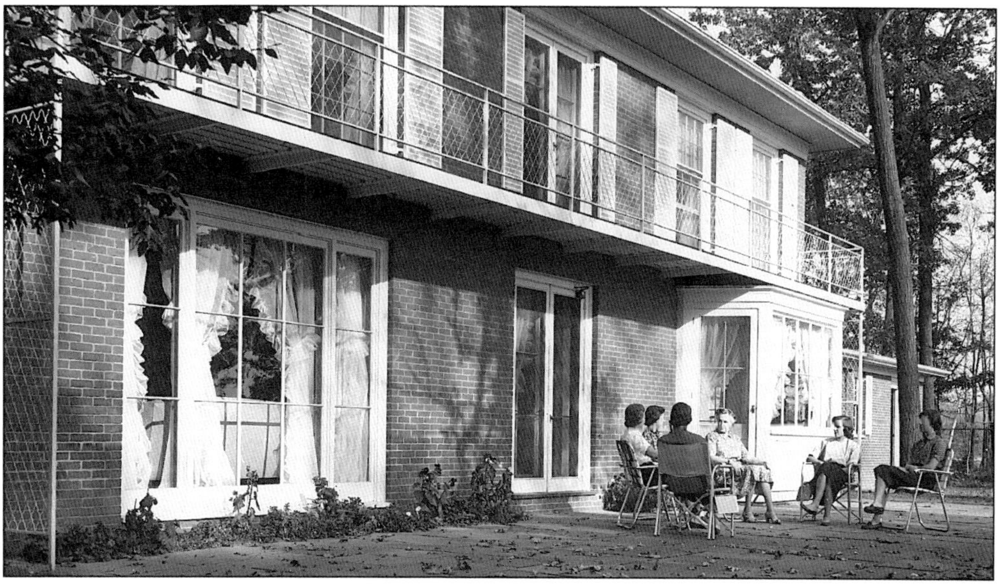

The President's House. The subject of a separate residence for the head of Bradford had first been broached by Principal Laura Knott. Despite her repeated plea, the trustees did not concur and the school's leaders continued to live in rooms in Academy Hall, except for a brief period when Marion Coats used a rented bungalow near the campus. The Coats House was used as the summertime residence. A major fund drive was undertaken in 1953 to commemorate Bradford's sesquicentennial with the goal of adding additional buildings. The President's House was the first building to be constructed. It was designed by alumna Laura M. Cox '17 and placed at the far end of the old picnic grove.

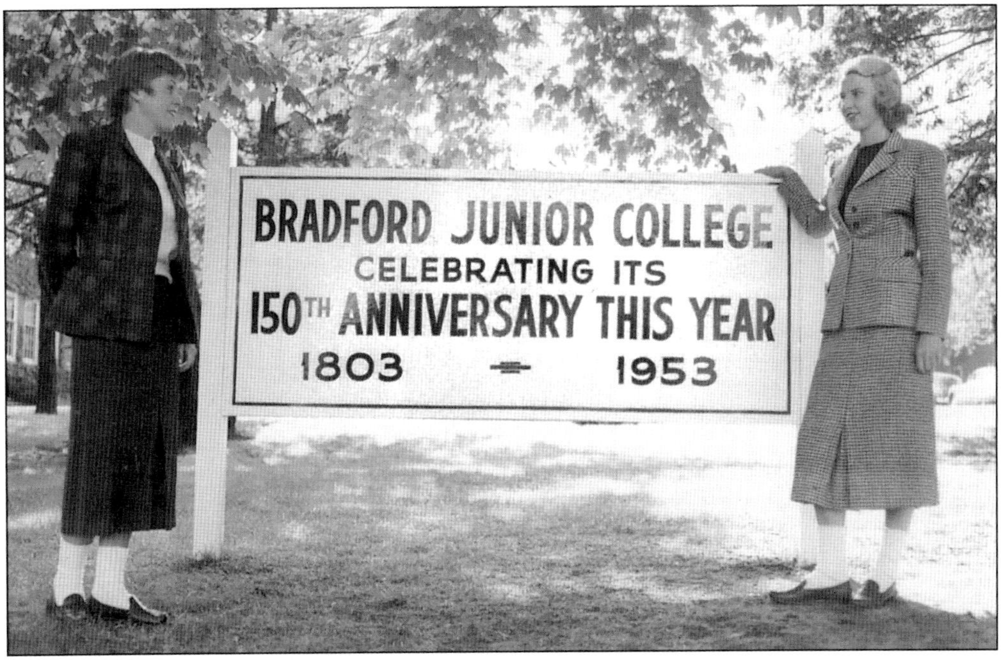

The Sesquicentennial. Bradford celebrated its 150th anniversary in the academic year 1952–53. The year was highlighted by three special ceremonies: a convocation in October, a Founders' Day observance in March, and a birthday party during June Commencement weekend. The constant theme through the entire series of events was the ties between Bradford and the local community.

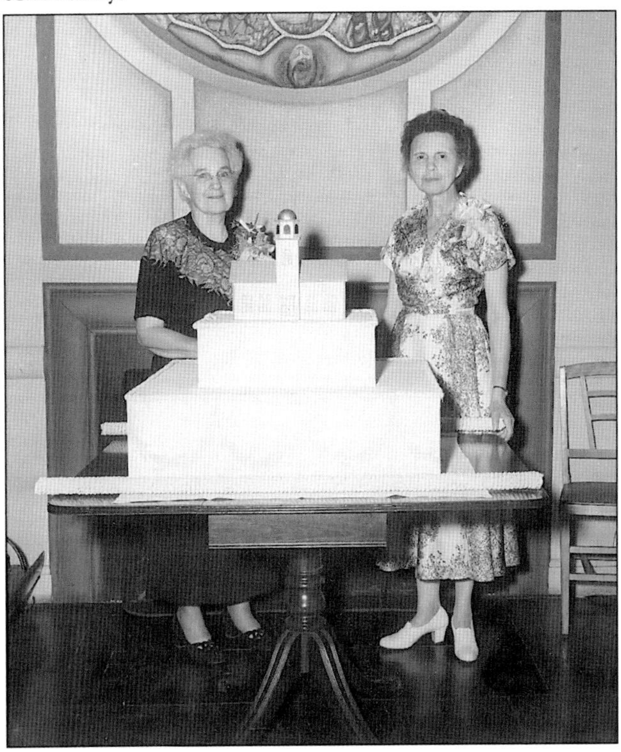

Former Leaders Return. A feature of 150th celebration was the return to campus of its only living ex-heads. (Laura Knott had died four years earlier.) Marion Coats, left, principal from 1918 to 1927, became the first president of Sarah Lawrence College after leaving Bradford. She returned to Bradford to serve as interim dean in 1950–51 and then retired with her husband Clifford Graves in the Haverhill area. Dr. Katharine Denworth, right, head of Bradford from 1927 to 1939, joined the faculty of the State Teachers College, West Chester, Pennsylvania, from where she retired in 1954. She died in 1984.

Dr. Dale Mitchell. Dr. Mitchell, right, had a long and productive career at Bradford, one in which he was called upon to play many parts. He arrived at Bradford in 1931, with a Ph.D. from Cornell, to teach English. He served as interim president in 1939–40, director of publications from 1943 to 1945, and dean of the college from 1946 to 1950. He taught until 1966, served on the library staff for a year, and retired with emeritus status. Mitchell updated Jean Pond's history *Bradford: A New England School* for the sesquicentennial. He is shown with President Bell at the 1956 commencement, for which he was the principal speaker. He died in 1981.

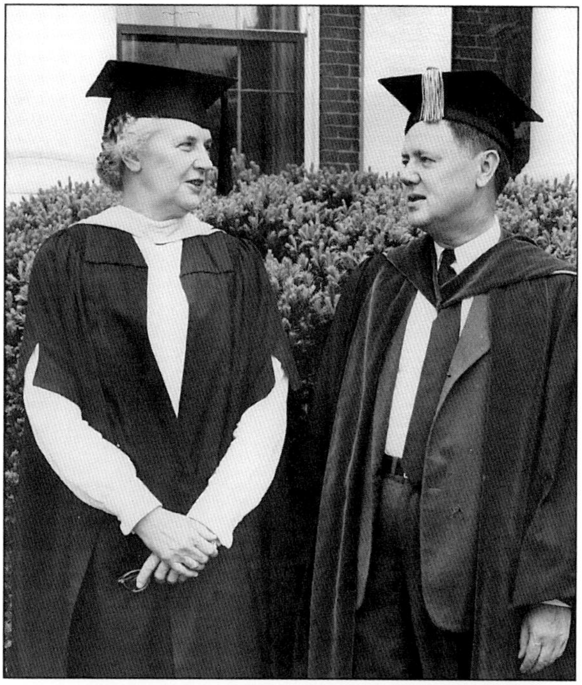

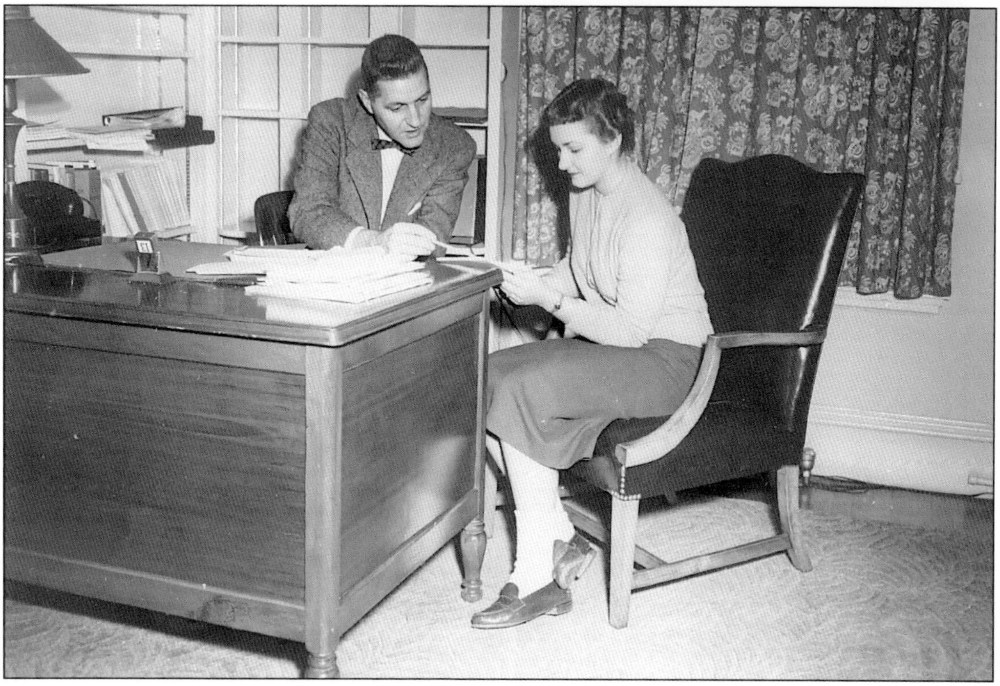

Dean Ferry. Dale Mitchell's successor as dean of the college was Frederick C. Ferry Jr. Ferry served in that position from 1951 to 1956. He had an M.Ed. from Harvard. During his tenure as dean, the college acquired a fine Tuscan Villa-style house at the corner of Chadwick and South Elm Streets as a residence for its deans; however, only Ferry and his successor lived there. Ferry left Bradford to become the president of Pine Manor Junior College. This photograph was taken in 1954.

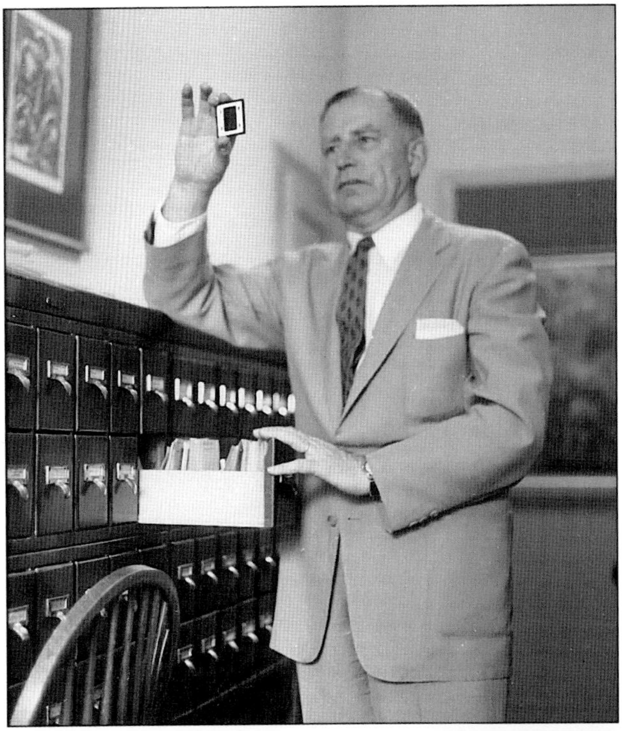

Dr. Nathan, Art History and Psychology. Walter Nathan had fled his native Germany in 1933. He had a Ph.D. from the University of Bonn, and came to Bradford in 1946. He is shown with the slide collection he developed and donated to the Art Department. He was stricken while on sabbatical in Greece in 1962 and died a few months later in Haverhill at the age of 55.

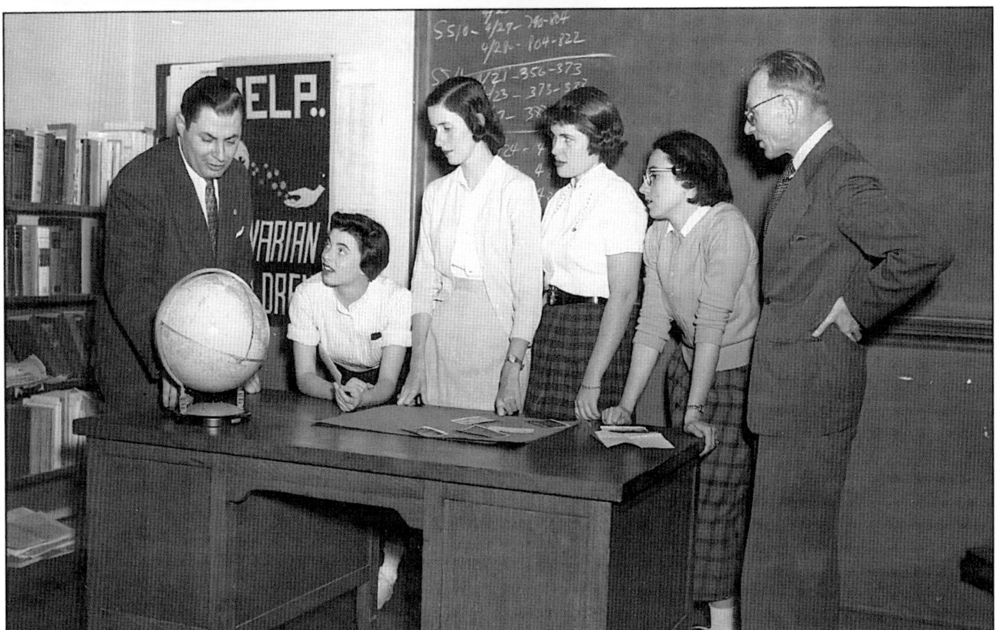

Dr. Weishaupt and Professor Knights. Lorenz Alois Weishaupt, right, with a Ph.D. from the University of Wurzburg, came to Bradford in 1946. He and his wife, Doris, had fled to Italy from Nazi Germany to escape persecution, but they were captured; they were on their way to Auschwitz when Allied bombing saved them. Weishaupt taught a variety of courses including German, mathematics, and art until his retirement in 1961. He was given the title of emeritus professor. Robert E. Knights, left, was an instructor in the physical sciences from 1952 to 1958.

Dr. Harold "Hap" Davis. Dr. Davis succeeded Bertha Clough as resident historian in 1944. His Ph.D. was from Columbia University. A quiet, retiring man, he is remembered each year at Bradford's commencement because the prize to the top student in history is named in his honor. Davis died of a heart attack in England in 1968 while on holiday.

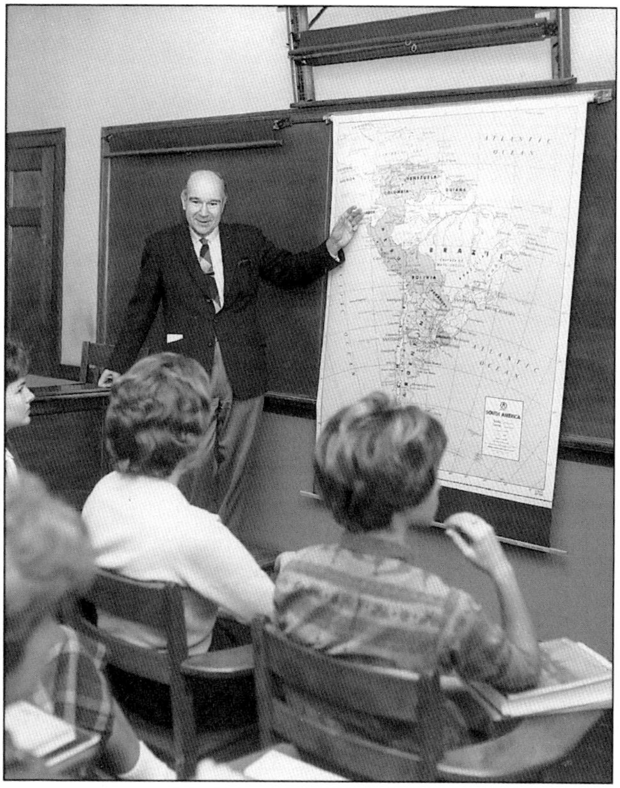

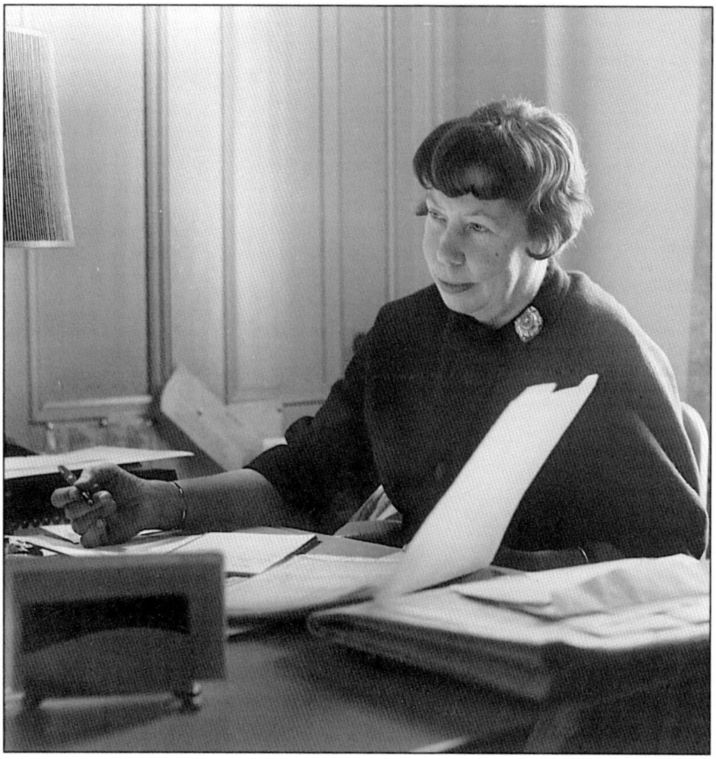

Dorothea L. Smart. Professor Smart arrived in 1951 to join Dr. Davis in teaching history and political science. She had an A.M. from the University of Pennsylvania. Smart was appointed assistant dean in 1957, dean of the college from 1966 to 1972, and dean of seniors until her retirement in 1975. She was awarded emeritus status. She died in 1998.

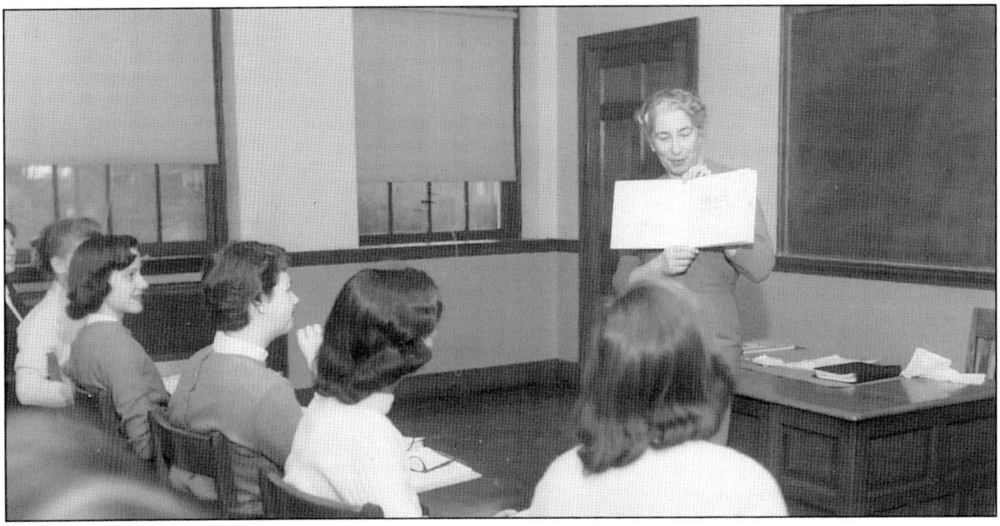

Flora Pinkham. Bradford started a cooperative preschool in 1951. Its director was Flora Pinkham, who was also an instructor in child psychology. She came to Bradford in 1950 with a B.R.E. from Boston University and taught until 1970 when Bradford discontinued the preschool. She became a professor emeritus and died in 1986.

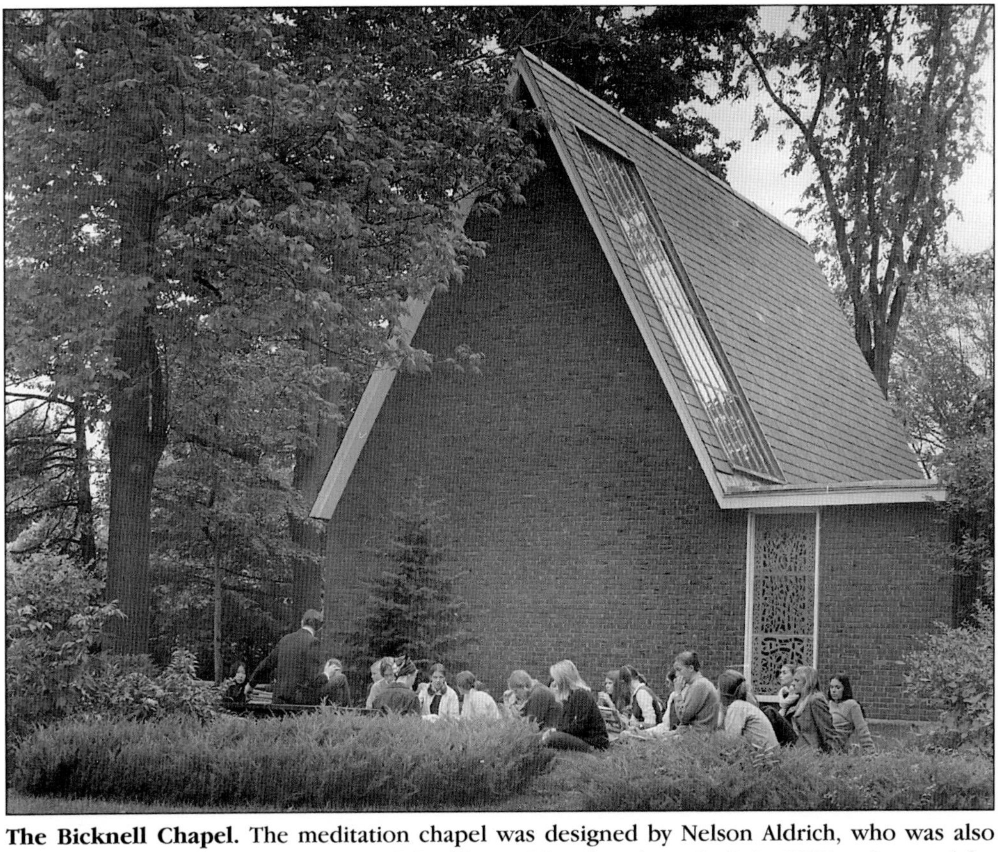

The Bicknell Chapel. The meditation chapel was designed by Nelson Aldrich, who was also responsible for the cluster houses and the library. The chapel was built in 1957 and named for Helen Grove Bicknell '17, who had been a trustee from 1948 to 1955.

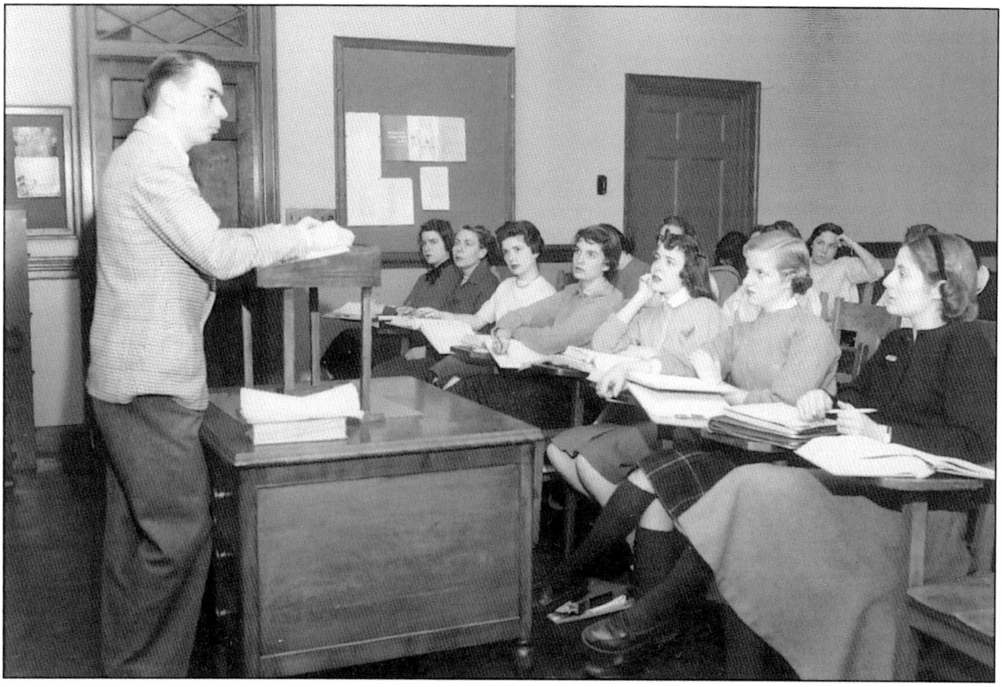

George E. Brown, English. Professor Brown succeeded Professor White. Robert Clarke White had been appointed by Dr. Denworth in 1935. He resigned in late August 1954, just before classes began. George Brown, with a recent M.A. from the University of Connecticut, got the call to replace him. He served as moderator of the yearbook and was a published poet. He resigned in 1968 to join the faculty at Ricker College in Maine.

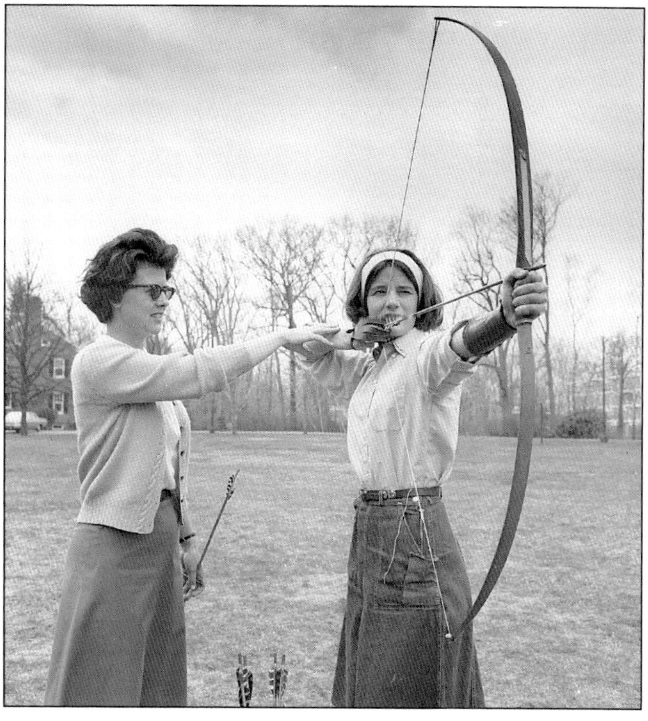

Prof. Ann Fowler Chesebro, Physical Education. In each decade of Bradford's history, there seem to be one or two professors added to the faculty who will dedicate their entire career to the school. In the 1950s, Ann Chesebro filled that role. She arrived in 1955 with a degree from Bouvé-Boston School of Physical Education, a school that had been founded by one of Bradford's pioneer physical education teachers. Chesebro taught and coached the women, and later the men, of Bradford in a wide variety of athletic activities. She retired in 1981 and became director of alumni activities.

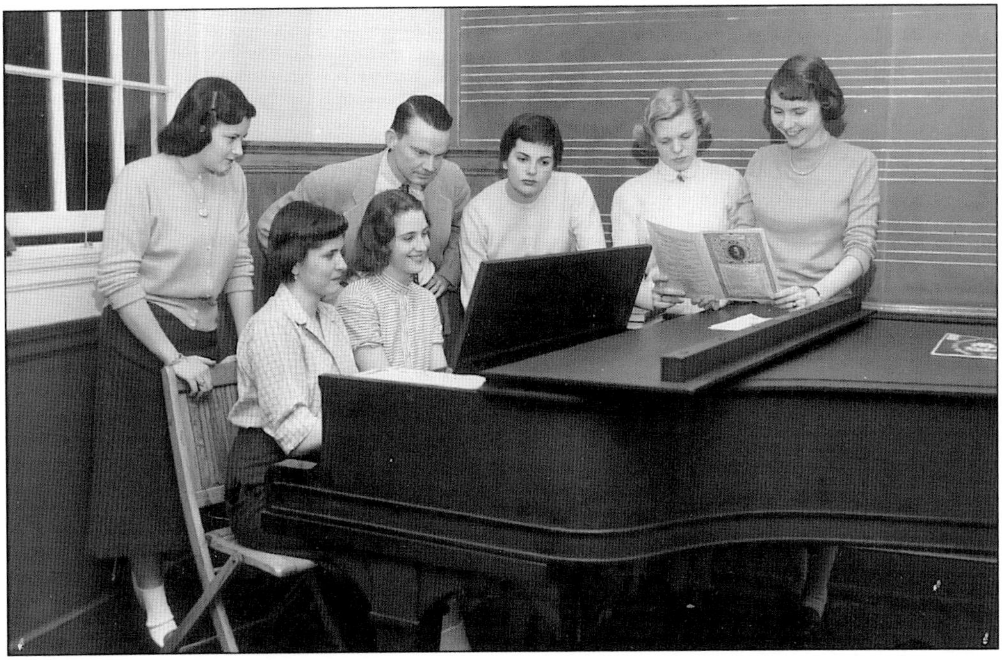

Prof. Glenn F. Welsh, Music. Professor Welsh was on the Bradford faculty from 1952 to 1957. He had a master's in music from Yale. He is pictured with two unidentified pianists and the 1954–55 choir officers, who are, from left to right, Cheryl Worthen; Nancy Barrott, president; Tony Upjohn, librarian; and Margie Bliss, vice president. The photograph was taken in the third-floor music room in Denworth.

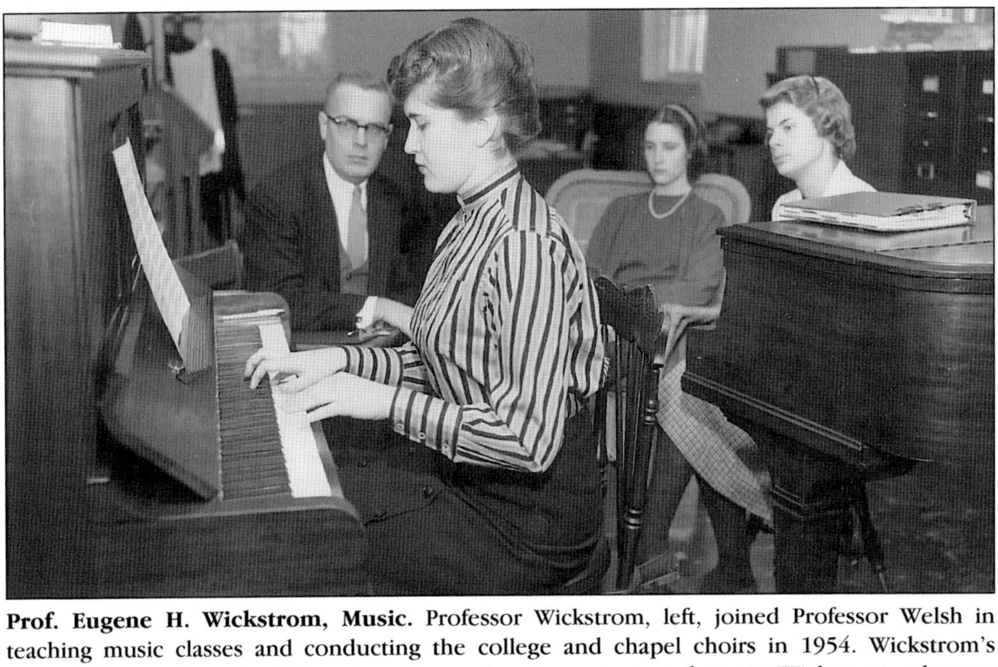

Prof. Eugene H. Wickstrom, Music. Professor Wickstrom, left, joined Professor Welsh in teaching music classes and conducting the college and chapel choirs in 1954. Wickstrom's master's degree from the University of Pennsylvania was in sacred music. Wickstrom, who was at Bradford until 1960, is shown with students in an advanced harmony class in the music room in Denworth.

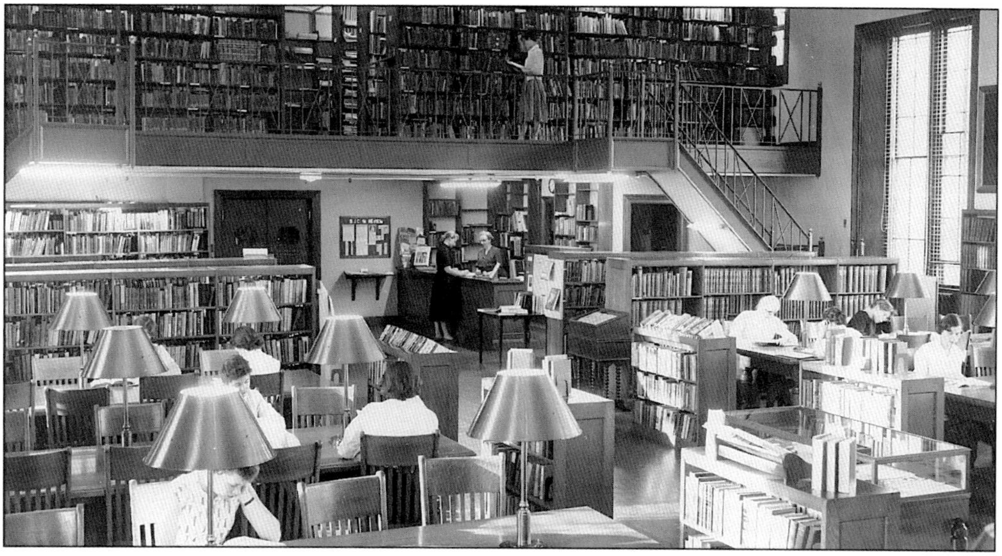

The Academy Hall Library. Bradford's second library was the former auditorium. The three rooms on the third floor were no longer adequate by 1939 and with the building of Denworth Hall, the auditorium was redundant. Eventually, this space had a third life as the dance studio, and a fourth life as dormitory rooms. The librarian behind the desk in the back is Mary Elvira Kauffmann, who served Bradford from 1942 to 1966.

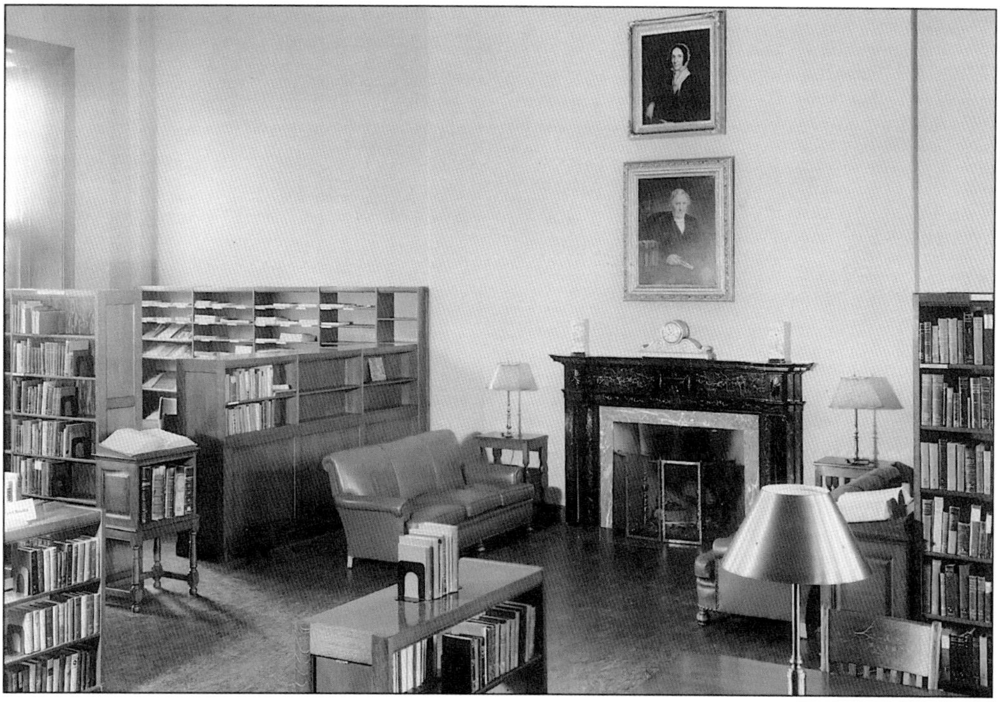

Inspiration from on High. Students using the library in the 1940s and 1950s could receive academic inspiration from the portraits strategically placed over the fireplace. They represent Bradford's pioneer leaders. The upper portrait is of Abigail Carleton Hasseltine, preceptress and principal from 1815 to 1858. The lower portrait is of Benjamin Greenleaf, preceptor of the male division from 1814 to 1836.

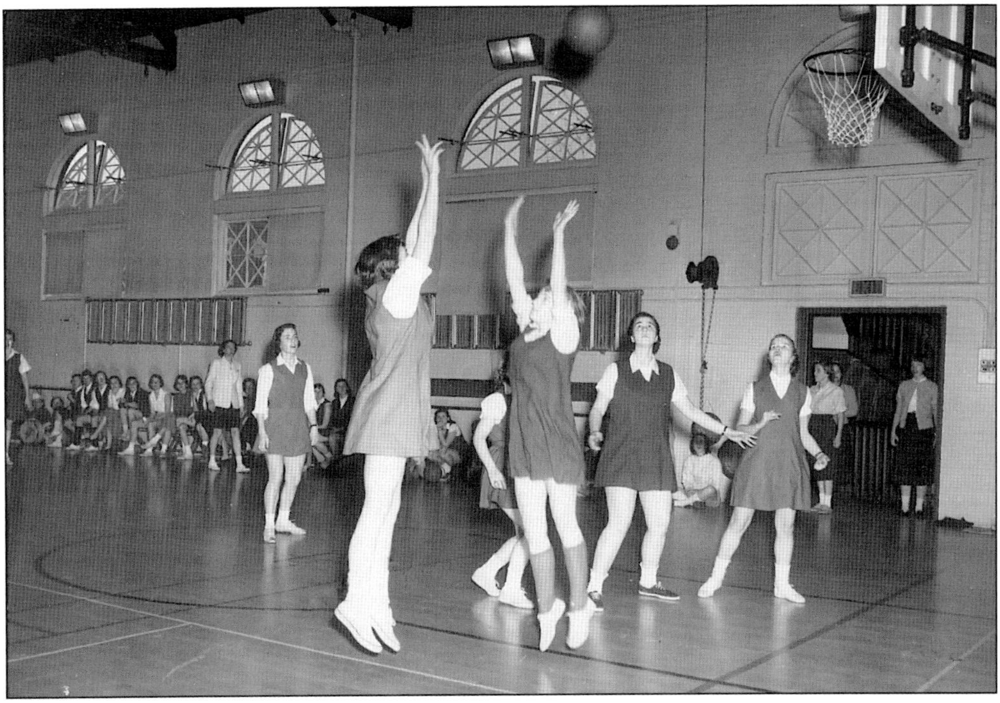

Basketball, 1954 to 1955. Old-style basketball, six to a side, was still being played in the 1950s. Three teammates stayed on one side of the court and three on the other side, because the rules makers did not think girls could handle full court play. Bradford's gym offered almost no sidelines, and energetic players risked running into a wall, a door, or the stage.

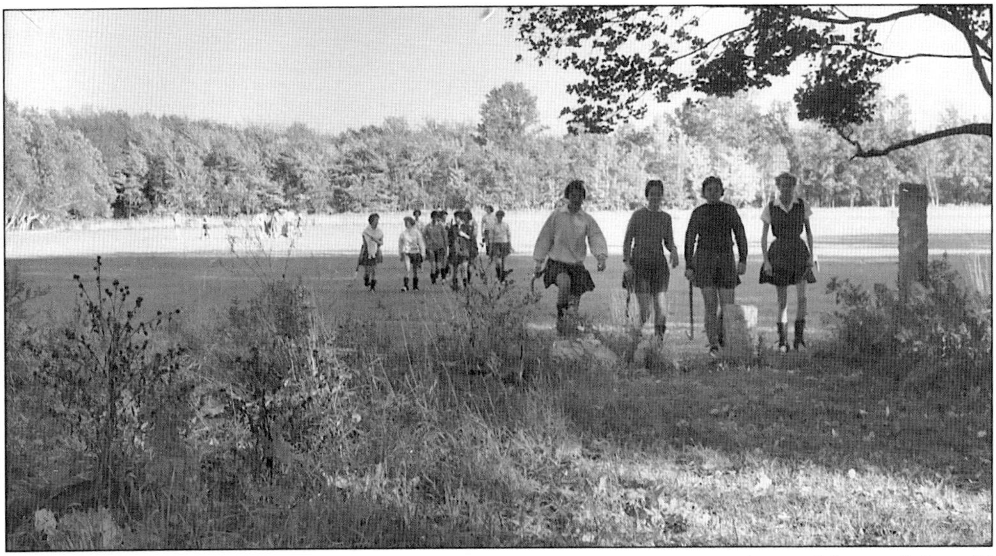

The Playing Fields. Principal Laura Knott acquired a 12-acre swamp located beyond the old picnic grove, at the end of what is now South Park Street, in 1909. Knott was determined that her girls develop into healthy women. It took five years of work to make the area usable, but it has served its purpose well, not only for the students but also for the local community, though its sogginess after heavy rain is a reminder of its swampy past. Here, field hockey players trudge back to their dormitories after a good workout.

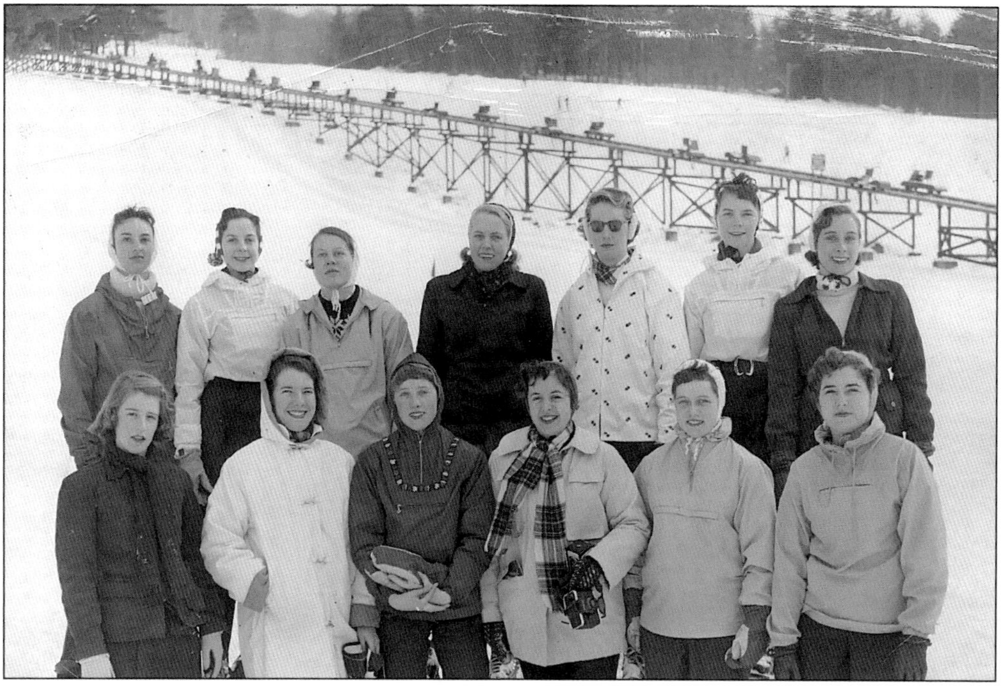

Ski Trip to Mount Cranmore. Each February, beginning in 1905, Bassett's Tours of Haverhill took groups of students to North Conway, New Hampshire, for "winter sports." By the 1950s, the ski trails in northern New England had become easily accessible and the rules on weekend visits liberalized, allowing the students freedom to make their own arrangements. The last organized ski trip by Bassett's was held in February 1954.

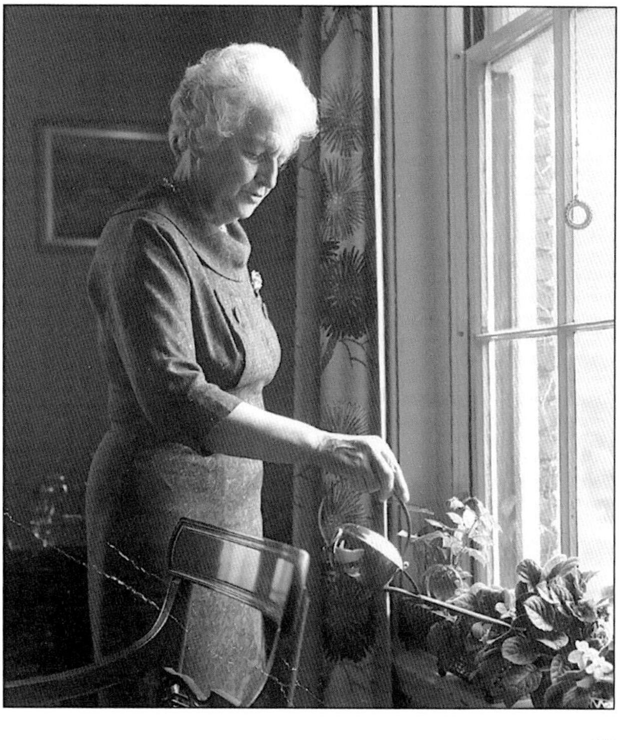

Susan Lacaillade, Receptionist. The first person to greet all visitors to Bradford from 1941 to 1973 was Susan T. Lacaillade. Her office was immediately off the entrance to Academy Hall. In the late 1960s, she also handled the switchboard, whose addition was a sign of Bradford's constant expansion.

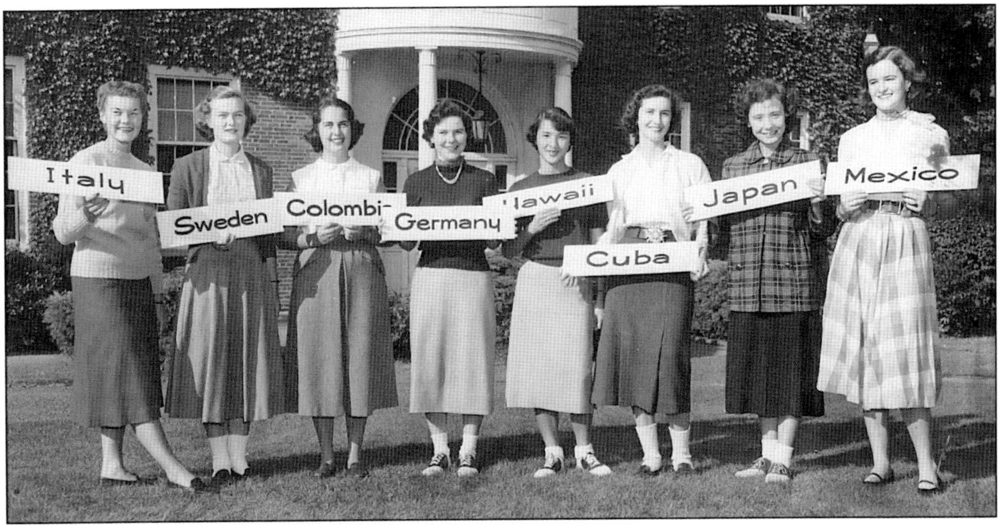

Bradford's International Students. Bradford presented a very homogeneous face during the middle of the 20th century. However, internationalization was a major goal of Pres. Dorothy Bell. Bell invited guest lecturers and visiting faculty from abroad, made study abroad at Reid Hall in Paris possible, and encouraged foreign students to attend the college. In addition, Bell created and taught a world literature course. These foreign students posing with the name of their homeland were enrolled at Bradford in 1952–53. They are, from left to right, Christina Mazzarrini '53, Ingrid Ehrnberg '53, Elvira Carmen Saenz, Margaret Kuhlman '54, Corinne Kong '54, unidentified, unidentified, and Elizabeth Ann Marquand '54.

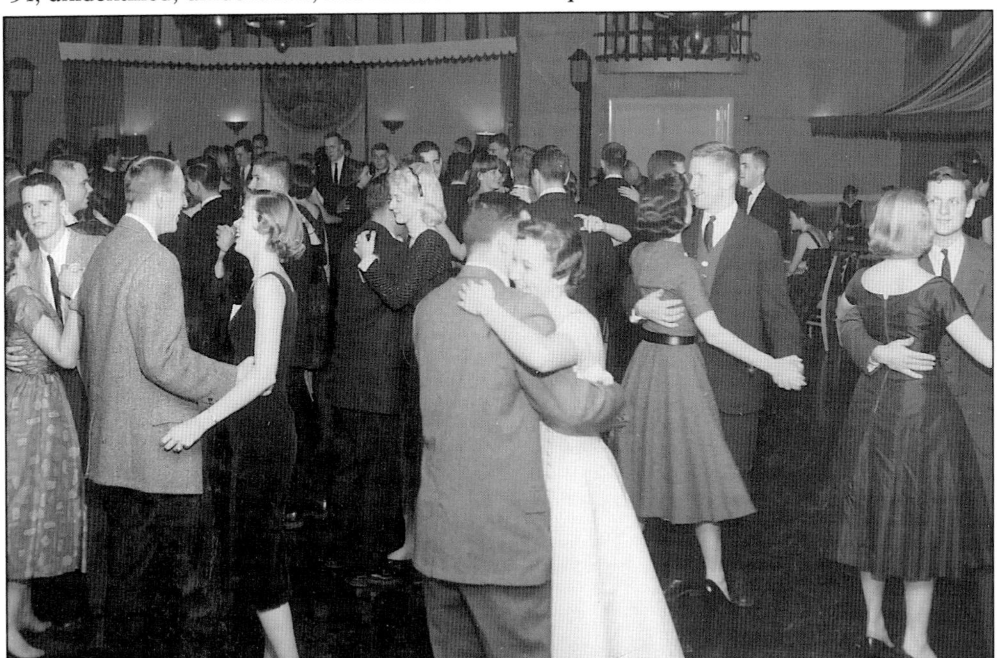

A Fifties Dance in the Rec Room. Lacquered and permed hair, dresses with waists and full skirts on the women; tweed jackets, close-cropped hair, and narrow ties on the men. Ah, the conservative, proper, uptight mid-fifties! Patricia Khouri, Class of 1957, center, helps date this photograph.

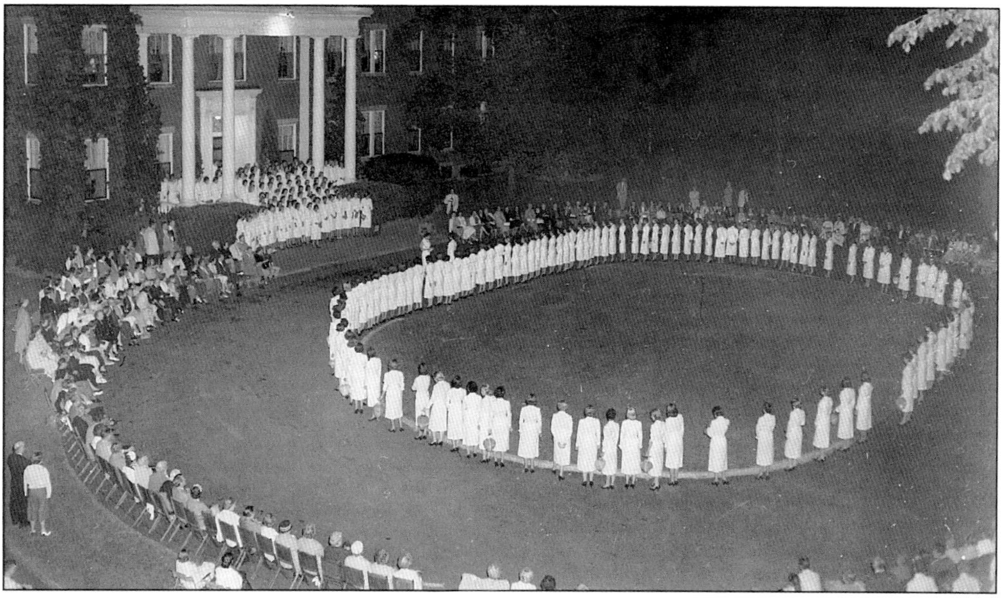

Class Night. For decades, arriving freshmen were taught that the oval green in front of Academy Hall was off limits to them. Only on Class Night, the day before graduation, were they finally permitted to step on the "sacred sod." It was all part of a charming ceremony. The seniors circled the "cookie," as the oval was called, while the freshmen filled the steps of Academy Hall. All were in their formal, required white suits. Each class sang to the other, and only at the end of the songfest did the seniors grant permission to the freshmen to join them.

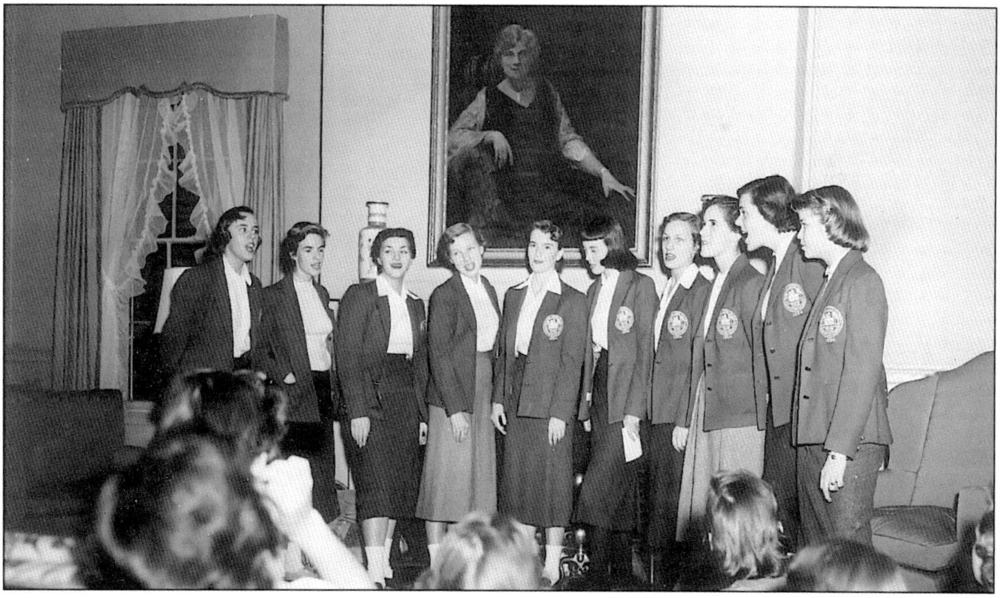

Tabooz—the 1954 Version. Members of the a cappella group are, from left to right, Susan Hunzicker '54, Joy Porter '55, Judy Hummel '54, Suzanne Shutz '55, Marian Green '55, Sally Redden '54, Dorothy Covell '55, Susan Lowell '55, Jane Logie '54, Harriet Hughes '54, and Betty Lackey '55. Missing are Nancy Lewis and Gertie Talcott. Each year Tabooz had six seniors and six freshmen to keep it a self-perpetuating group. The singers worked on their close harmonies on their own, without faculty assistance.

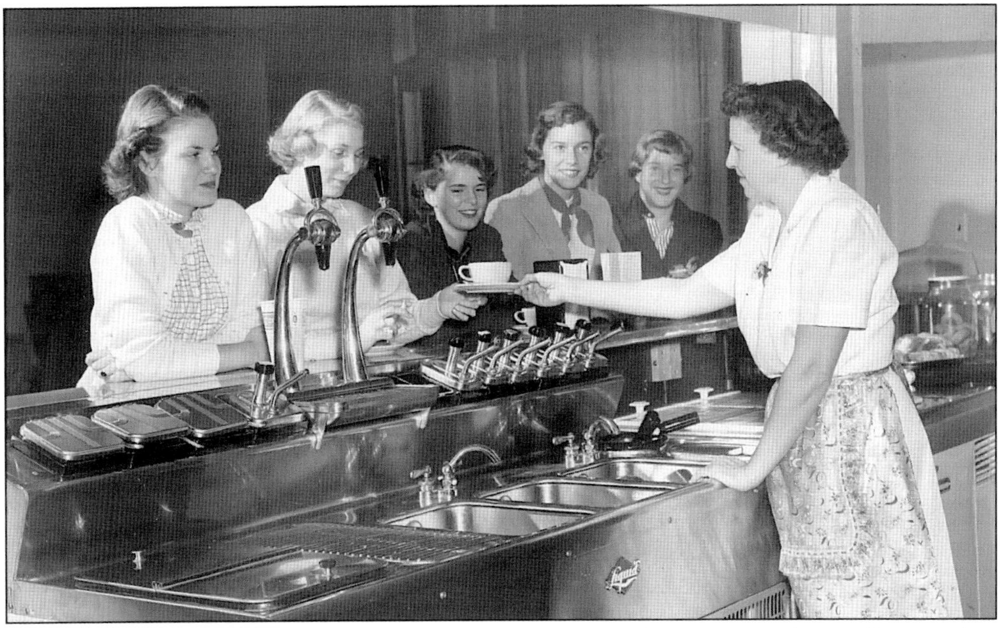

The Snack Bar. A number of new buildings were constructed during President Bell's term, but none was more welcomed by the students than the Snack Bar. The girls of the classes in the late forties initiated the fund-raising themselves. The building was designed by Laura M. Cox '17, a Boston architect, who also designed the President's House. It opened on Alumnae Day, June 10, 1950. The manager was Florence Kelly, shown here serving a cup of coffee. The Snack Bar offered treats such as freshly squeezed orange juice, hot cocoa, English muffins with peanut butter, and—on weekends—sticky buns, hot from the kitchen bakery.

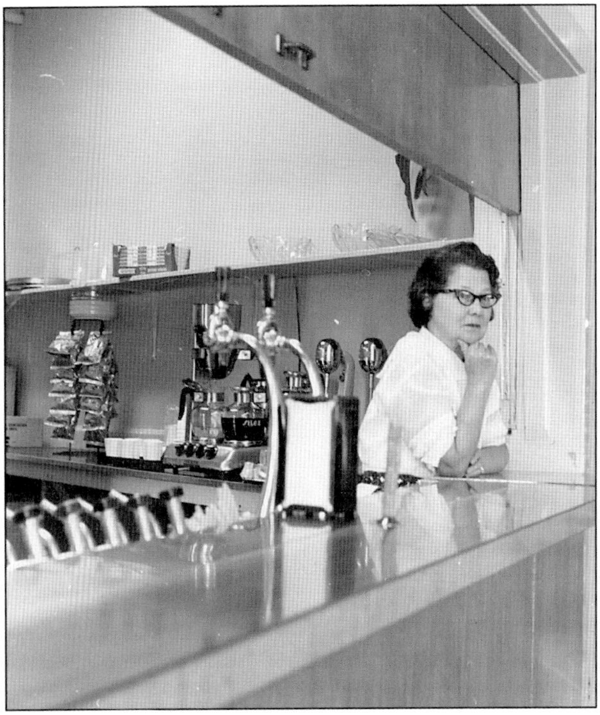

Gladys Bradshaw, Headwaitress. Bradshaw joined the house staff in the 1930s. As headwaitress, she was responsible for training the students who, under President Bell, were required to take turns serving their fellow students. She was the wife of chef Bernard Bradshaw. In later years, when waitresses were no longer in use, she helped to run the Snack Bar.

Four

The Sixties

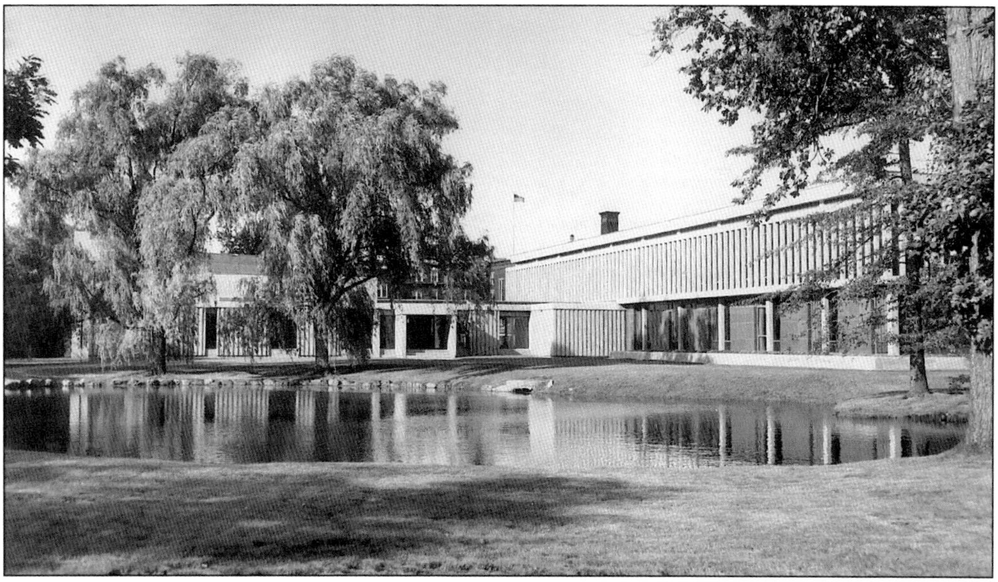

The Dorothy Bell Study Center. The decade of the 1960s carries a label of rebellion, riot, and great change. It is a misleading label—particularly when applied to a place like Bradford. Change and rebellion did come but not until very late in the decade, and never while Dorothy Bell was in charge! However, there was physical change early in the decade. New buildings transformed the campus. The Bell Center included, from left to right, Conover Hall, the Keller Foyer, the Carlson Art Wing, the Laura Knott Gallery, and the Hemingway Library. The building is in a Brutalistic modern style, quite at variance with the red brick front campus. The library and art wing were completed in 1964. Conover Hall and the Keller Foyer were added in 1966.

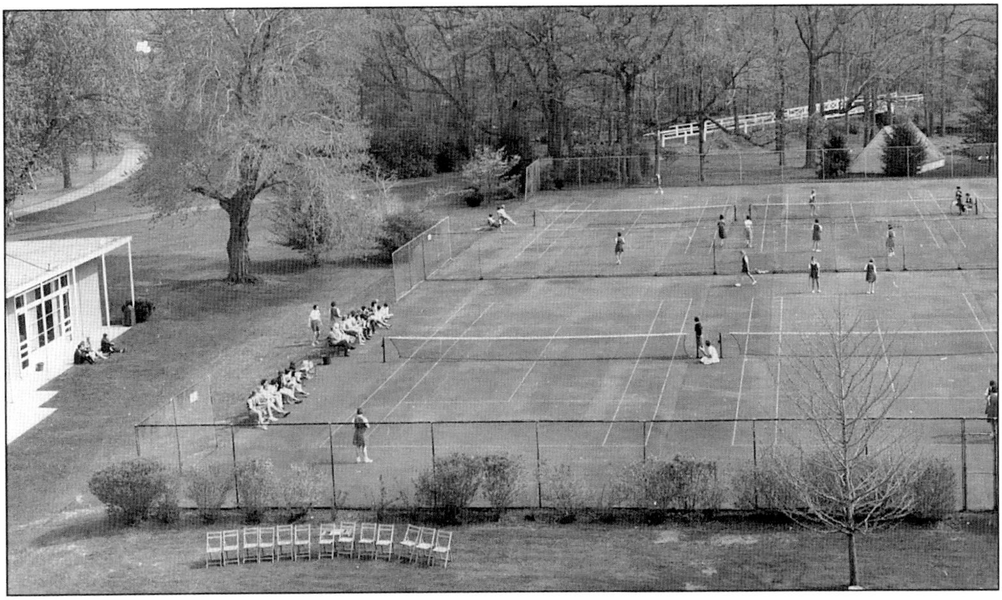

The Tennis Courts. This space by the Snack Bar, left, and Tupelo Pond was the site of the new Bell Study Center. When the center was built, it occupied the area of the back two tennis courts. The front courts were turned into lawns, which explains the flatness of that area. The tennis courts were relocated to the playing fields, but the former swamp was not congenial and the courts there had constant problems, making them unusable by the 1980s.

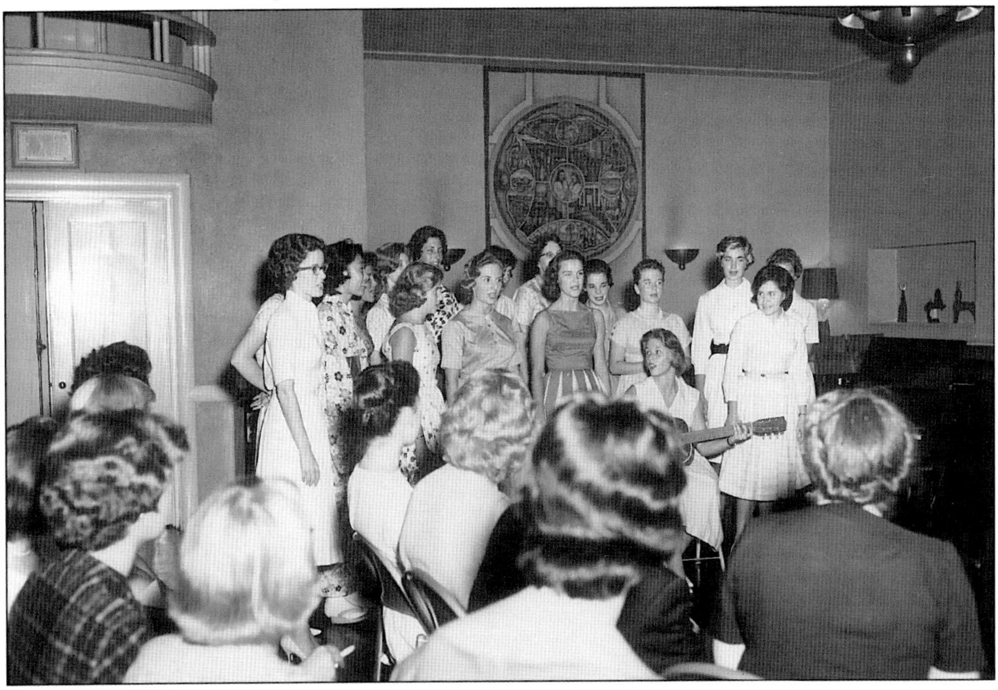

The Passports. Folk singing became very popular in the 1950s and early 1960s, perhaps as a balance to Rock 'n Roll. Bradford girls interested in folk and foreign song formed a new singing group, The Passports, in the early 1960s. Like the Tabooz, the Passports were self-directed. Both groups lasted into the 1970s.

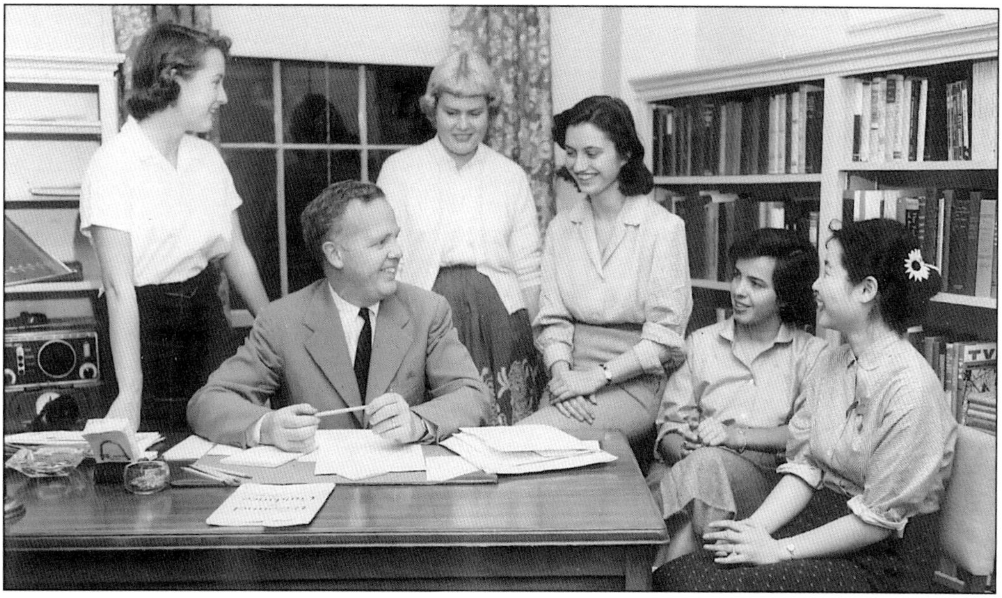

Dean Menand. Dr. Louis Menand III followed Frederick Ferry Jr. as dean of the college in 1956. Menand had a Ph.D. in history from Syracuse. He served as President Bell's right hand for ten years, until he left in 1966. Menand, who was very impressed by the English university tutorial system, introduced such a program to Bradford. Faculty and administrators offered a list of topics—there were 76 offered in 1968. Students could choose one topic on which to work in close association with a mentor.

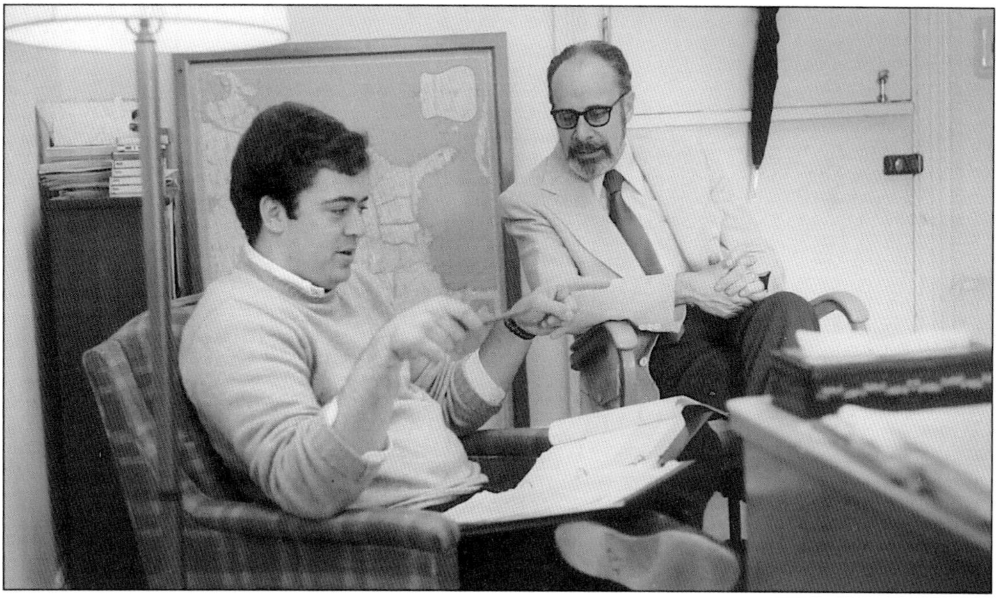

Prof. T. Downing Bowler. Professor Bowler, right, arrived at Bradford in 1959, after being a minister at the White Church on the Bradford Common. He taught religion and philosophy. He was a wise and beloved counselor who put his philosophy into action. He replaced Dorothea Smart as dean of the college in 1974. Bowler added admissions to his resume in 1977. After a sabbatical he decided to separate from Bradford and to go into business. Pictured with him is Tom Wilson, B.A., '76.

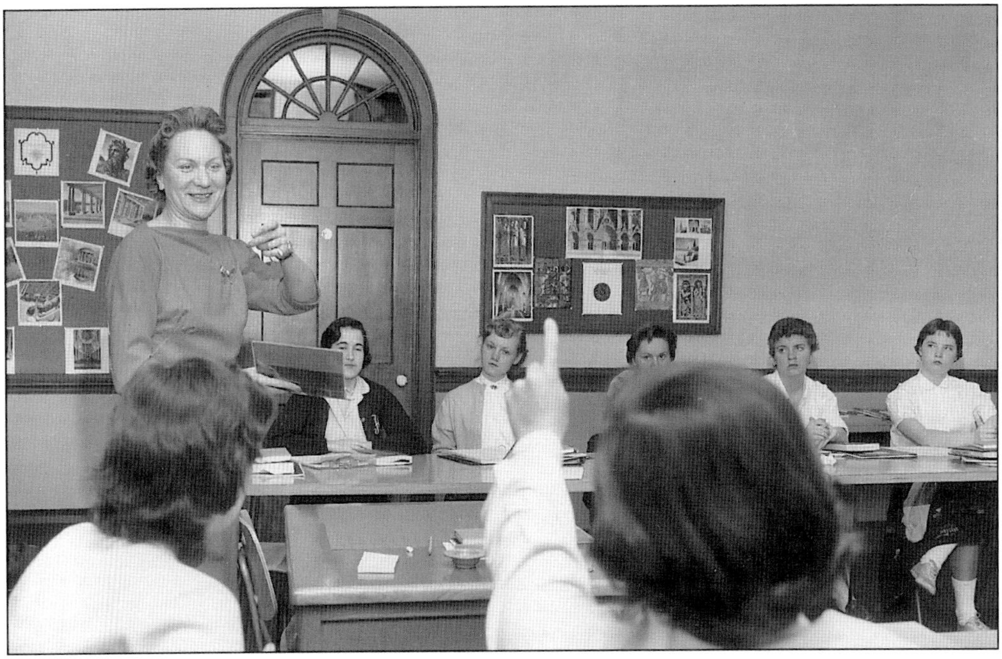

Mlle. Genevieve Wantiez, French. Professor Wantiez came to Bradford upon the retirement of Mathilde Boutron-Damazy in 1954. Wantiez had a baccalaureate and a licentiate from the University of Nancy, France. She is shown in Room 102 in Hasseltine, which was traditionally reserved for French classes. She left Bradford in 1971.

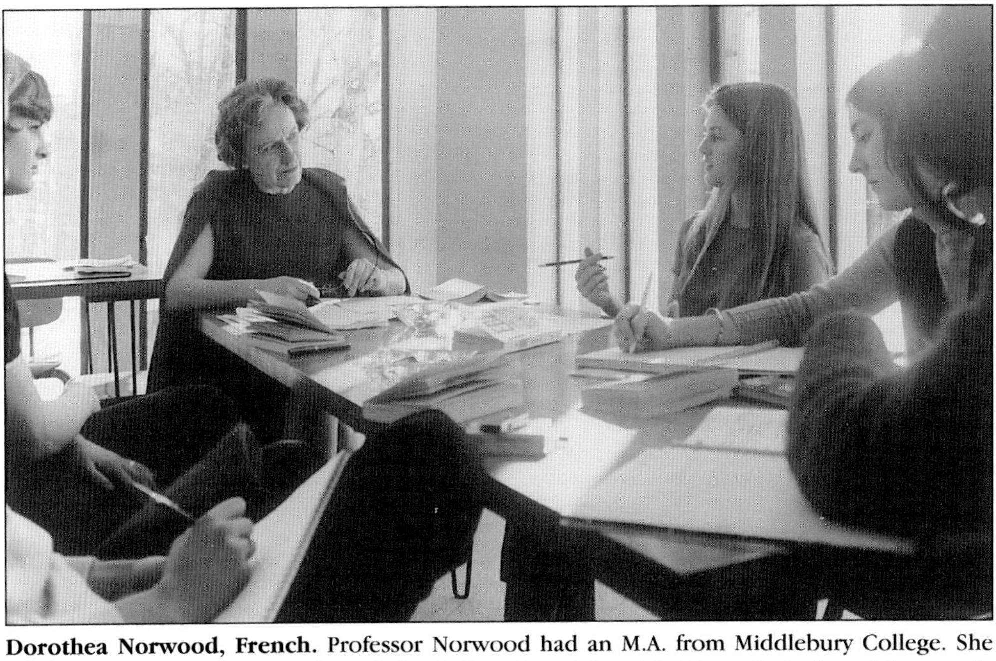

Dorothea Norwood, French. Professor Norwood had an M.A. from Middlebury College. She came to Bradford in 1957 and taught both French and Spanish. Her principal teaching was in French language and literature. She is shown with a class in Seminar Room D in the library. This was one of four rooms available in the library for the small classes that made Bradford a special educational experience. Norwood retired in 1975 as an emeritus professor.

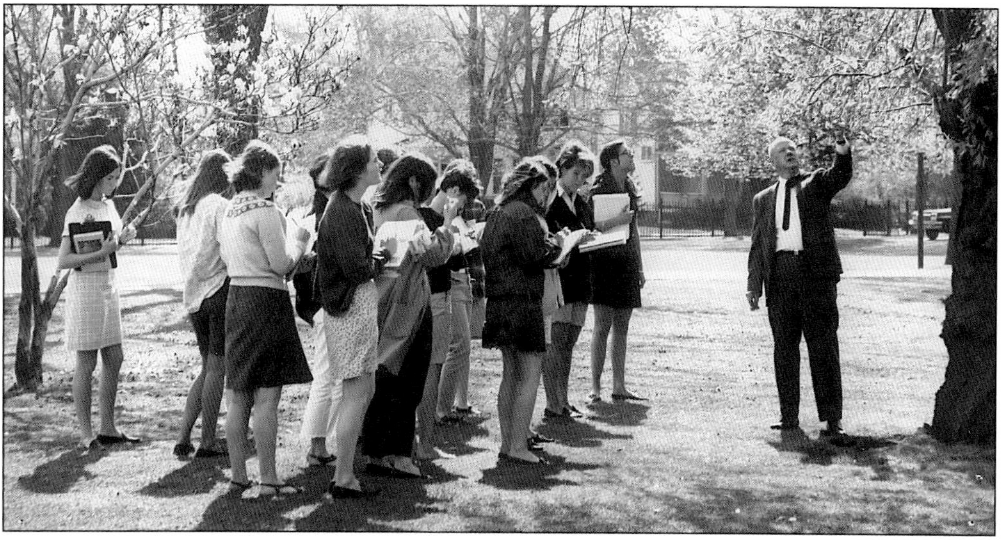

A Botanical Tour. Dr. Norman Sprague Bailey arrived at Bradford in 1956 to teach biology. He continued to do so until 1975. He had a master's from Boston University and a Ph.D. from Harvard. This photograph, taken in the late 1960s, shows Bailey taking his class on a tour of the many rare botanical specimens on campus. In the 1870s, Samuel Warren, a trustee, had given the academy a great variety of plantings, including over 300 trees, such as hawthorns, Japanese gingkos, and tulip trees, which were then rare in New England. Bailey retired to Swans Island, Maine, as professor emeritus.

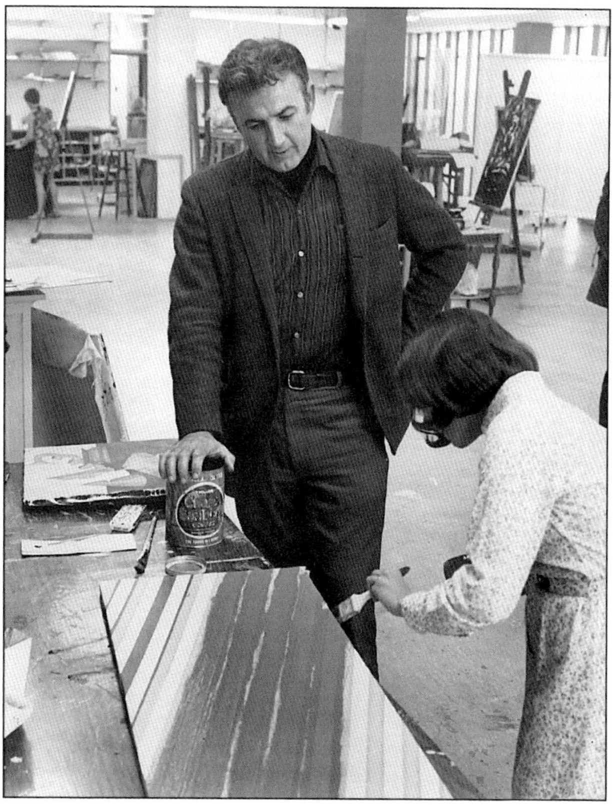

Charles Douglas Huebler, Art. Doug Huebler replaced Francis Merritt in 1957. He possessed a M.F.A. from Michigan and was considered one of America's leading conceptual artists. In 1957, he was the only studio artist on the faculty. In 1964, when the art program moved into the new Carlson Art Wing, which he had helped to design, there were three artists on staff. Huebler went to California Arts School in 1974 but returned in 1981 to give the commencement address. He died in 1997.

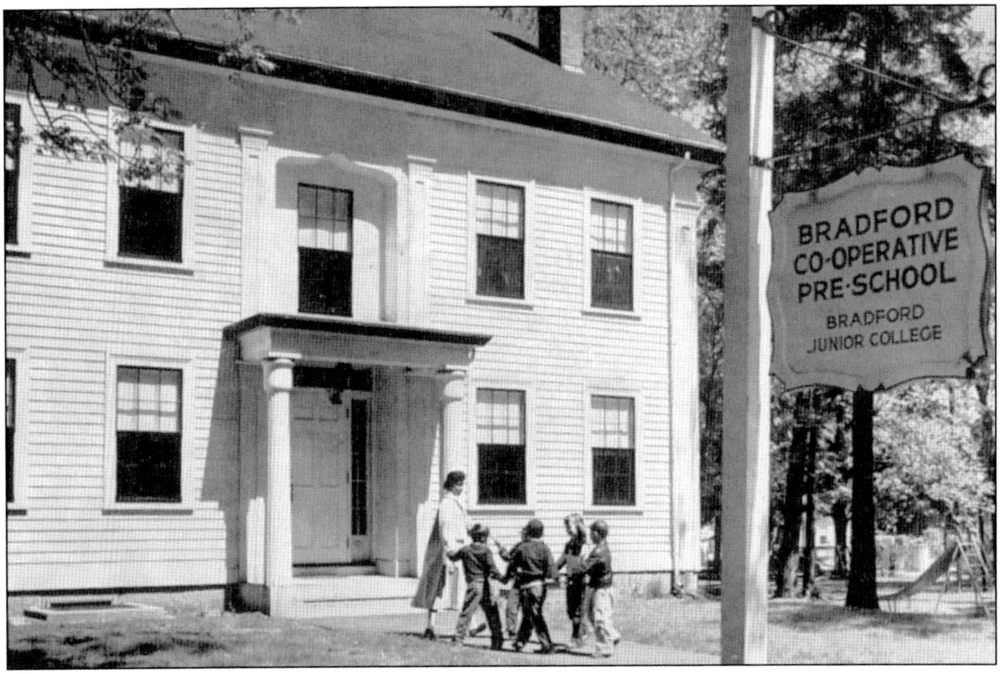

Bradford Co-operative Pre-School. The Daniel Kimball House on South Main Street, not to be confused with the Kimball Tavern or the Alfred Laburton Kimball House, was acquired by Bradford in the late 1940s. It was put to use in 1951 as a cooperative preschool for local children. The 1846 Kimball House was designed in a Greek Revival style with Egyptian Revival pillars. This was not Bradford's first use of the house. From 1851 to 1856, girls boarded here, before Academy Hall was built.

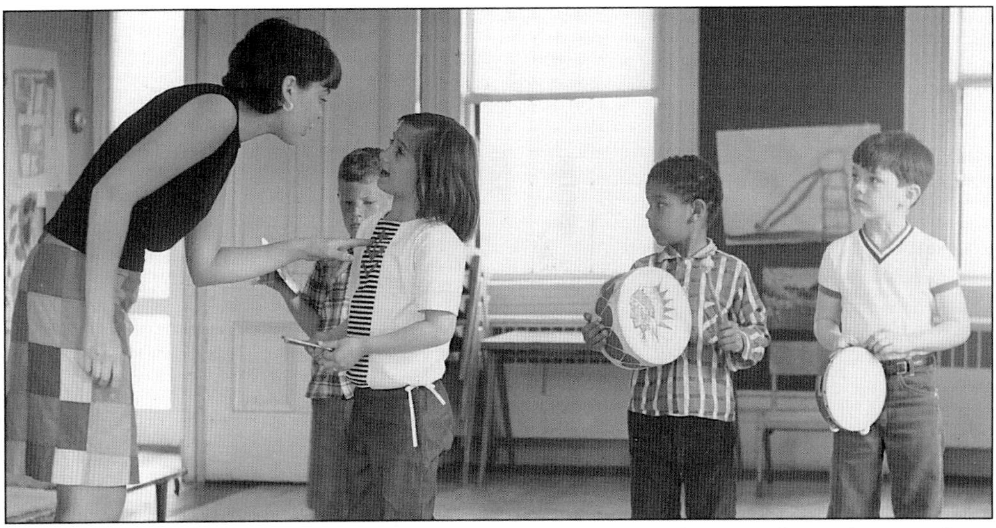

Student and Preschoolers. The preschool served as a learning laboratory for students studying child development. It also brought the Bradford girls into closer contact with the community, since parents of the children enrolled were required to contribute their time to the running of the play school. When Bradford discontinued its child development courses in 1970, the preschool was turned over to the Haverhill Day Nursery, now the Haverhill Day Care Nursery and Kindergarten.

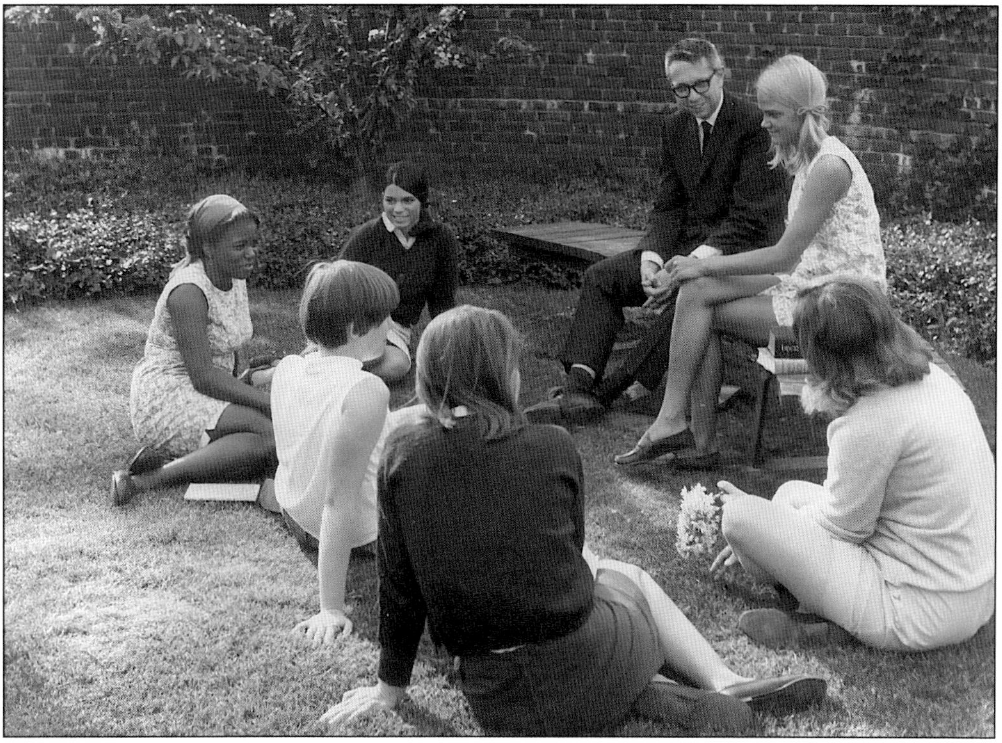

Dr. Matthew Melko, History and Political Science. Dr. Melko arrived at Bradford in 1959. He succeeded Dr. Franz Gross, who taught from 1953 to 1959. Melko achieved his degree from the London School of Economics and Political Science. He taught at Bradford until 1971 and then returned in 1974 as associate dean and director of the B.A. program until 1975. He is shown with his students in the chapel garden.

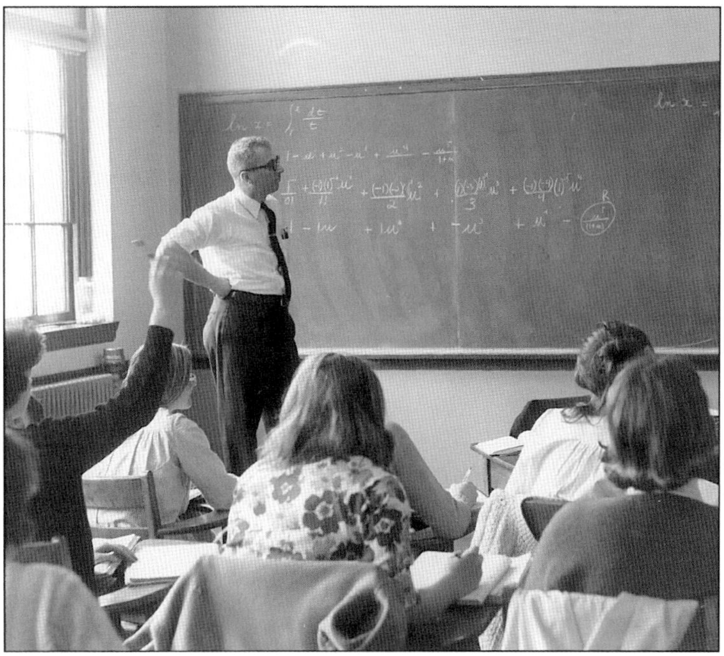

Prof. Lionel Poulin. Professor Poulin taught mathematics at Bradford from 1961 to 1973. He had a bachelor's and a master's degree from the University of Montreal and an M.Ed. from Harvard. Mathematics was an elective (only the tutorial was specifically required in the revised curriculum of 1970) and was principally for students interested in doing advanced work in social, behavioral, or physical sciences.

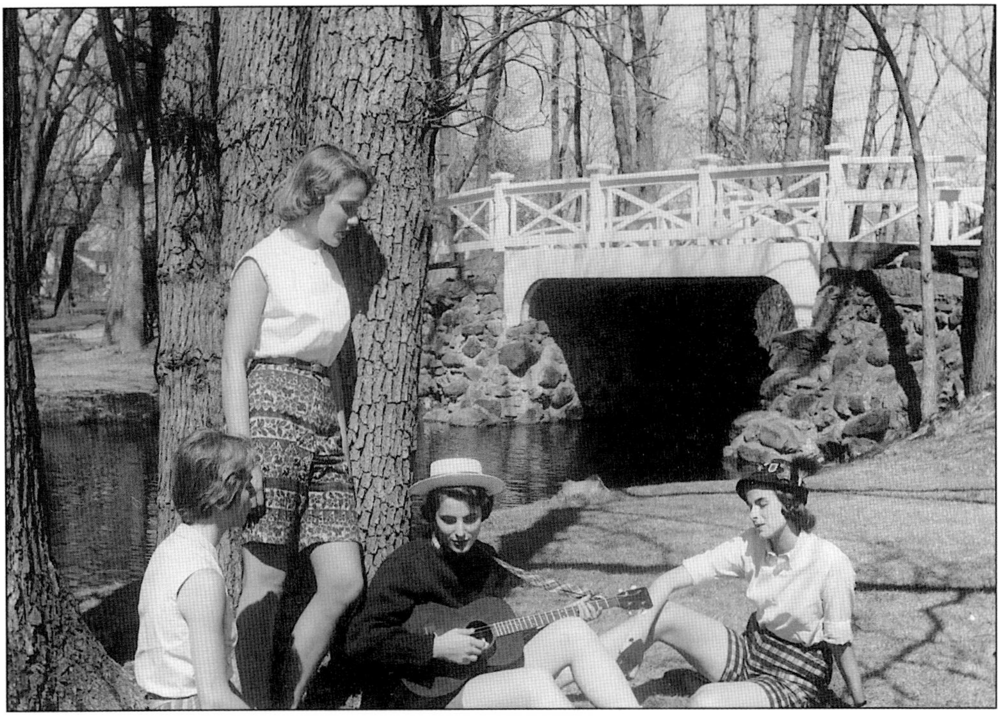

A Tranquil Moment by Tupelo Pond. Frances "Dee" Manning '60 strums her guitar by the banks of the lovely Tupelo. Her friends, in their colorful Bermuda shorts, seem quite wrapped up in the music and the moment.

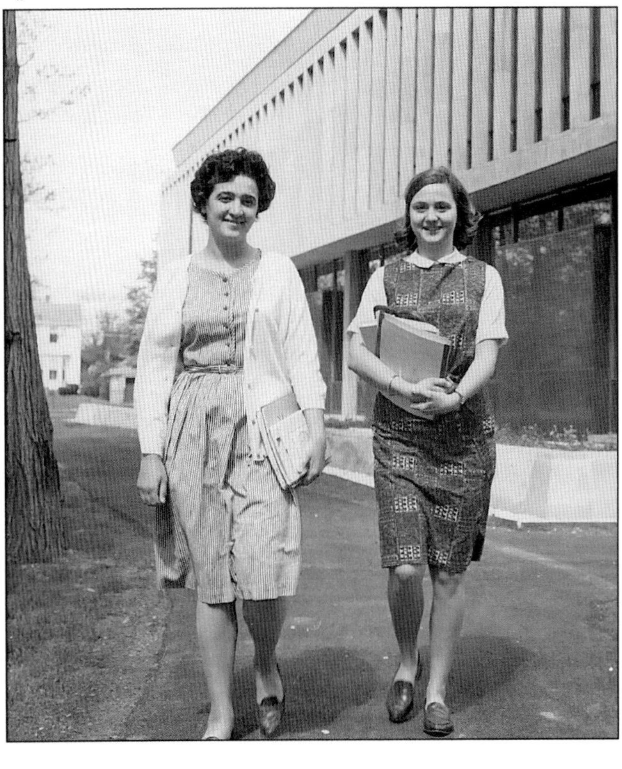

Rena Bizios and Barbara Zoukis, Class of 1964. Rena Bizios, left, and Barbara Zoukis were day students. Bizios, a native of Greece, lived with relatives in Haverhill. Zoukis lived near the college. They had the best of both worlds, fully involved in student life but free to go to nearby family homes in the evening. They were often invited to stay overnight with classmates in the dormitories. Bizios was a cousin of Prof. Jim Valhouli. Until the 1970s, there were never more than a few day students.

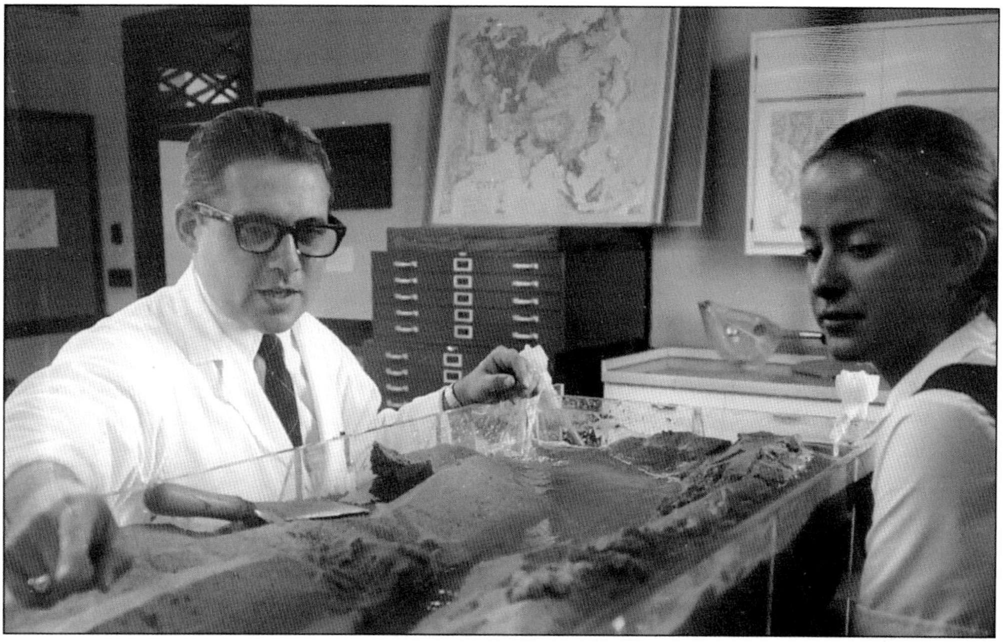

Prof. John Roberts, Geology and Geography. Prof. "Tony" Roberts began teaching at Bradford in 1963 and continued to do so until 1995. He had a master's in science from Penn State and did graduate work at Harvard. In addition to his geology and geography courses, he was also the first director of Bradford's Computer Center.

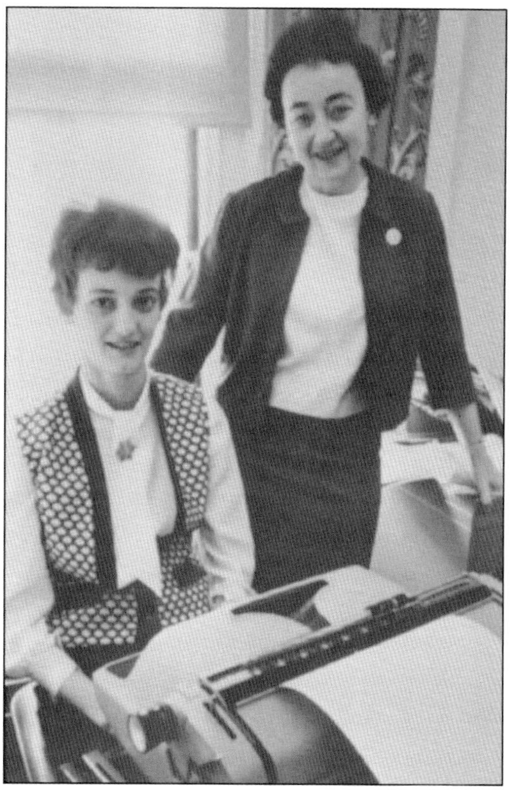

Connie Leighton and Judy Bologna. These two women were institutions at Bradford. Constance Leighton, right, came in 1947 to handle public relations. She was named assistant to the president in 1972. Technically, she retired to her home in Warner, New Hampshire, in 1980 but in reality, she continued to handle Bradford's publications until 1985. In that year she was awarded the Dorothy Bell medallion. Judy Bologna, left, came to Bradford in 1962 as a 22-year-old secretary. From 1968 to 1980, she was Leighton's assistant and then her successor. Since then, she has worn many hats, from director of financial aid to academic support adviser. She won the Bradshaw award in 1990 (see p. 122).

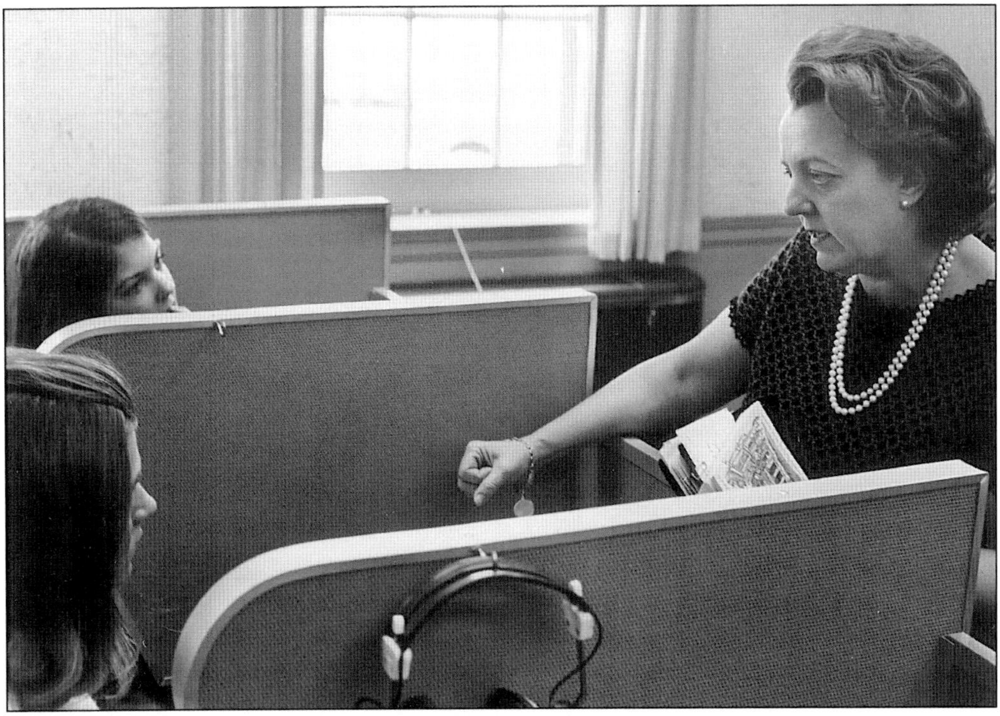

Mme. Helene Hall, French. Professor Hall held a baccalaureate from the University of Paris. She came to Bradford in 1963 with her husband H. Albert Hall, who served as school photographer and was in charge of audiovisual equipment. Professor Hall was one who truly earned the title of "much loved." She and her husband retired in 1978, and she was granted the title of professor emeritus. She died in 1986.

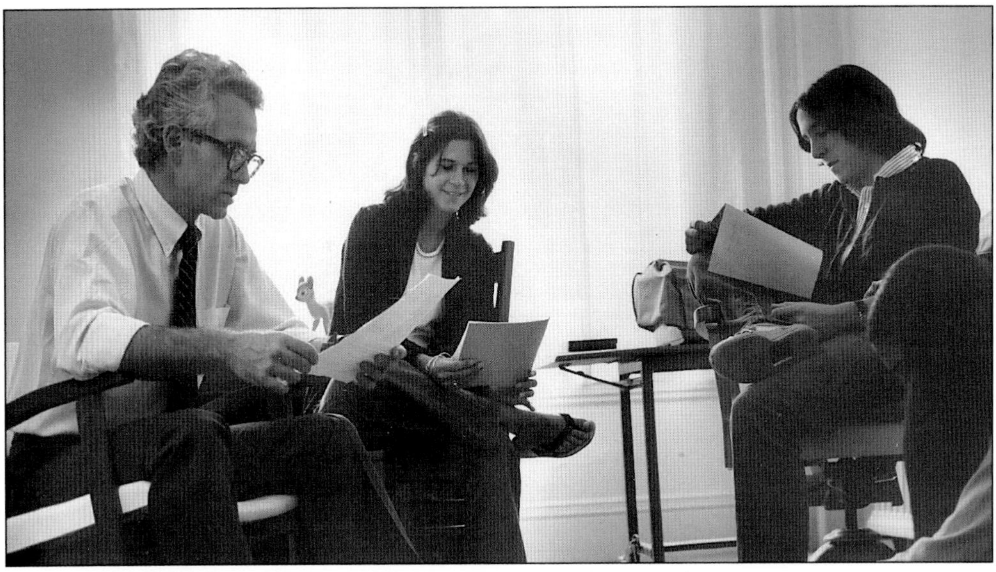

Prof. Edward Spicer, Spanish. Professor Spicer joined the Modern Language Department in 1963, along with Helene Hall. He also had studied at the University of Paris, and he had an M.A. from Middlebury College. In 1972, he replaced Professor Genevieve Wantiez as chairman of the Modern Language Department. He left Bradford in 1981 to teach in Florida.

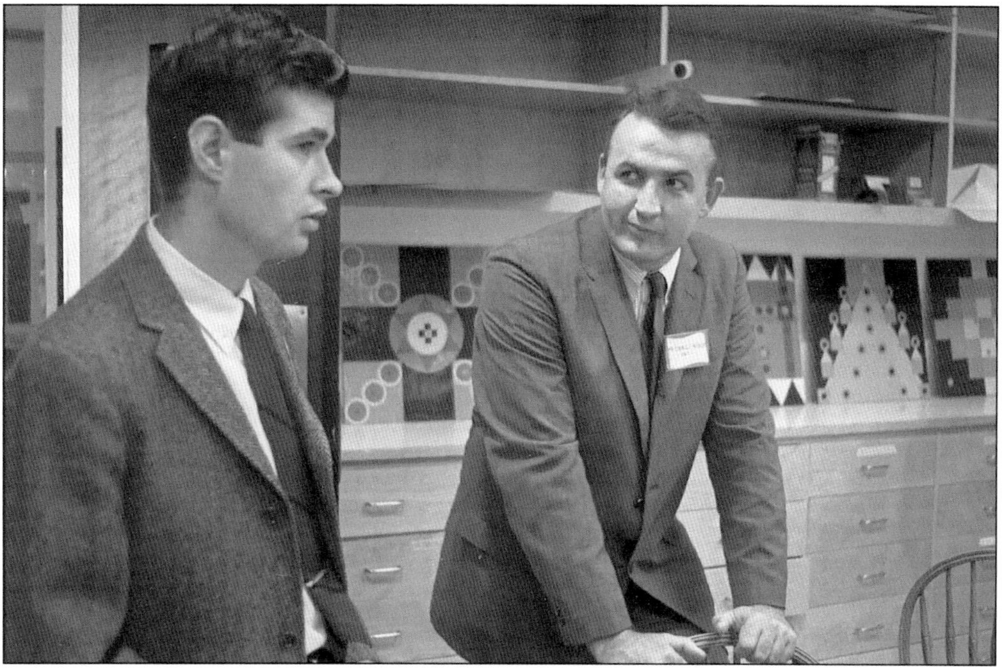

Richard Newman, His First Appearance. Dick Newman, left, almost unidentifiable without his trademark goatee, is shown with Doug Huebler. Newman arrived in 1965 with a M.F.A. from Cornell. When Huebler left, Newman took over the creative arts program and served as its chairman. When academic titles were first assigned to faculty in 1983, Newman was granted the highest title of professor. He was honored in 1993 as the first recipient of the Jane Walker Kopf Chair in Art History and Theory. Newman retired in 1999 with the status of emeritus.

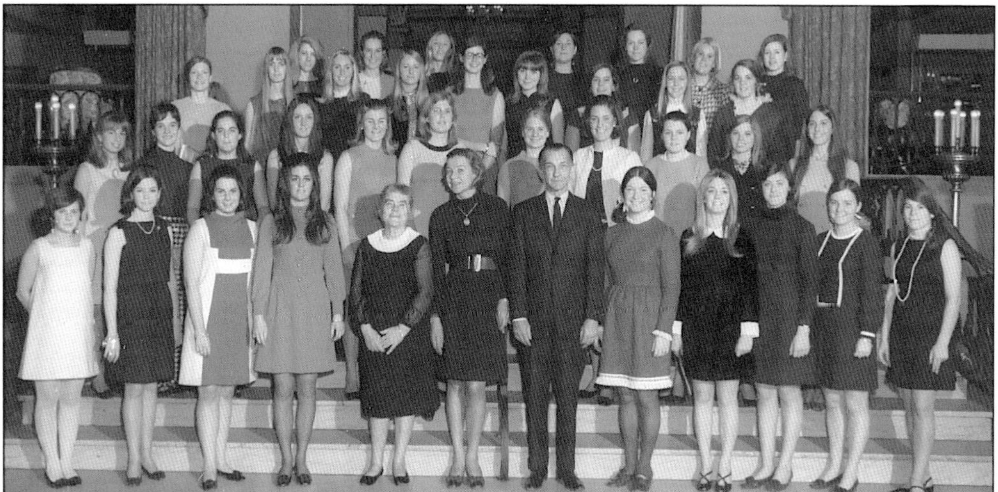

Professor Gittes and the Glee Club. Cecily Foster Gittes, fifth from the left in the front row, came to Bradford in 1960 to teach piano. She held a diploma from the Ecole Normale Musique in France and had extensive training with private piano teachers. She retired in 1969, soon after this picture was taken, and became professor emeritus. With her in the photograph, taken at the Shoreham Hotel in Washington, D.C., in February 1969, are Pres. and Mrs. Robert Vogel and the Bradford Glee Club.

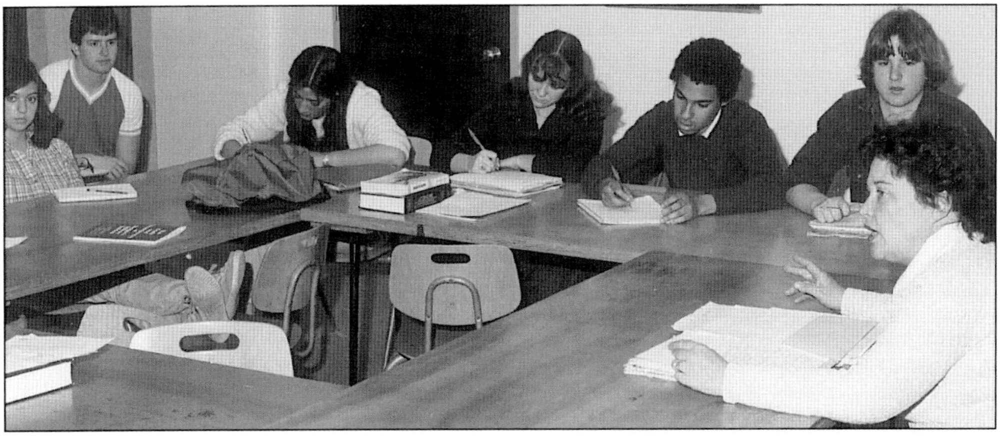

Carolyn Morton, History and Political Science. Professor Morton joined the social science faculty in 1963, teaching courses in European history and American government. Students from the 1970s and 1980s will remember her as Lynn Whitaker. She was a political activist in the community and many of her students acquired first-hand experience in elections and campaigns. She had a master's degree from Boston University. In the 1980s, she became the internship coordinator before deciding to go to law school. She became a practicing attorney in Bradford. This photograph was taken in the early 1980s in one of the seminar rooms in the library.

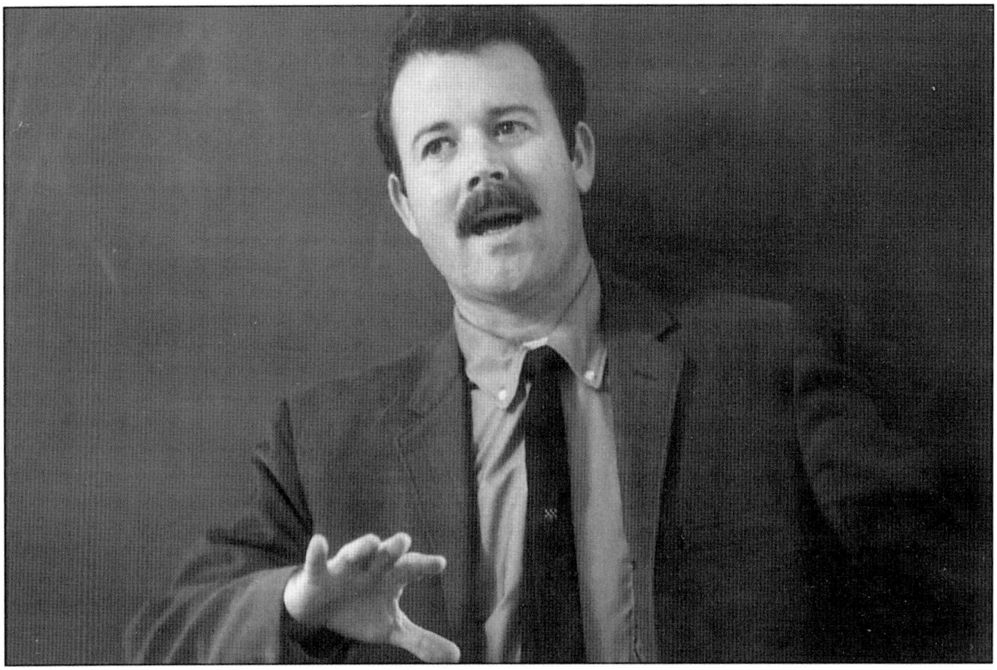

The Legendary André Dubus II. André Dubus was one of the most acclaimed short story writers in America. Whenever he was published, given an honor, or recognized for his superb talent, people were reminded of his ties to Bradford. He arrived in 1966 with a M.F.A. from the University of Iowa. He taught courses in fiction but also taught students how to write fiction. The creative writing program that he put together remained one of Bradford's strengths. Soon after he left Bradford in 1984, he was badly injured in an auto accident; he later received a Macarthur Genius Grant. He died suddenly in 1999 of a heart attack; all the obituaries mentioned his links with Bradford.

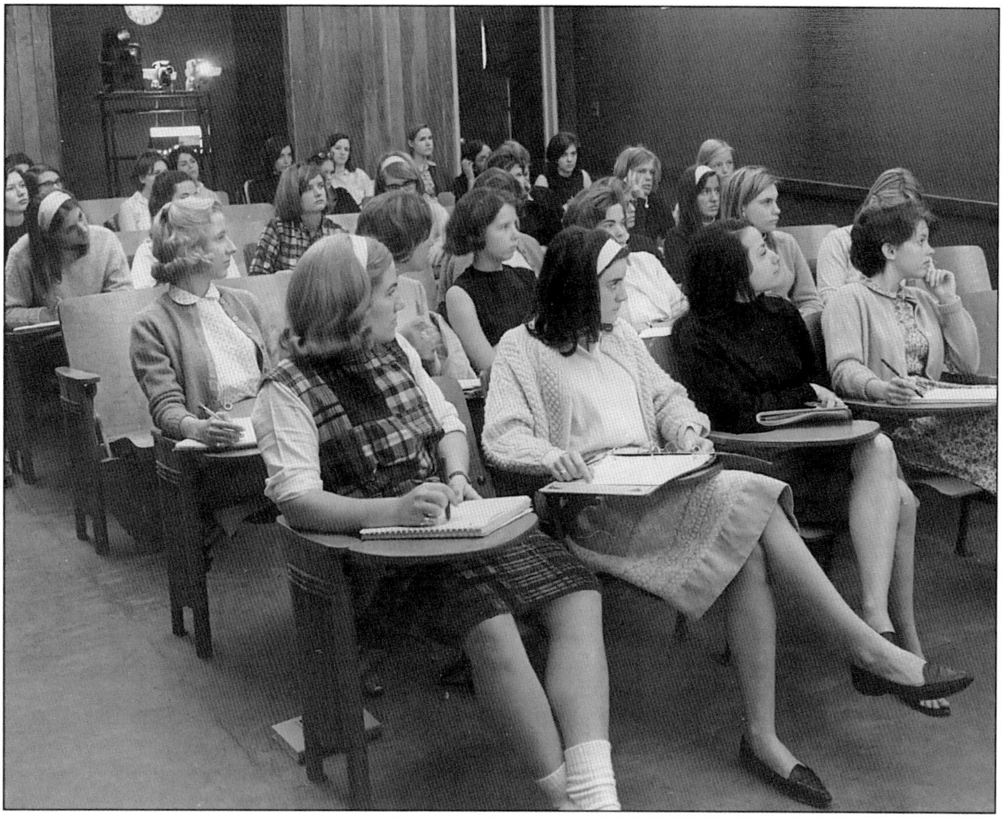

"The Black Hole of Calcutta." Room A-4 in the Carlson Art Wing of the Bell Center had a deserved reputation as a place to be avoided. It was intended to be used for art history lectures and was equipped with the appropriate audiovisual equipment. However, the walls were painted black and there were no exterior windows, presenting a most claustrophobic atmosphere—or quite possibly, the perfect place for a catnap during a class!

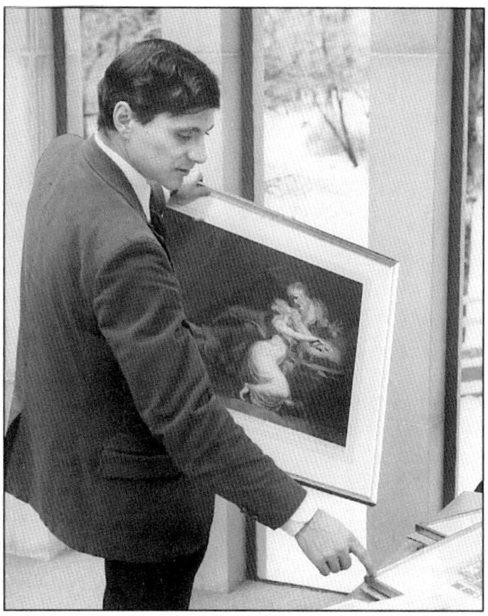

Vernon Hinkle, Speech and Drama. Hinkle, with a M.F.A. from Yale, came to Bradford in 1961. Though speech was not a required subject, students were encouraged to take one of the many classes available, so that they would become articulate as well as educated. Hinkle resigned in 1971 to become a full-time playwright.

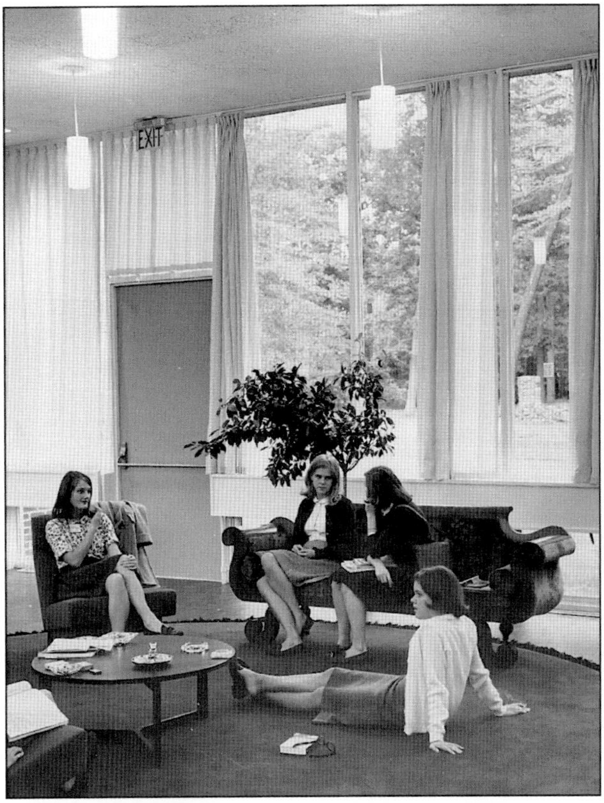

The New Dormitories. Bradford was bursting at the seams by the early 1960s. Four houses—Greenleaf, Hatch, Johnson, and Cogswell—supplemented Academy Hall, but still more room was needed. Offices and classrooms on the first floor of Academy were put into use as bedrooms, and more rooms were created in what had been the stacks area of the old library. It was still not enough. Finally, two new dormitories, named after the tupelo trees around Tupelo Pond, went up in 1964 and the off-campus houses were closed. This is a view of one of the commons rooms in the new dormitories.

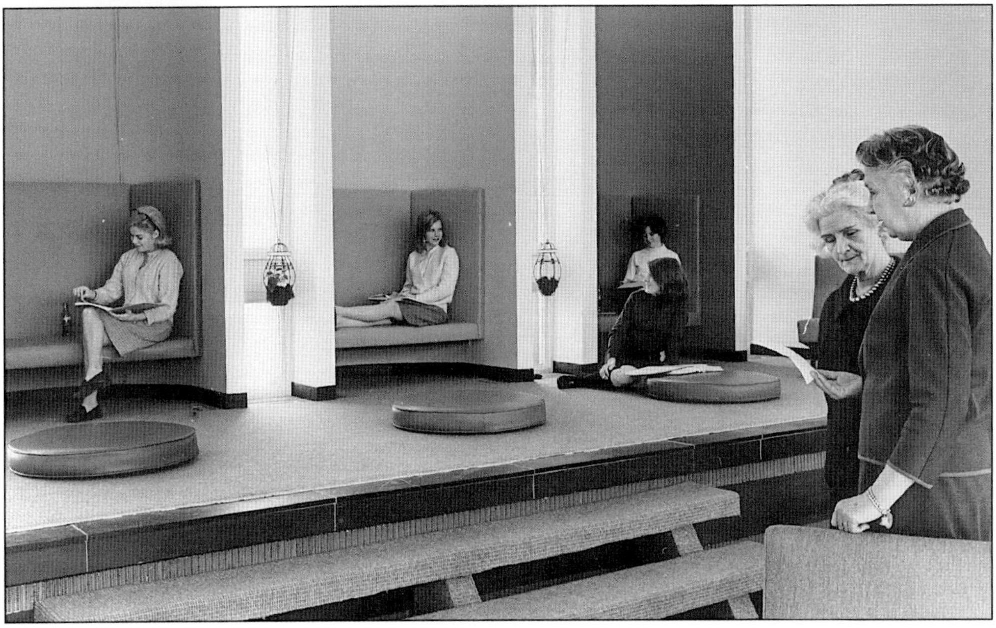

President Bell and Mrs. Curry. Supervision of resident students rested in the hands of older women, usually widows, throughout the Bell and Vogel presidencies. House fellow for the new Tupelo West dorm was Kathleen Curry, right, widow of the famed artist John Steuart Curry. She worked at Bradford from 1962 to 1968. With her is Pres. Dorothy Bell.

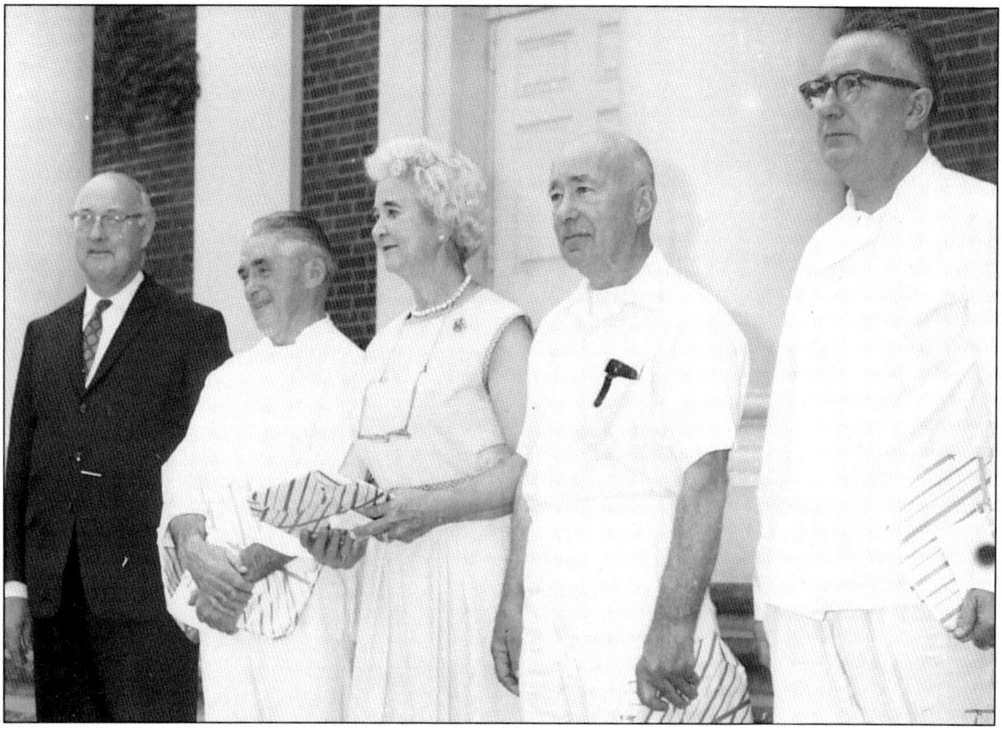

Honoring the Senior Staff. During Dorothy Bell's final days as president, she took the time to honor five of the staff veterans. The gesture was both gracious and well deserved. It was also a reminder of how important such people are in the operation of a small residential school. The five honored employees are, from left to right, Herbert Noel of the household staff; chef Bernard Bradshaw; housekeeper Helen Walker, who was employed at Bradford from 1917 to 1923 and again from 1939 to 1968; baker Ralph Carrington; and Carrington's brother Joseph Carrington, who became chef in 1936 and died in 1972.

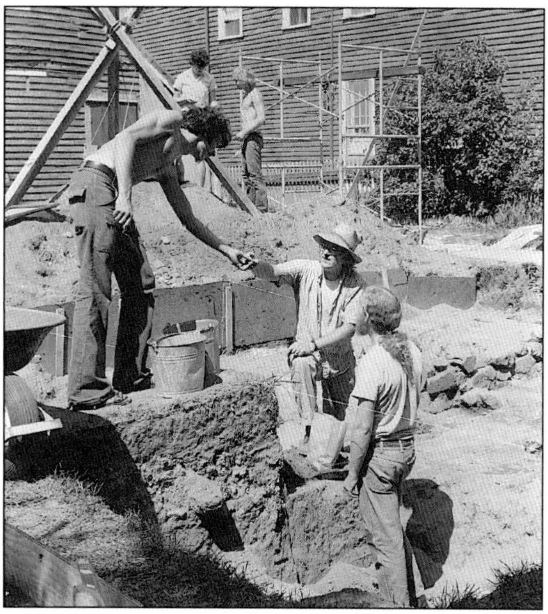

Prof. Geoffrey Moran, History. Moran came to Bradford in 1968 as a Ph.D. candidate from the University of Massachusetts. In addition to his history classes, he also taught courses in historical archaeology. Moran, seen here with the straw hat, had a grant in 1974 to conduct this excavation at the 17th-century Narbonne House in Salem, Massachusetts, which he carried out with his students.

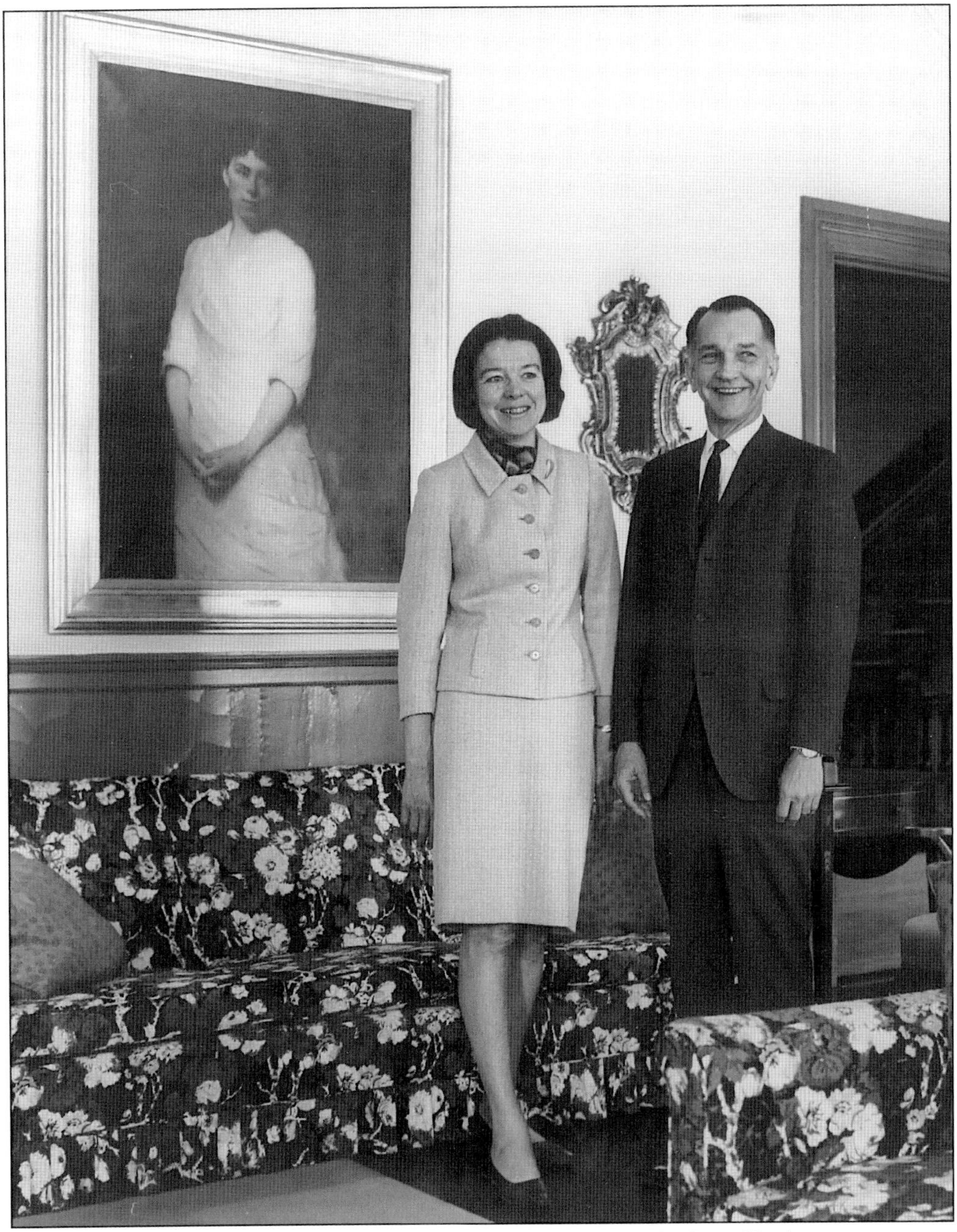

Pres. and Mrs. Robert Vogel. Vogel was the first married head of Bradford since Benjamin Greenleaf in the early 19th century. He was a graduate of Wabash with a master's from Michigan and a doctorate from Columbia. During Vogel's term as president, Bradford became both a coeducational and a B.A.-granting college. Vogel also initiated a program of accelerated admissions and created a School of Urban Studies. His wife, Caroline Vogel, was his trusted assistant and took on the many obligations expected of a presidential spouse. He resigned his office in January 1972 and died in 1991.

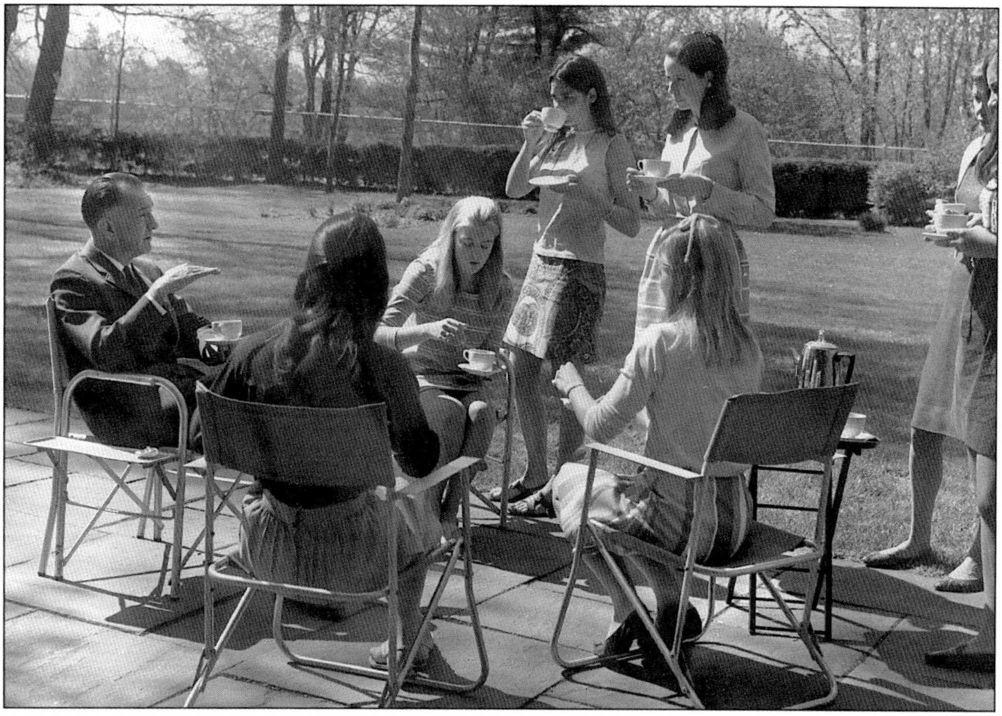

Pres. Robert Vogel, 1967-1972. Bradford's third President is joined by students for coffee on the patio at the rear of the President's House. Vogel had the misfortune to be president during a period of great social disruption and change, including the Vietnam War moratoriums, social rebellion, and attacks on the establishment. He took the challenges to his authority quite personally. There were great changes in campus life throughout America's academic world, and Bradford was not immune. One by one, the long-standing rituals and traditions were scrapped; Bradford was permanently changed.

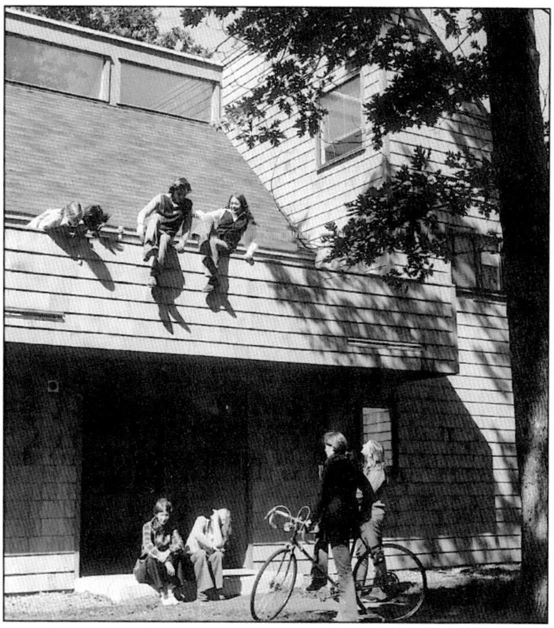

The Cluster Town House Dormitories. Bradford's enrollment continued to grow throughout the 1960s. It reached 425 in 1969. Once again, there was a housing crunch, and Greenleaf House had to be reopened to handle the surplus. The Cluster Houses were erected in 1968. The five double houses and two single ones represented both a new concept in student life and in student governance. Each house unit, complete with its own kitchen, accommodated ten students, who were expected to supervise themselves. The houses presented an interesting design, but they were plagued with problems from the start, most having to do with the vagaries of New England winters.

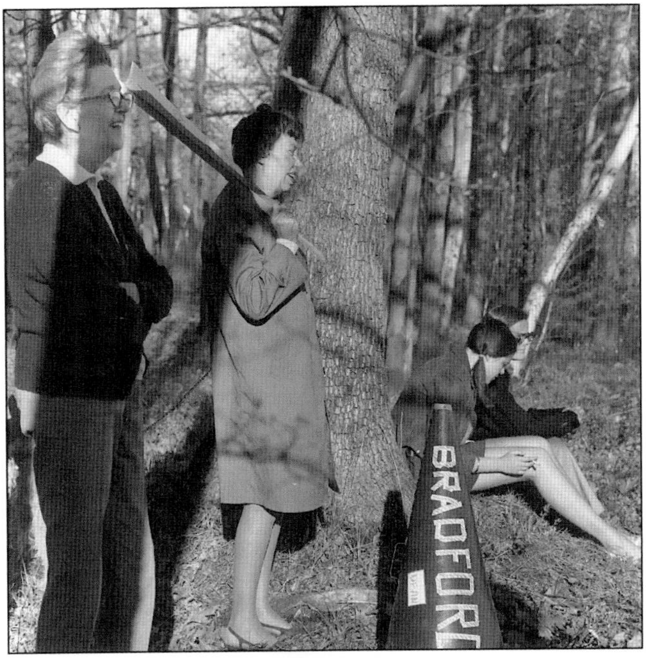

Cheering on the Girls. Lucy Messer, left, head house fellow, and Dorothea Smart, dean, provide moral and vocal support—with megaphone and poster—to Bradford's team at the playing fields on May 1, 1969.

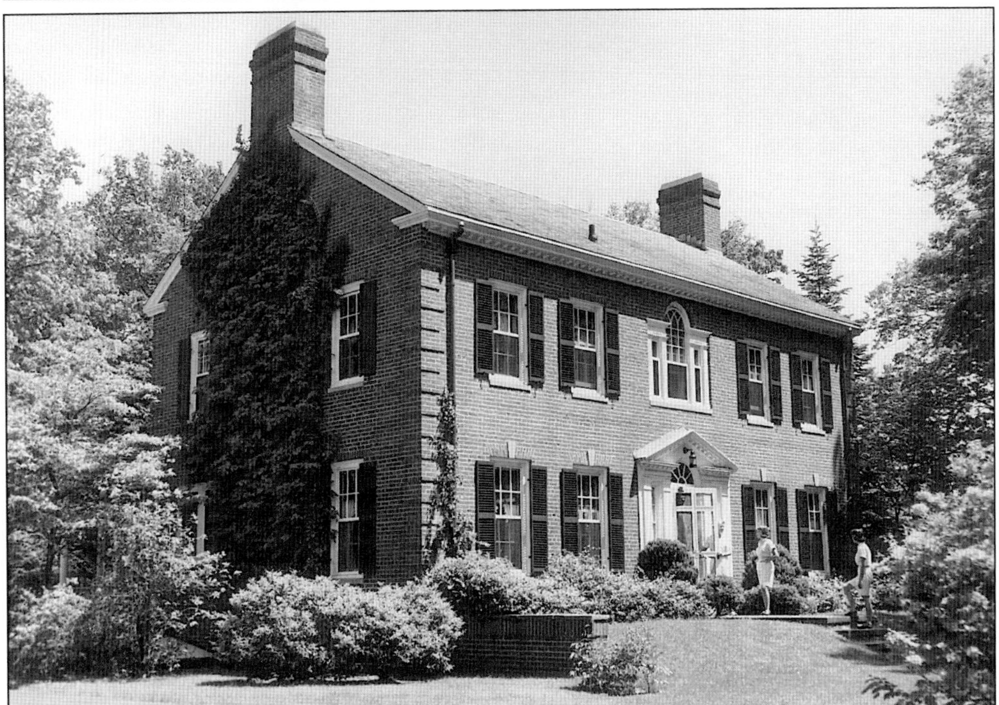

The Coats House. In 1926, Principal Marion Coats expressed her concerns about the lack of an adequate health facility during a chapel talk to the students. Immediately, students began a fund drive and a year later, this Federal-style brick building was completed near Tupelo Pond. The building, named in honor of Coats, served as an infirmary, a summer home for Pres. Dorothy Bell, offices for the development staff, offices for the humanities division, and—its last incarnation—the health and counseling facilities.

Five

The Seventies

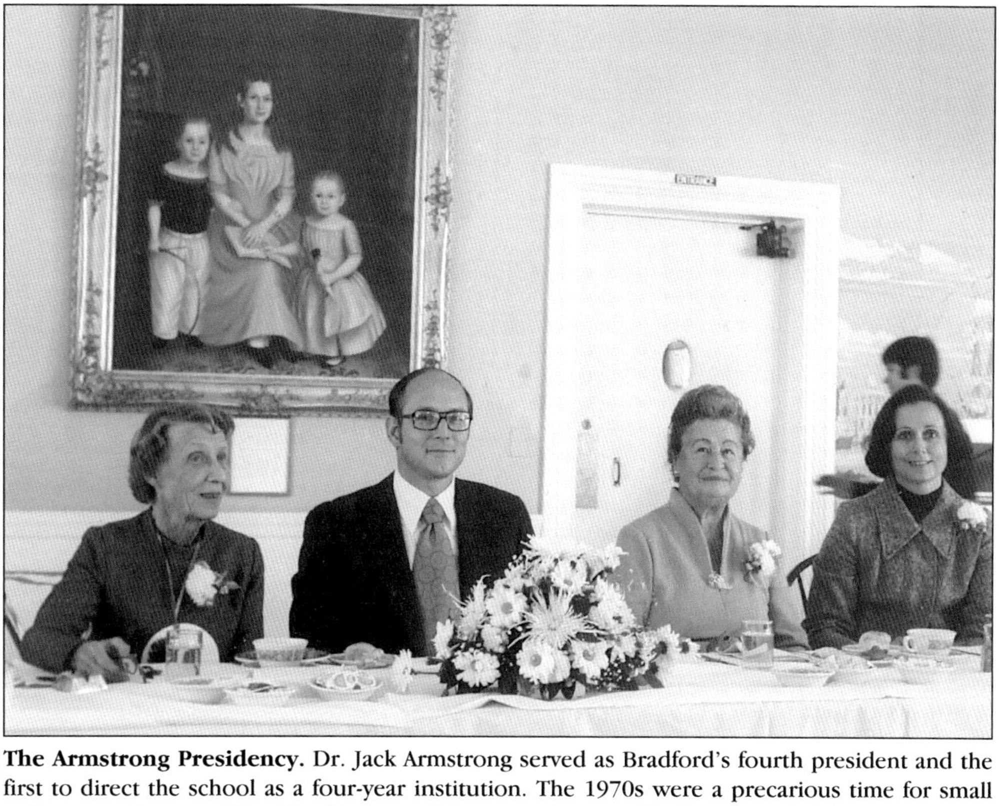

The Armstrong Presidency. Dr. Jack Armstrong served as Bradford's fourth president and the first to direct the school as a four-year institution. The 1970s were a precarious time for small colleges, and many of Bradford's peers did not survive. Bradford College did, but it struggled with falling enrollments, limited endowment, and the need to carve out its new identity as a B.A. degree-granting college. Alumnae support was demonstrated on occasions such as this 1976 reunion. Shown with Armstrong at the head table in the dining room are Udell Redmond White '26, president of the Alumni Association; Florence Eisenhardt Dangerfield, emeritus professor; and Ann Faubion Armstrong.

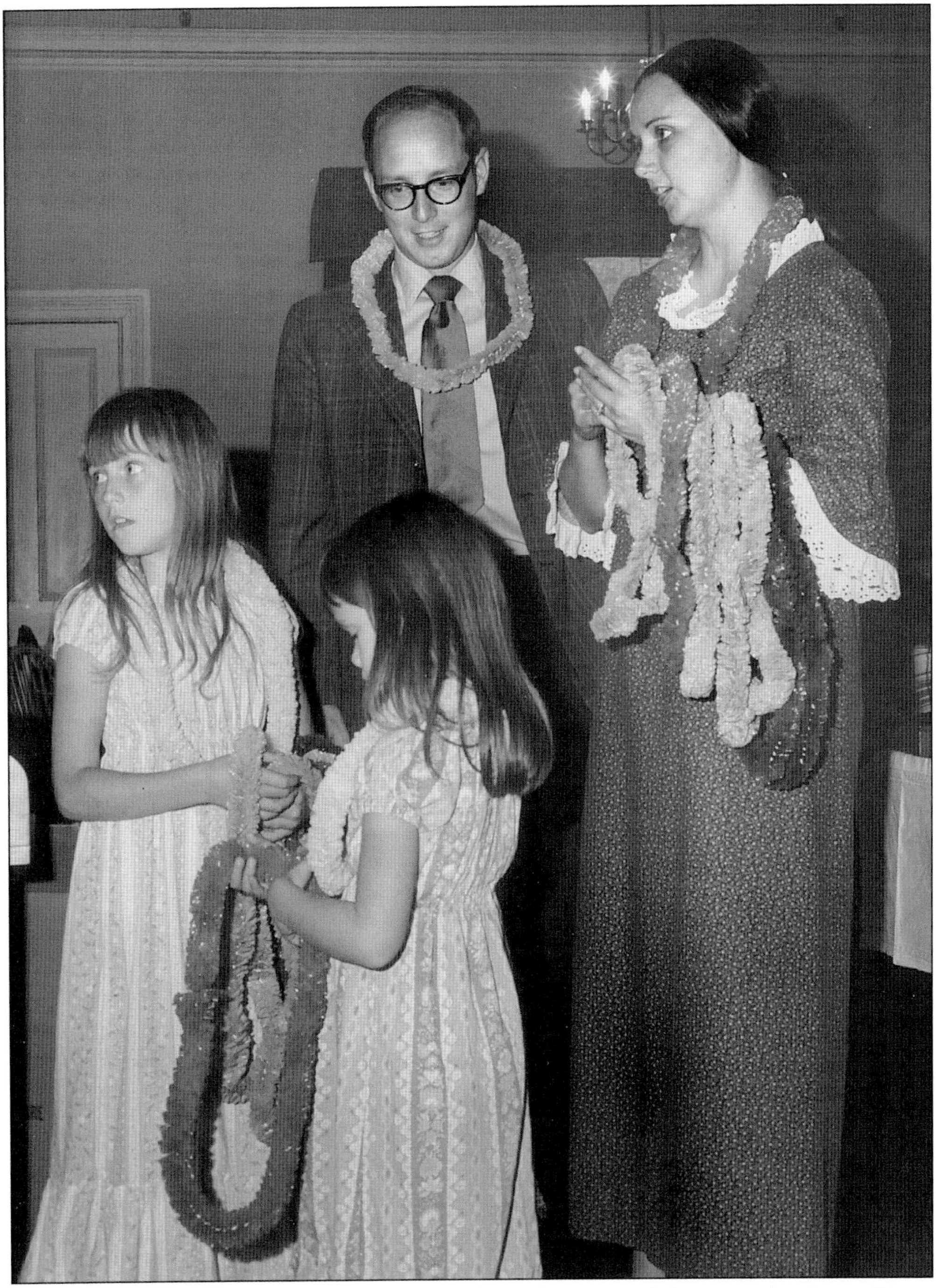

The Armstrong Family. Pres. Jack Armstrong, his wife, Ann, and their two daughters, Diane, left, and Katherine '93, brought youth and vitality to the campus. Armstrong, who had a Ph.D. in psychology from Minnesota, had been the dean at Macalester College. He was 35 years old when he became president. Like Armstrong, a significant part of the faculty and all of the house fellows were young and new to Bradford. It was a time of great change and boundless energy. The Armstrong family wear the leis given to them at the 1972 alumni reunion.

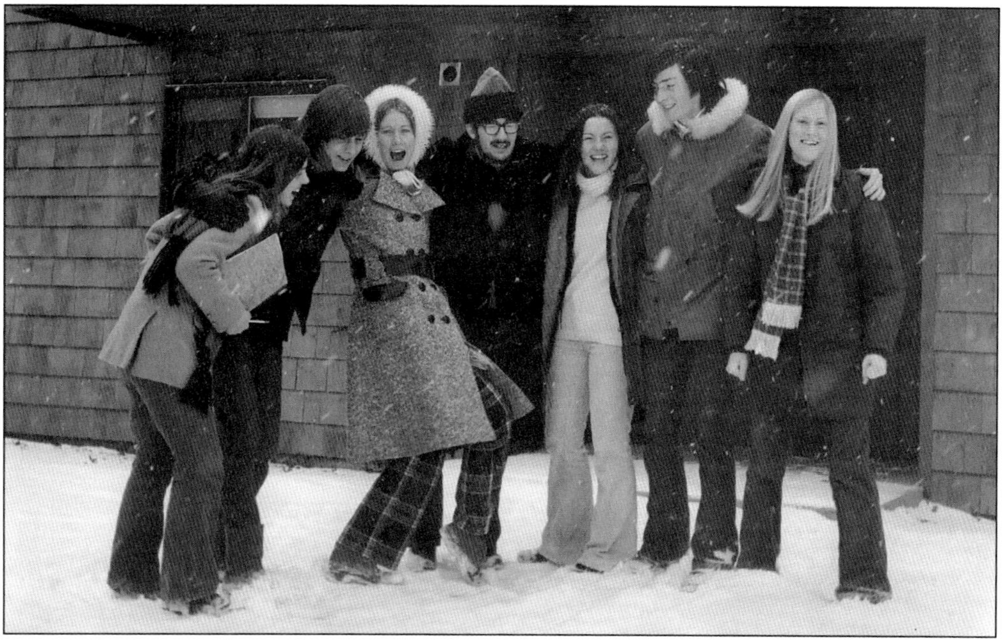

Coed Again after 135 Years. There was no more visible sign of change at Bradford than the first appearance of males in the student body. Eight young men arrived in 1971, the first of their gender since 1836. They lived together in Cluster House E and jokingly referred to themselves as the school's mascots. The three in this picture, from left to right, are Stewart Wolfe, John Danner, and Todd O'Connell.

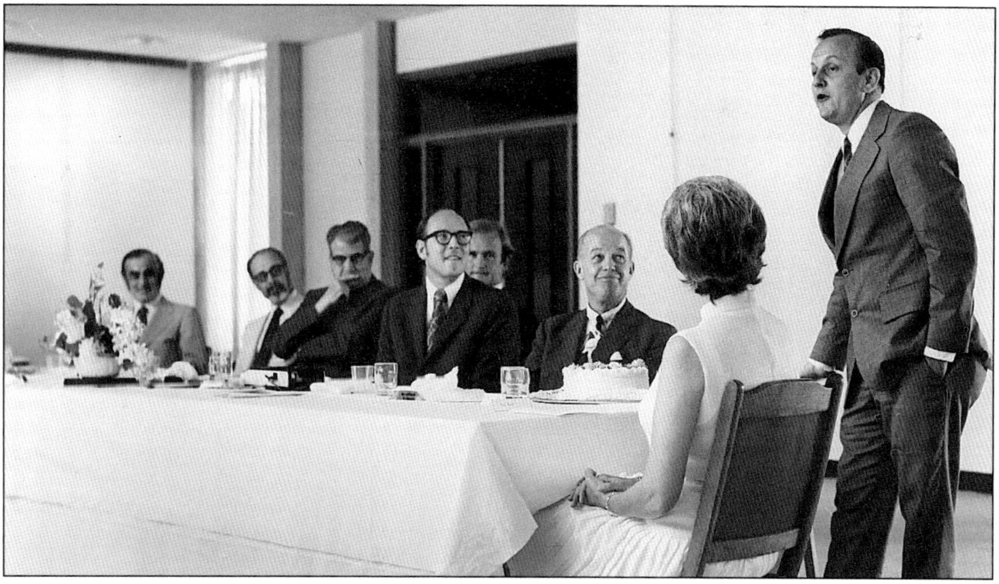

The Reception for the First B.A. Graduates. Bradford's initial B.A. program was in urban studies. An intense curriculum, including summer school, had the first candidates earning their degree in August 1973. At the head table during the ceremony held in the Laura Knott Gallery are, from left to right, George Katsaros, mayor of Haverhill; Downing Bowler, dean; Fred Scribner, trustee chair; Pres. Jack Armstrong; Congressman Michael Harrington; Charles Cheever, trustee; Marion Runt, registrar; and Dr. Albert Whitaker, director of the program.

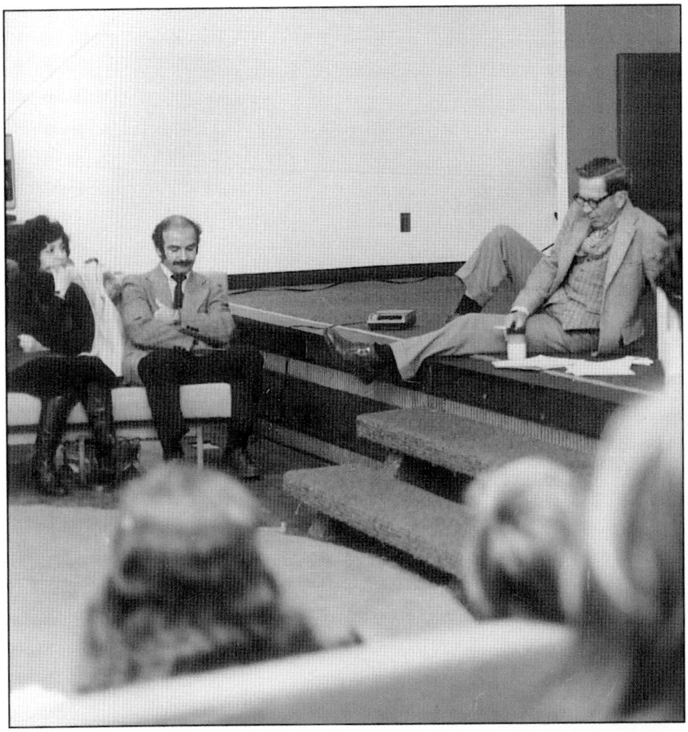

John Cheever Visits Bradford. Novelist John Cheever, right, came to Bradford in 1977 to give a reading as a favor to "his good friend" Dr. Jim Valhouli. Valhouli had written his doctoral dissertation at Wisconsin on Cheever's works. Valhouli, shown seated with Prof. Mary O'Brien in a Tupelo commons room, had come to Bradford in 1969 and was an inspired teacher and scholar. He became associate dean under Downing Bowler and also acting dean. Valhouli left to teach at Phillips Exeter Academy, where he died in a tragic skating accident in 1994.

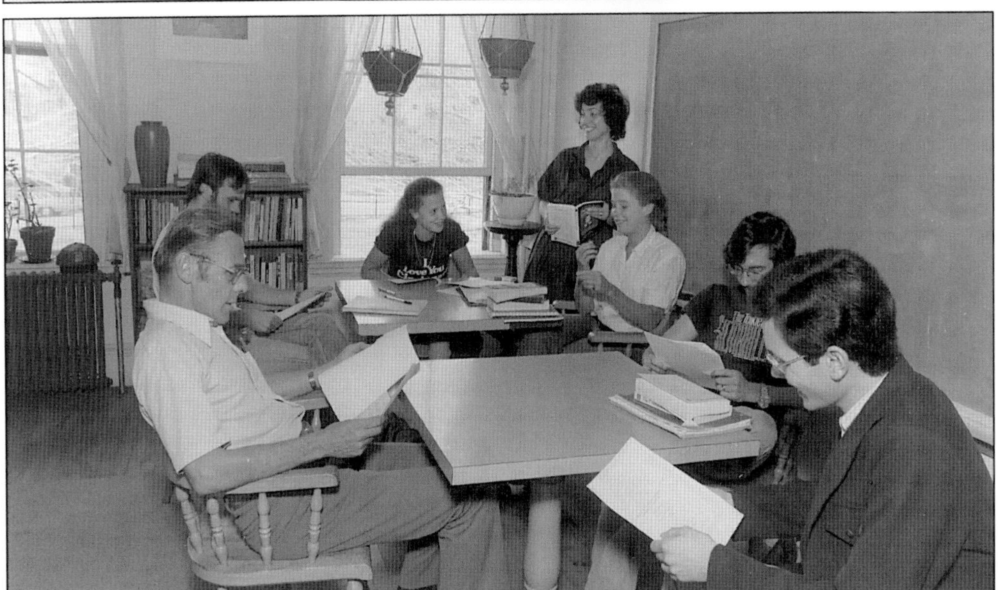

Mary Bevilacqua O'Brien, English. Like her colleague Jim Valhouli, Mary O'Brien called Haverhill her home. She came to Bradford in 1971 with a master's from Tufts University and made such an impact that she was selected by the graduates of the Class of 1974 to address them at commencement. She is shown standing in her office in Hasseltine, which she had turned into a seminar room. The students in the foreground are Ralph Hansen, A.A., '79 and Frank Oberti, B.A., '80, which dates the picture to the late 1970s. O'Brien returned to Tufts in 1982 to work on her Ph.D.

Prof. Forbes Bryce, Psychology. Bryce had been a commander in the U.S. Navy. After retiring, he decided to return to college. He earned an M.A. in sociology from the University of New Hampshire in 1968 and taught sociology and psychology at Bradford from 1970 to 1975. By popular acclaim, he returned in 1976 to address the graduates at commencement.

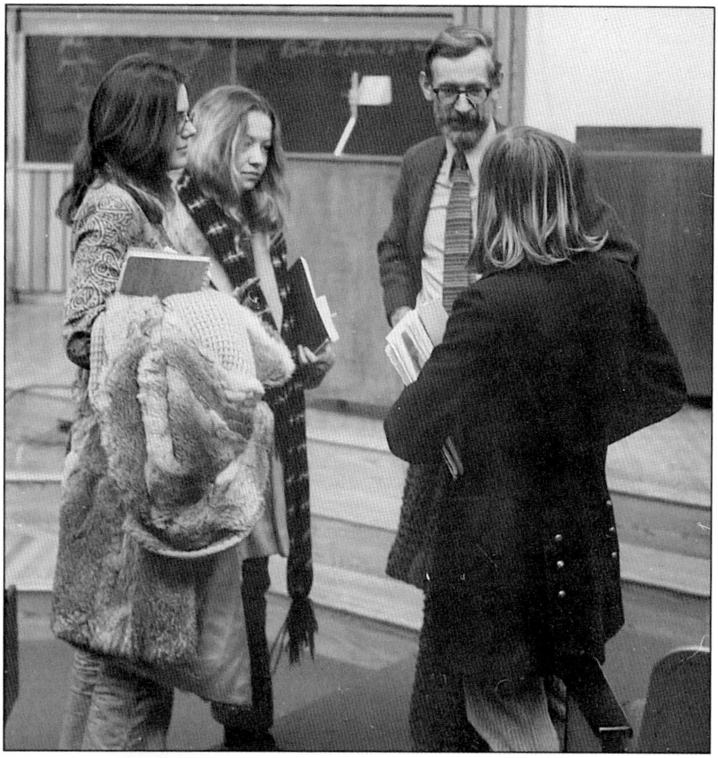

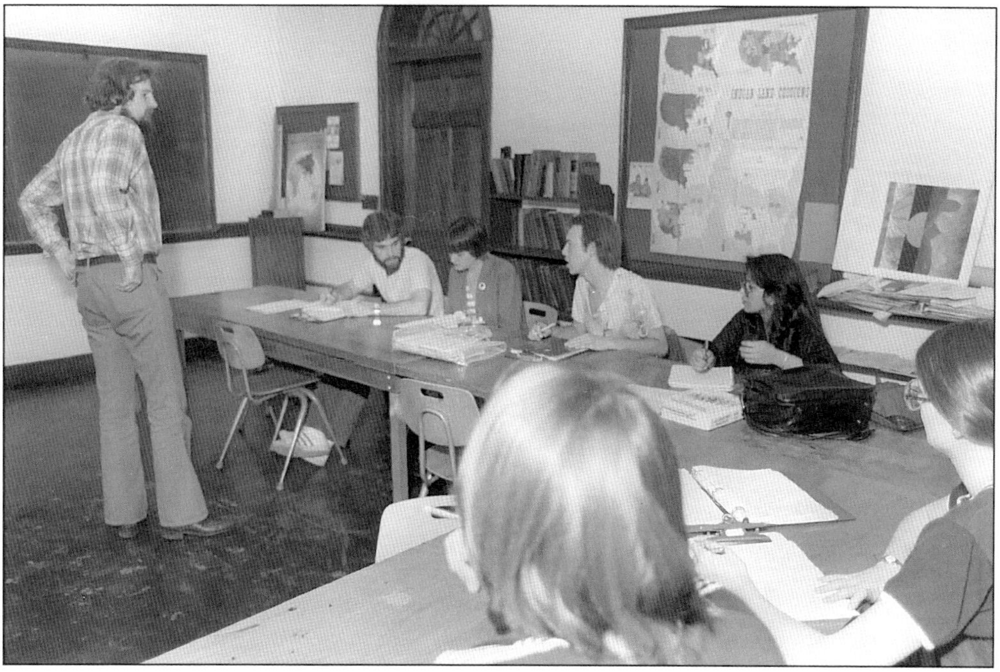

Prof. Tom Cheetham, Sociology. Cheetham came to Bradford in 1971. He had an M.A. from Brown and completed his Ph.D., also from Brown, in 1981. His area of expertise was in Romanian cooperative farms. This classroom photograph dates from the early 1980s. Cheetham left Bradford in the mid-80s to pursue a career as a novelist.

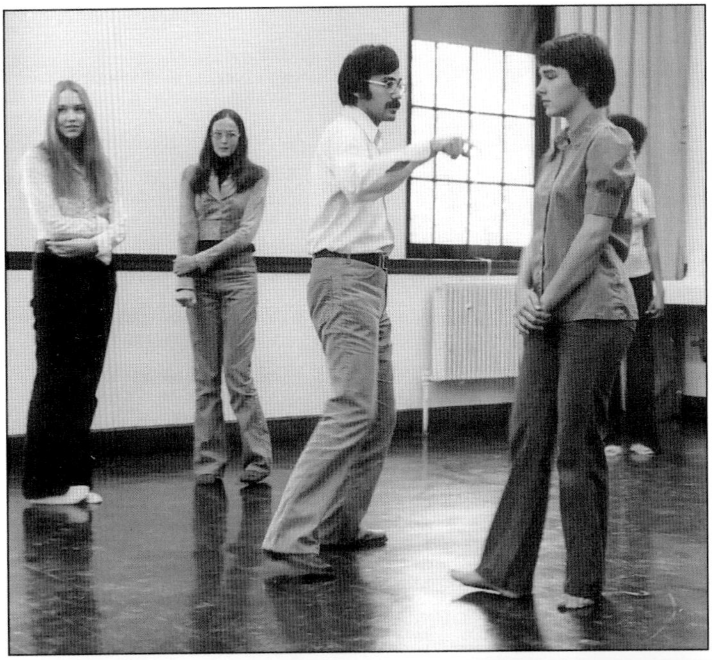

Mark Weisstuch, Drama. Professor Weisstuch replaced Prof. Vernon Hinkle in 1971. He had an M.A. from City University of New York. He is shown putting his acting students through their paces in the theater practice room on the third floor of Hasseltine. Weisstuch left Bradford in 1982 to pursue a doctorate in rabbinical studies but returned in 1985 to offer a course as an adjunct.

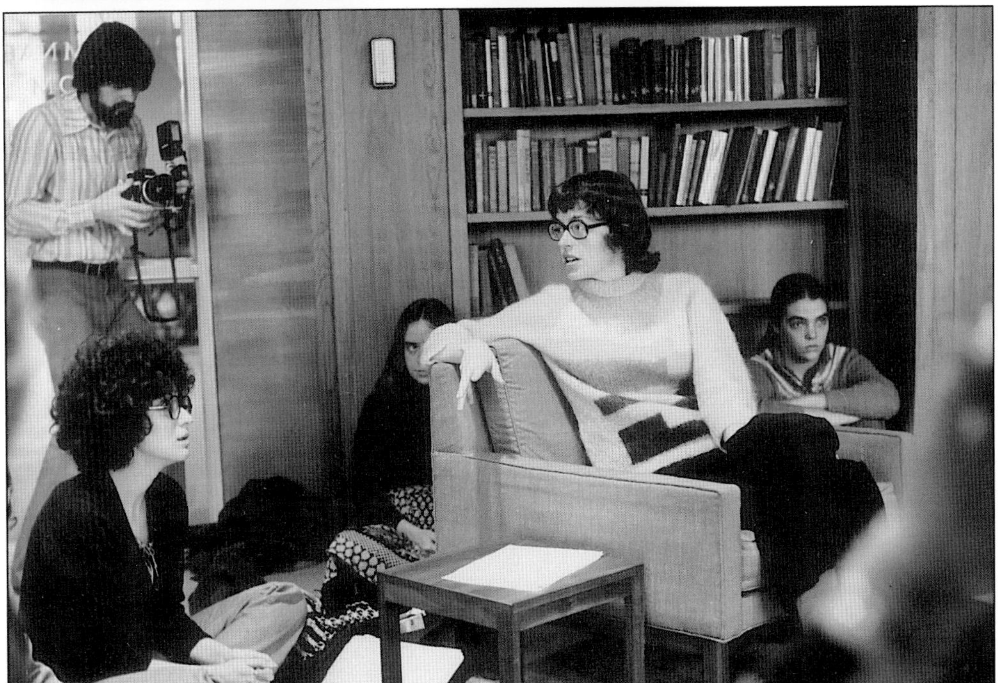

Dr. Margaret Walsh, Philosophy. When Downing Bowler gave up his philosophy courses in 1972 to take on the position of dean of the faculty, his replacement in the classroom was Dr. Walsh. Walsh had a Ph.D. from Duquesne University. She was the recipient of many honors at Bradford: chairman of the Humanities Division, promotion to professor in 1988, first recipient of the Christian Johnson Chair in Ethics and Values, and Professor of the Year in 1996. She is shown, seated in the chair, talking with students in the Alumni Room in the library, *c.* 1980.

Prof. Martha Boles, Mathematics. Marty Boles, right, came to Bradford in 1973 with a master's in science from the University of Oregon. She was a dynamic teacher. She was also a very creative one, as demonstrated by a unique course she created with Rochelle Newman entitled Mathematics in Art and Nature. Boles was promoted to professor in 1989. She was selected as Professor of the Year and the second recipient of the Johnson Chair in Ethics and Values in 1994. She took an early retirement in 1999. With her is student Kimberley Snow, B.A., '81.

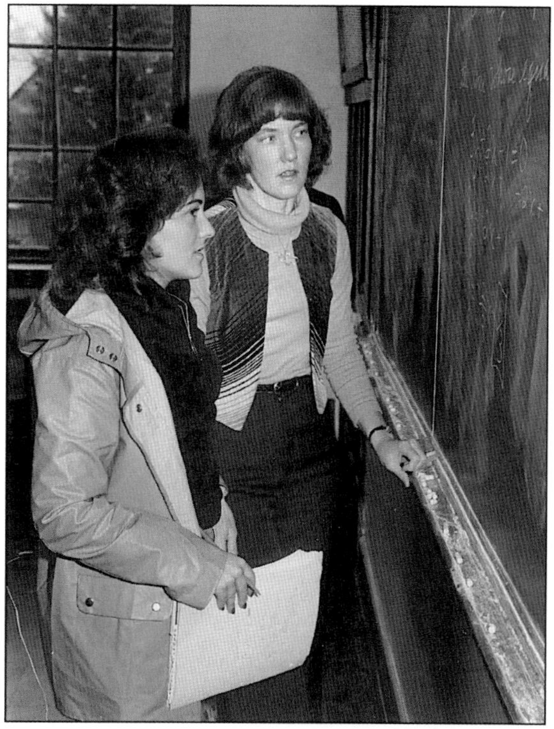

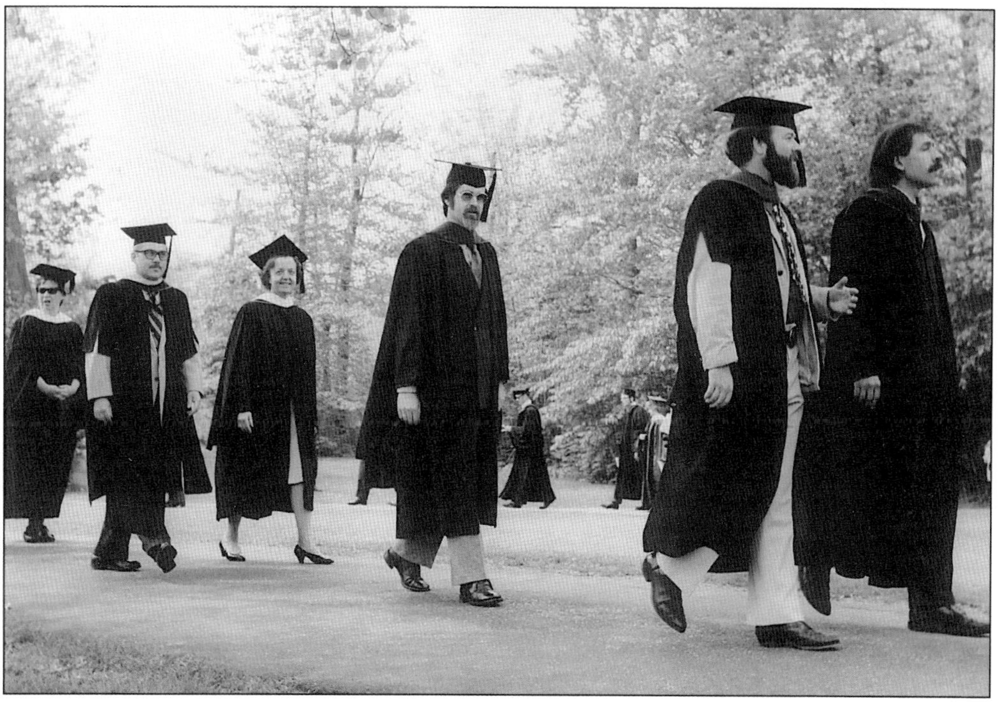

The Faculty of the Seventies. There are many familiar faces among this group of veteran faculty processing during commencement 1973. Seen here, from left to right, are Carolyn Morton Whitaker, John Roberts, Helene Hall, Richard Newman, André Dubus II, and Donald Burgy. All had been hired in the 1960s during the Bell presidency.

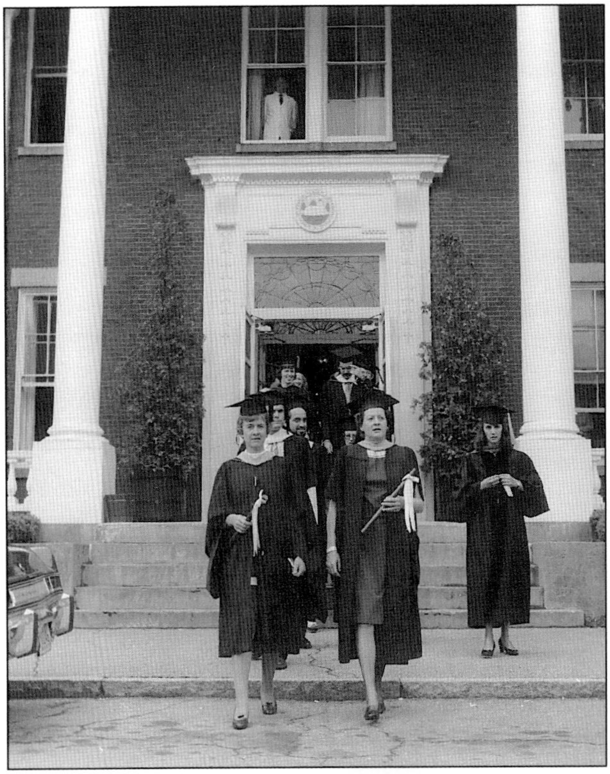

Commencement 1975. Ann Chesebro and A. Elizabeth Weber are the marshals leading the faculty out of Academy Hall to commencement exercises in Denworth Hall. Ann and Betty earned their honor by virtue of being the senior faculty members. Joining the procession on the right is Dr. Grace Baron, psychology professor from 1974 to 1978. Visible in the doorway is Dr. Peggy Walsh.

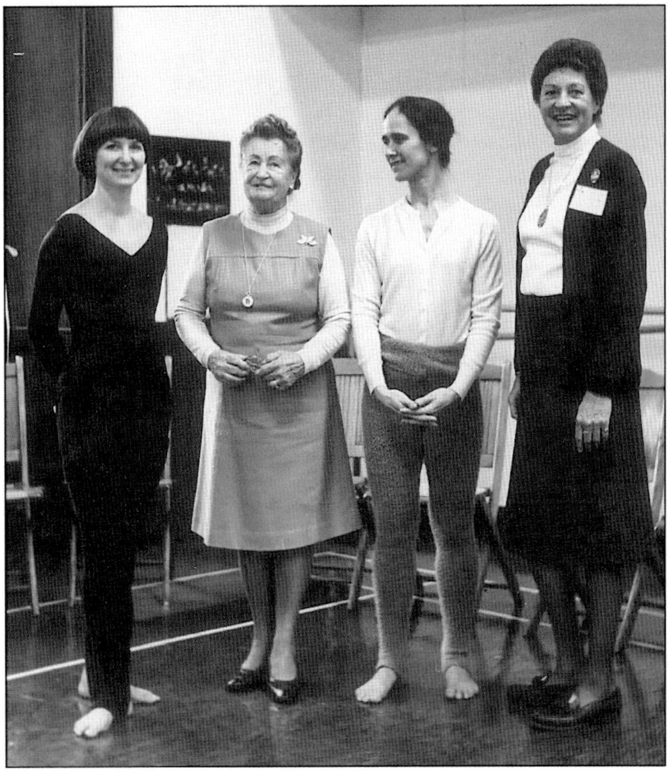

The Return of Mrs. Dangerfield. Florence Eisenhardt Dangerfield, second from left, had retired from Bradford in 1952, after three decades of teaching dance. It was she who had conceived the idea in 1924 of honoring each year's outstanding dance student and had even contributed the silver cup, which eventually carried her name. She returned to Bradford in 1977 to help direct a master class in dance. With her, from left to right, are June Gobelein Finch, dance instructor Janet Craft, and Prof. Betty Weber. Dangerfield's long and productive life ended in 1991 when she died at the age of 97.

"Gretta" Hourihan Morrissey. Margaret "Gretta" Hourihan, right, came from Ireland with her sister Bridey soon after World War II. They both began to work at Bradford Junior College as waitresses. Bridey became the housekeeper for President Bell. Morrissey became assistant director of the Food Service Department. She was honored in 1988 with the Bradshaw Award. With her in this photograph is Pres. Jack Armstrong. She died suddenly in 1991.

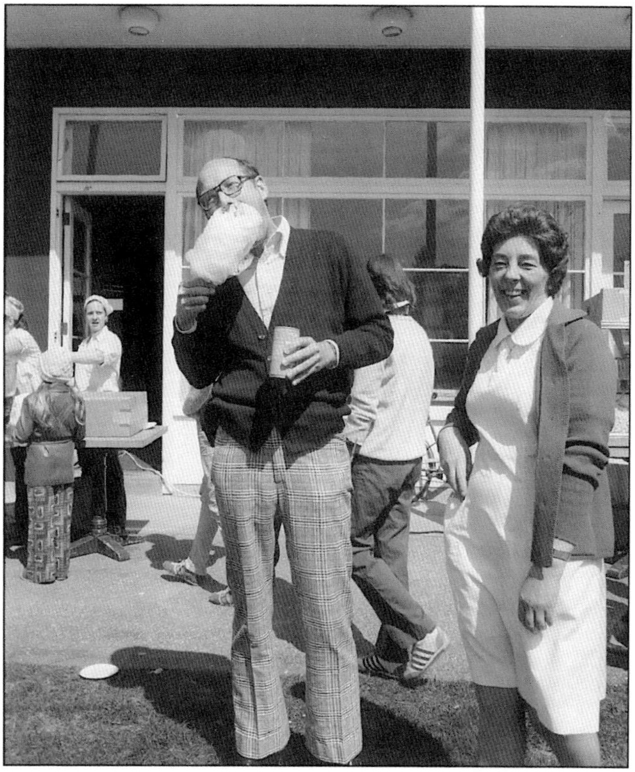

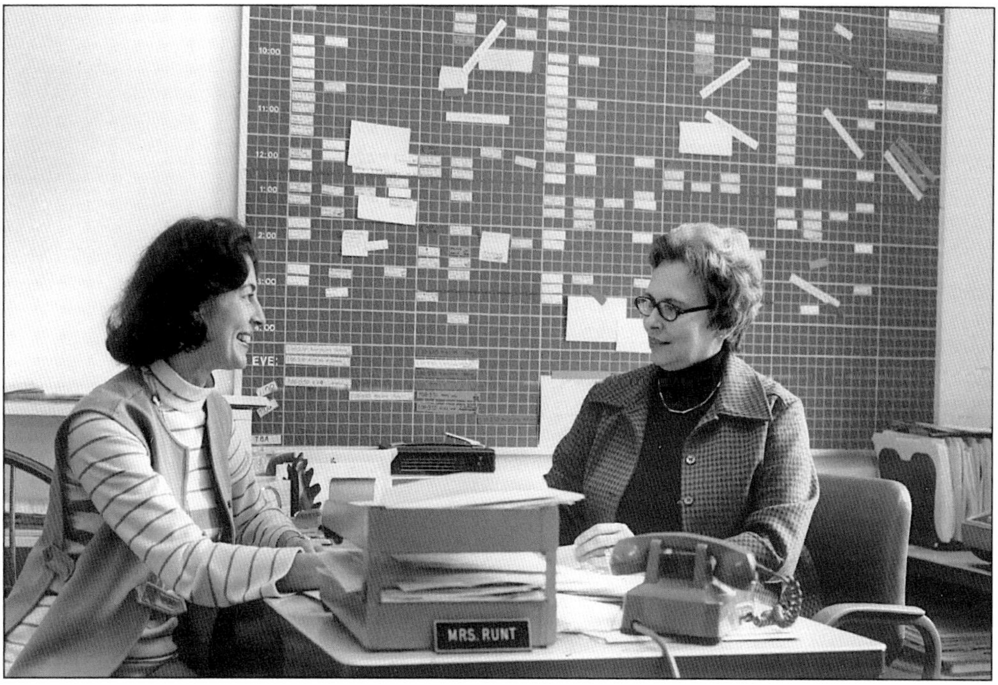

Marion Runt and Dorothy Mann. Marion Runt, right, was registrar at Bradford from 1963 to 1978. Her assistant Dotty Mann began working at the college in 1972. Mann was also secretary to the dean of the college from 1978 to 1982.

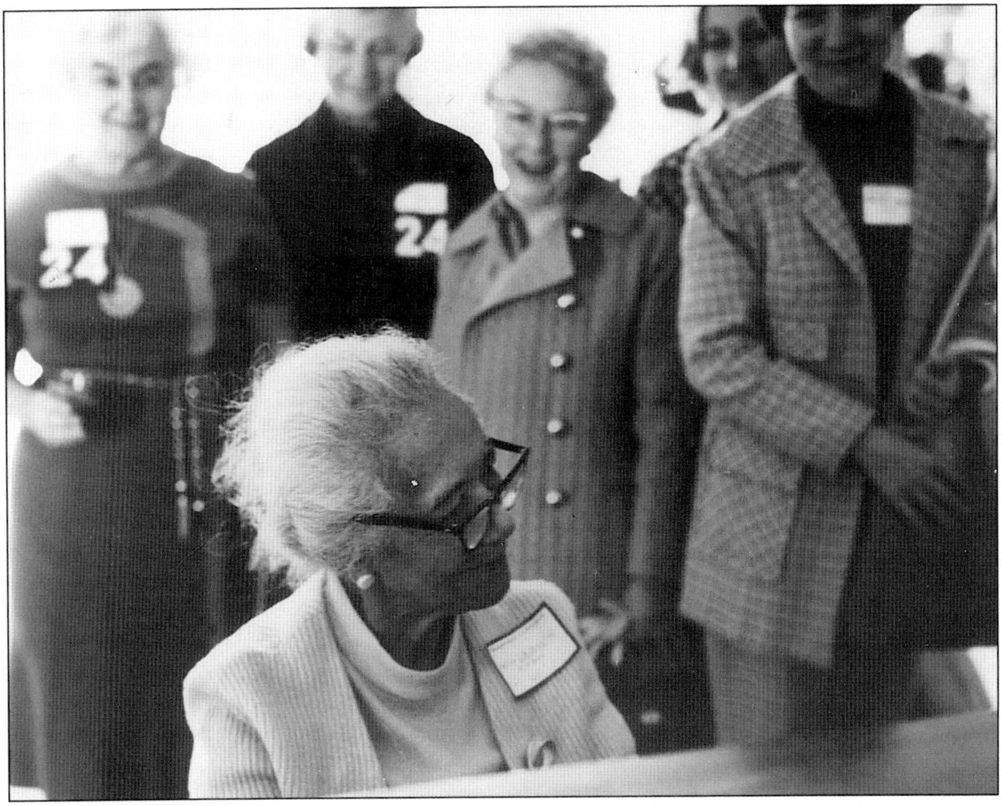

Portia Washington on Campus Again. Portia Marshall Washington Pittman '05, daughter of Booker T. Washington and the first person of color to attend Bradford, attended the 1974 alumni reunion. A student of piano while at Bradford Academy, she entertained her fellow alums by playing for them. She died in 1977.

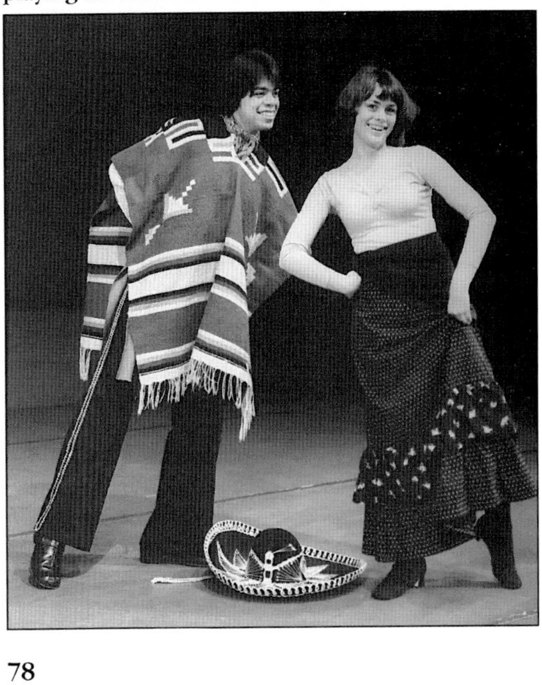

International Day Celebration. With an increasing number of foreign students on campus, Bradford inaugurated International Day. The foreign students, with a little help from some American friends, supplied the entertainment after dinner in the dining room. Mario Garza, A.A., '75 of Mexico demonstrates the Mexican Hat Dance with Mary Lou Gallagher, B.A., '79 of New Hampshire.

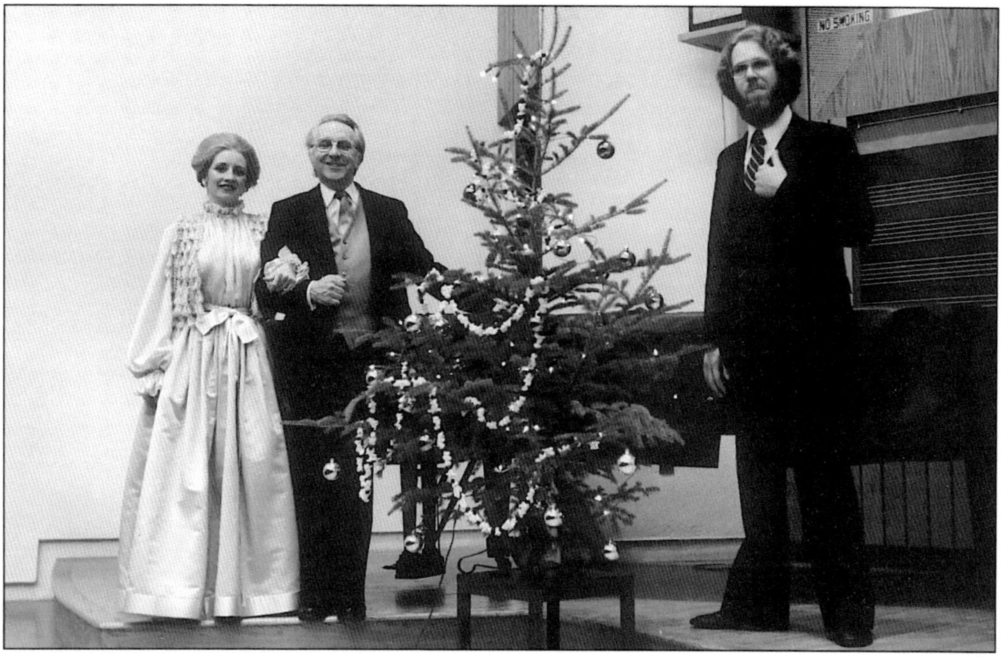

Prof. Ludington and the Music Faculty. Charles Ludington taught music to Bradford students through three decades. He arrived in 1960 with a M.F.A. from Princeton and retired as professor emeritus in 1986. In addition to music theory and voice classes, he also led the glee club—which became the Bradford-Pentucket Chorale and included community members—and began the very successful Music Theater program. For the chorale's Christmas concert in 1977, Ludington was joined by voice teacher Frances DeMoulas Kettenback '71, left. Standing to the right is accompanist Prof. Mark Peterson, who succeeded Ludington in 1983 as director of the chorale. Peterson earned a master's from the University of New Hampshire.

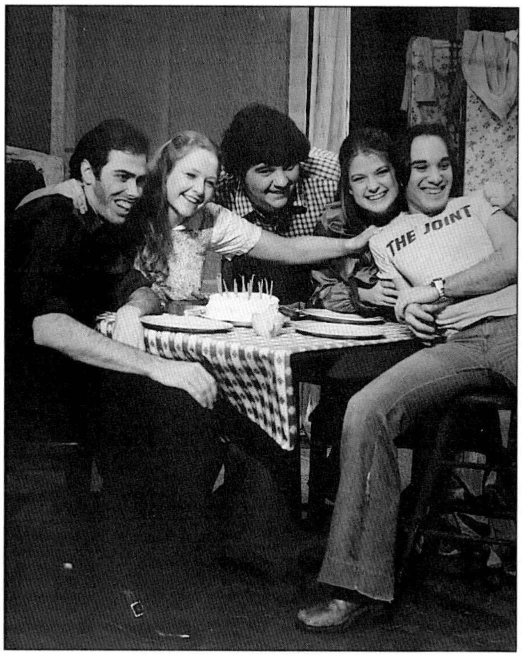

The Cast of *A Streetcar Named Desire*. Theater has been a significant part of the Bradford experience since the late 1800s. The Denworth Hall auditorium provided a better performance area than those early students had known, and the addition of male students in the 1970s added some range to the plays that could be presented. These students are part of the 1978 production of *A Streetcar Named Desire.* They are, from left to right, cast members Cliff Travers, B.A., '78; Joan Fox, B.A., '79; John Buzzell, B.A., '79; and Allison Henry, A.A., '79; and stage manager Mike Roth, A.A., '79.

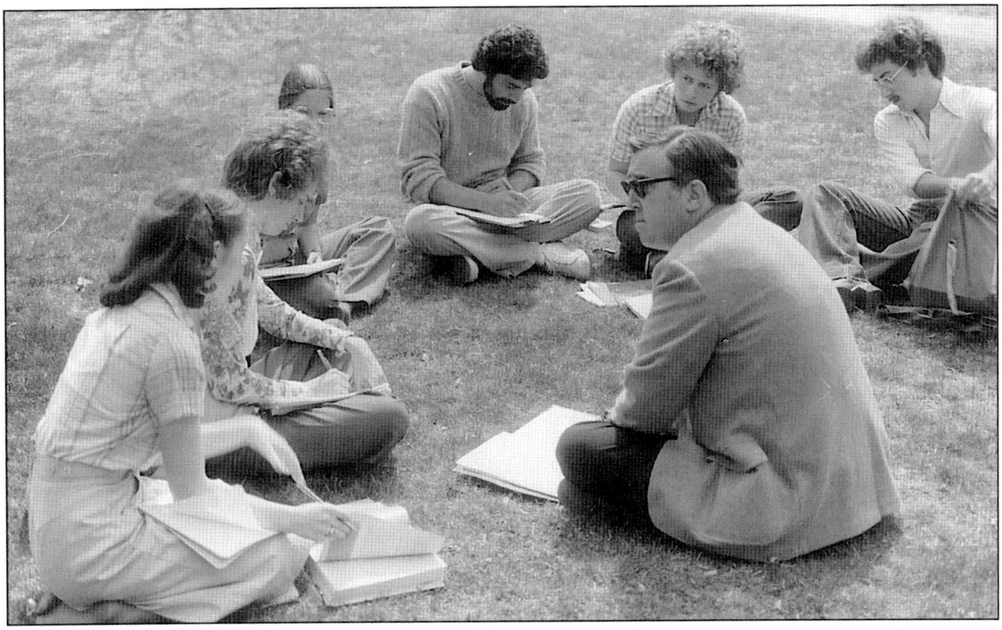

Prof. Richard Broadhurst, Biology. Dick Broadhurst joined the faculty in 1975, replacing Dr. Norman Bailey. He had an M.S. from Boston College and had done graduate work in Vienna and Paris, as well as at Tufts University. Broadhurst developed the introductory science course for the Bradford Plan curriculum revision of the 1980s. He is shown with students Cindi Carbone, A.A., '79; Janet Bologna, A.A., '79; Geri Bergstein, B.A. '81; Ron Simonian, B.A., '78; Paige Allner; and Ron Soucy, A.A., '79. Dick Broadhurst died suddenly in 1986.

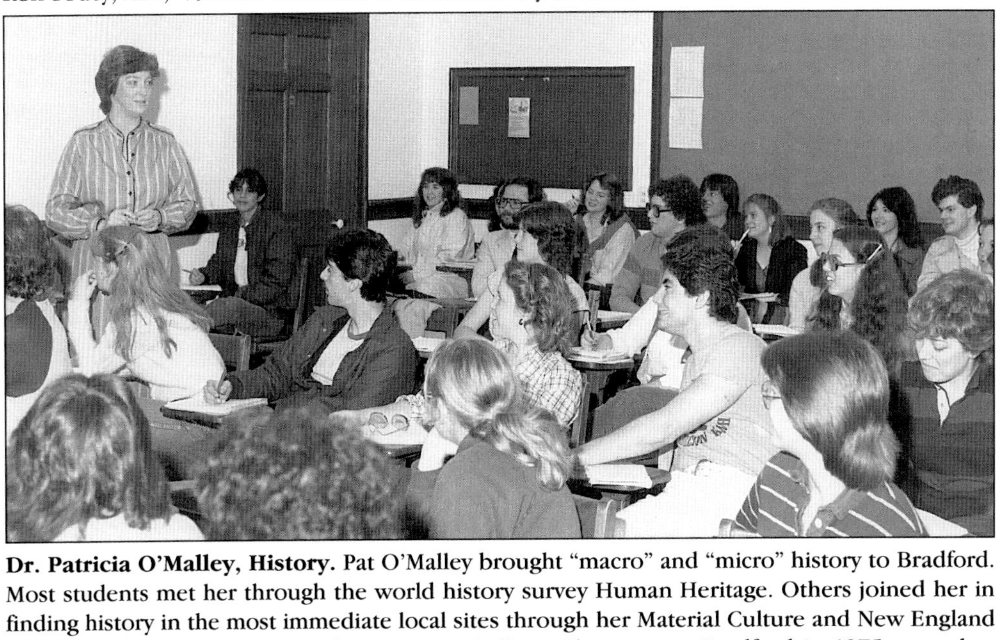

Dr. Patricia O'Malley, History. Pat O'Malley brought "macro" and "micro" history to Bradford. Most students met her through the world history survey Human Heritage. Others joined her in finding history in the most immediate local sites through her Material Culture and New England courses. O'Malley had a Ph.D. from Boston College. She came to Bradford in 1975, served as first chairman of the Humanities Division, and was the Abby Milton O'Neill Distinguished College Professor from 1986 to 1990. She was promoted to professor in 1988 and chosen Professor of the Year in 1999.

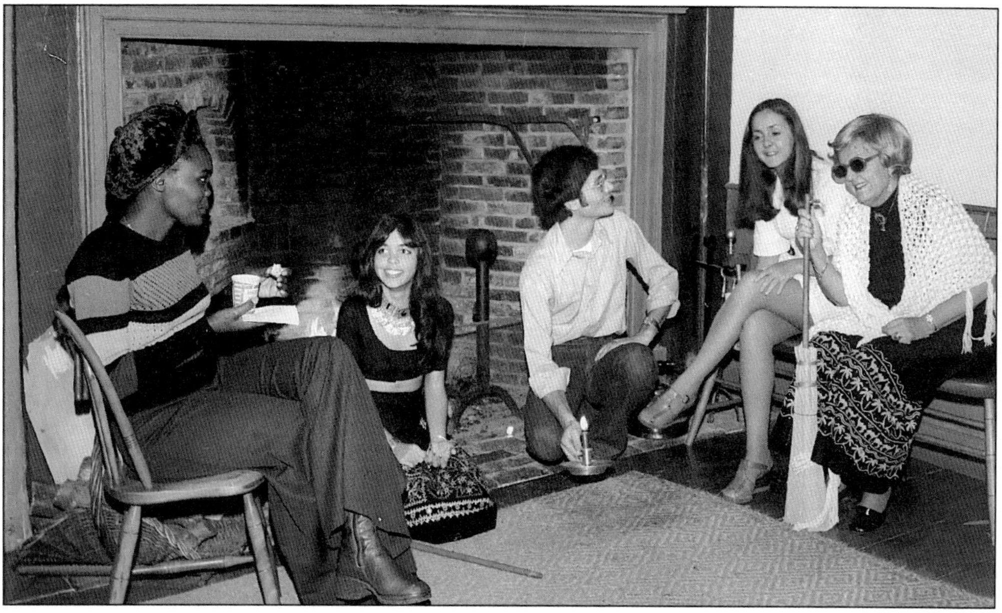

The International Club. The place is the Tavern Room at Kimball Tavern; the date is November 1976; the event is a Halloween party for the International Club. In disguise on the right is Helene Hall. With her are students Nyammeru Wazuhiu, Parul Baahat, Frank Oberti, and Leslie Archambault. The tavern, where Bradford was founded in 1803, was purchased by the college in 1967.

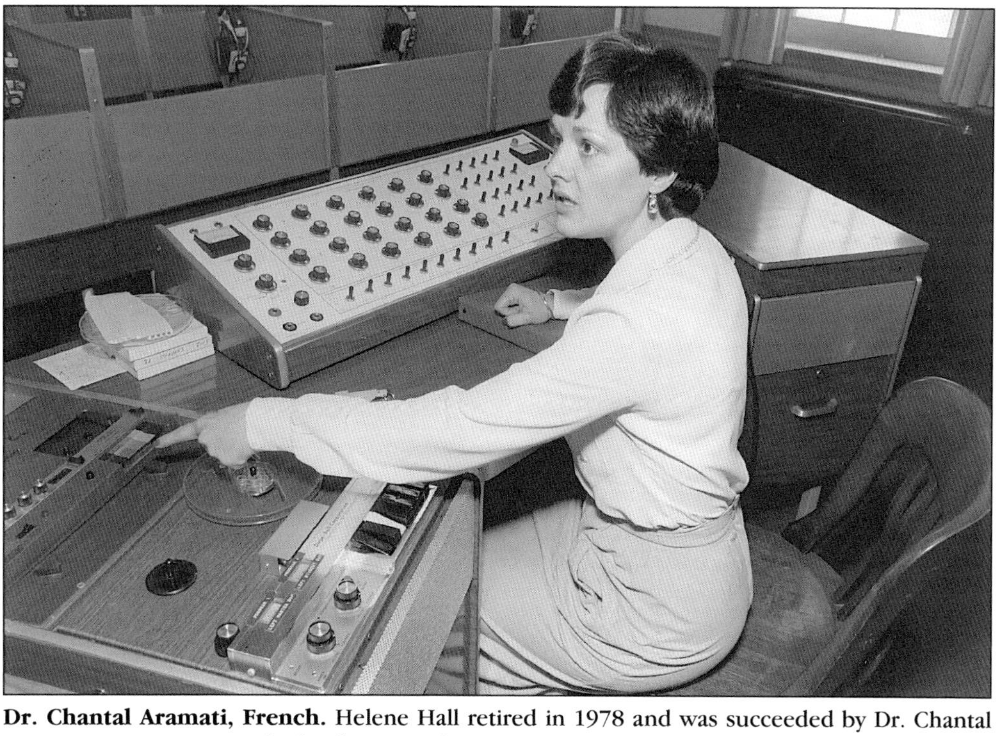

Dr. Chantal Aramati, French. Helene Hall retired in 1978 and was succeeded by Dr. Chantal Moreau Aramati. Aramati had a doctorate from Boston College. She was at Bradford until 1982. She is shown at the console in the language laboratory in Hasseltine Room 101.

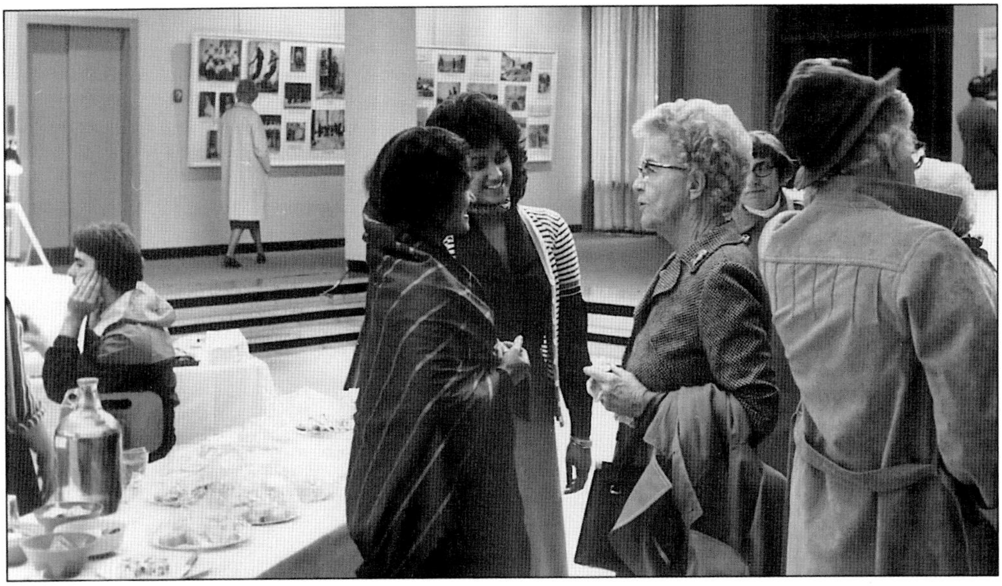

Reunited at the 175th Anniversary. Bradford celebrated its 175th anniversary in 1978, and it was an opportunity for old friends to return to the campus. Latika Ramsden Rajpal, front left, of Delhi, India, who had been a guest lecturer at Bradford in 1957, and her daughter Premanjali Rajpal, B.A., '80, center, greet Jane Runyon '18, front, second from the right. Runyon, to whom the Alumni Room in the library was dedicated, served as secretary of the Alumnae Association from 1948 to 1967. On the right, with her back to the camera, is Dorothy Bell, president emerita.

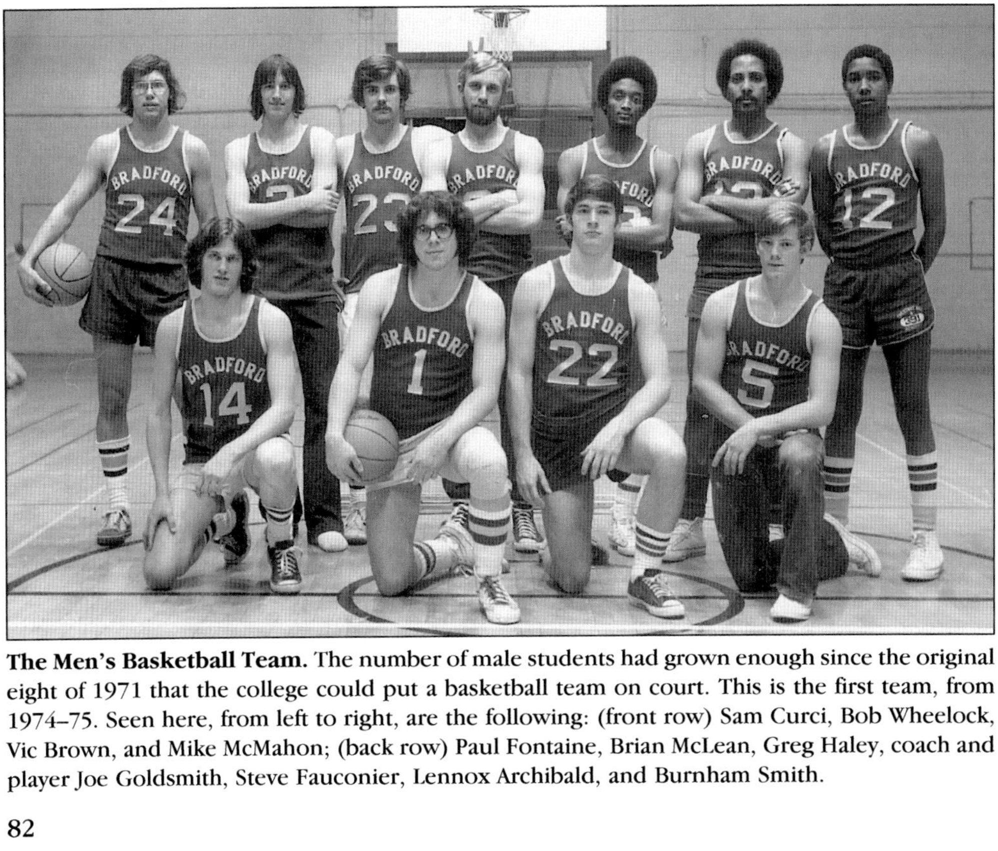

The Men's Basketball Team. The number of male students had grown enough since the original eight of 1971 that the college could put a basketball team on court. This is the first team, from 1974–75. Seen here, from left to right, are the following: (front row) Sam Curci, Bob Wheelock, Vic Brown, and Mike McMahon; (back row) Paul Fontaine, Brian McLean, Greg Haley, coach and player Joe Goldsmith, Steve Fauconier, Lennox Archibald, and Burnham Smith.

Grant Peacock, Physical Education. Peacock succeeded Prof. Betty Weber in 1978 and thus became the first male to teach physical education at Bradford. He had a master's degree from Springfield College and a national reputation as a volleyball player. Peacock left in 1982 to pursue a doctorate.

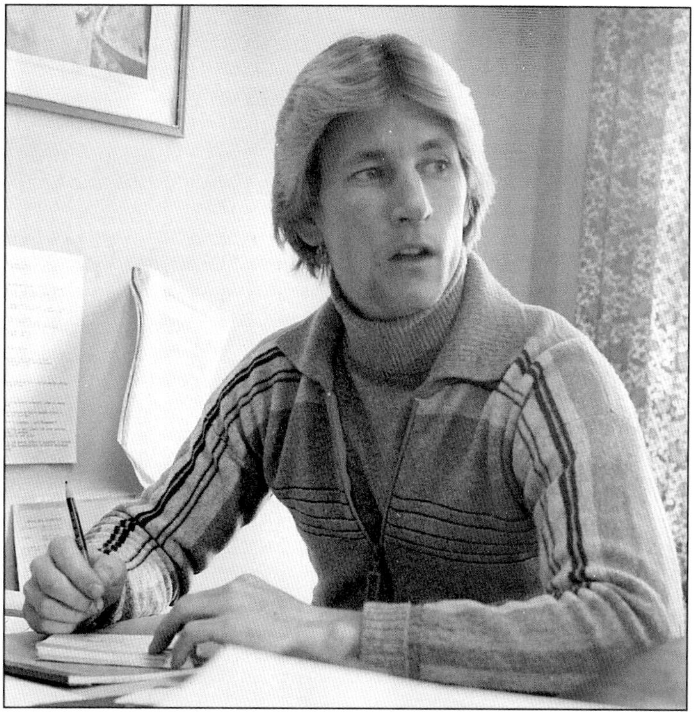

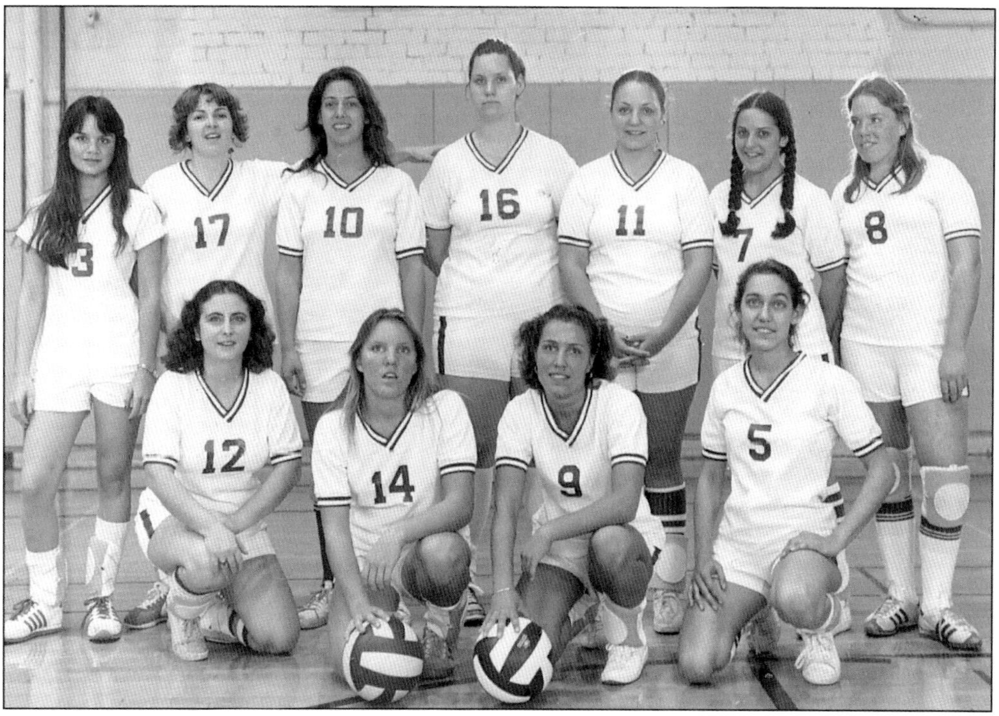

The Women's Volleyball Team. This is the 1979–80 volleyball team. Team members, from left to right, are as follows: (front row) Jean Breidenback, Josie Adams, Renate Krivanek, and Cindy Robertson; (back row) Nuri Dib, Irene Kelsey, Candace Baker, Paula Ridley, Reuki Bhavnani, Jeannette Kelting, and Sally Steinbreder.

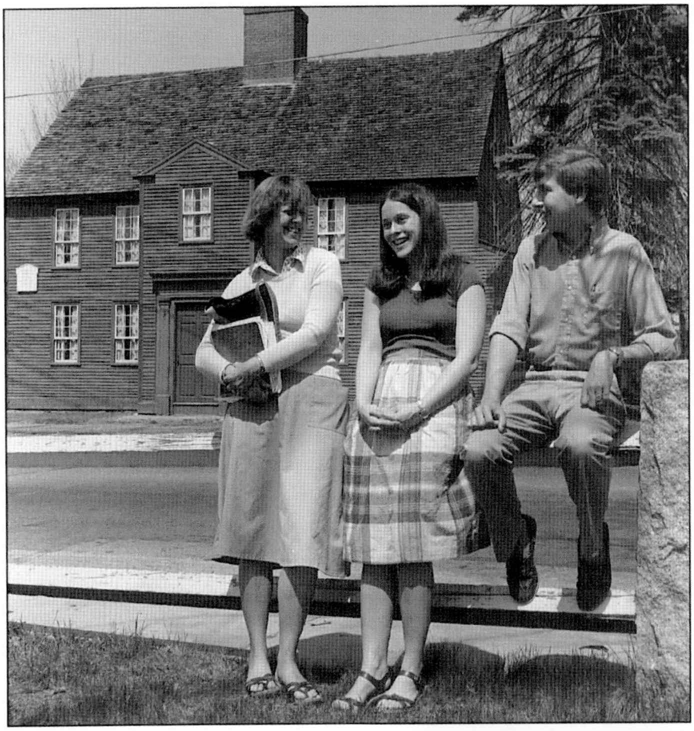

American Culture Majors. Bradford College began to expand the number of interdisciplinary majors it offered beyond the original urban studies. One such major was in American culture, which included a historic preservation component. Kimball Tavern, in the background, served as a learning laboratory. Students in the program, from left to right, are Lindsay Cavanaugh, B.A., '82; Monica Glass, B.A., '79; and David Schure, B.A., '80

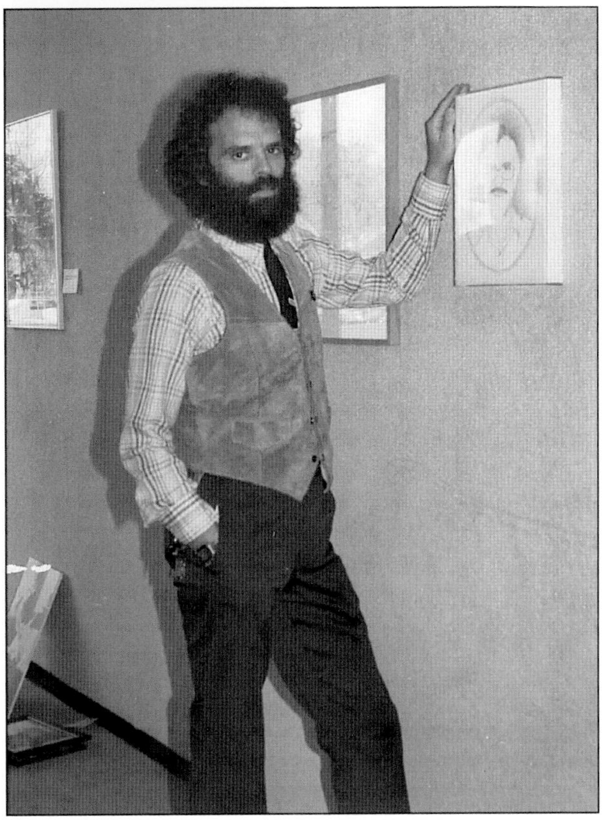

Marc Mannheimer, Art. Professor Mannheimer came to Bradford in 1979 with a master's from New York University and a flair for the unconventional. He was promoted to professor in 1991 and was the Abby O'Neill Distinguished College Professor from 1993 to 1996. He also held the Kopf Chair in Art.

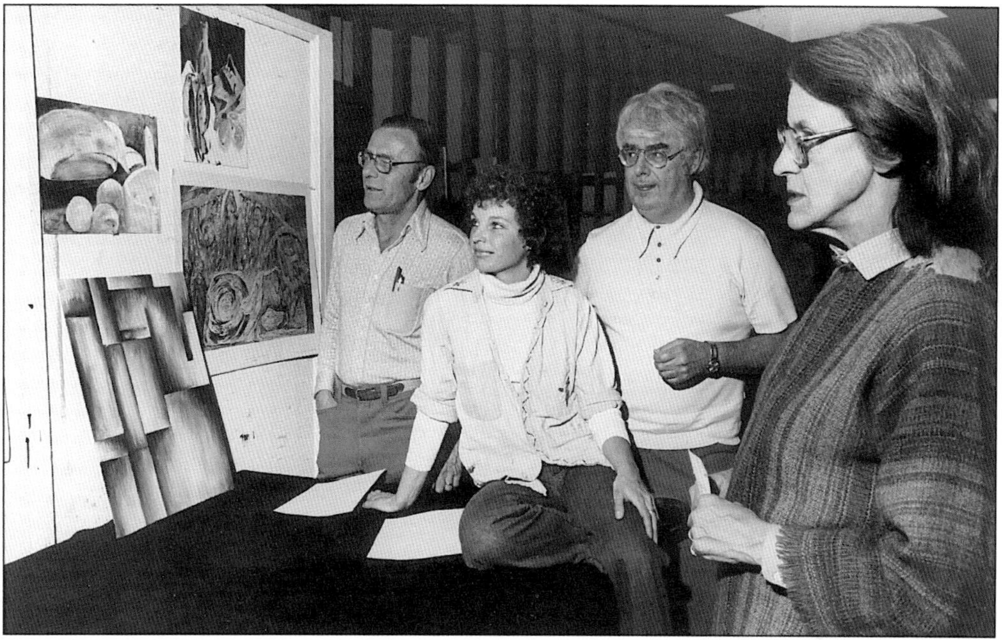

Prof. Jan Watson, Art. Professor Watson, right, came to Bradford in 1973. She had a M.Ed. from Harvard and a fifth-year certificate from the Museum of Fine Arts, Boston. When Bradford began to open its courses to part-time students, many were drawn to the art courses—among them, from left to right, Ralph Hansen, A.A., '79; Stephanie Simmons; and Louis Jameson.

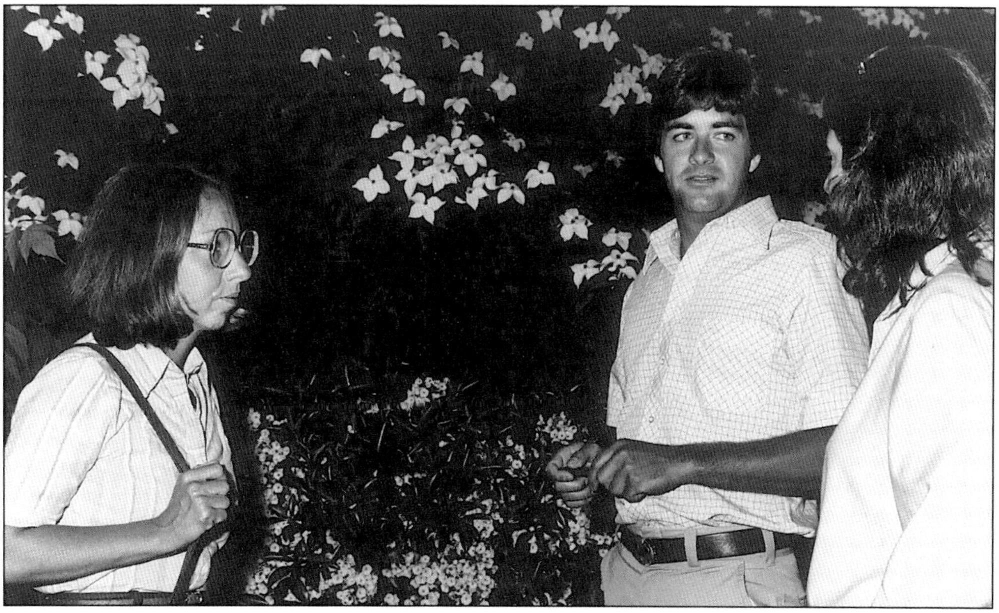

Continuing Education Students. For a few years, Bradford attempted a separate program of courses in the evening for community residents of nontraditional age. Eventually, the program was discontinued and all courses were opened to part-time students. Eleanor Grillo, left, came to Bradford with a nursing degree; Dennis Pare, center, was a state police officer. Both of them completed their B.A.s through the continuing education program in 1980. With them is "traditional" classmate Betsy Middlemus, B.A., '80.

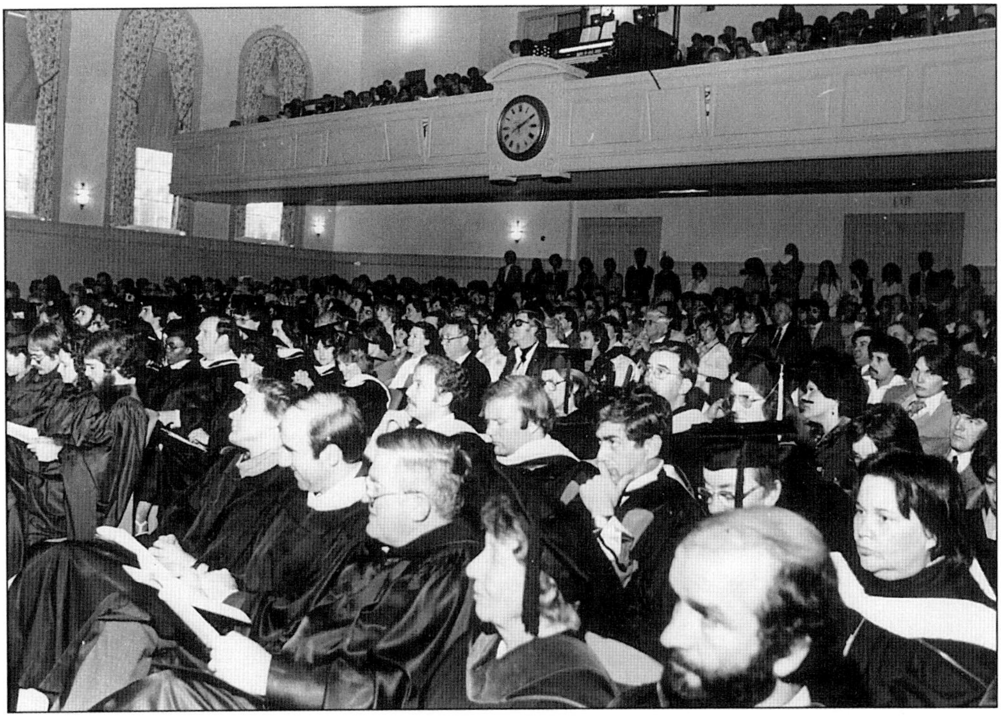

Commencement 1979, Denworth Hall. Among those attending commencement exercises in 1979 are the following: (front row, right) James Valhouli, acting dean; and from left to right, (second row) Joseph Forgiano, dean of students; Gary Horton, counselor; Dr. Anthony DeLuca; Connie Leighton; and Prof. Carolyn Morton Whitaker; (third row) Prof. Jan Watson, Prof. Richard Broadhurst, Dr. Patricia O'Malley, Dr. Chantal Aramati, and Prof. Don Ryujin.

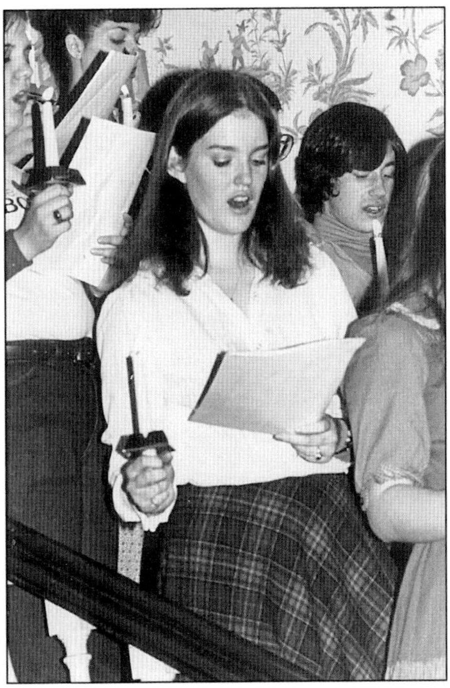

Step Singing, December 1979. Traditions fell by the proverbial wayside all throughout the 1970s. But one that survived was the ceremony of Step-Singing, which began in 1902. Just before Christmas vacation, students lined both of the main staircases, and with lighted candles in hand, sang a repertoire of carols and popular songs. Identifiable in this 1979 group of singers are, from left to right, Kathi Smith, Holly Margeson, and Kathy O'Malley—each of whom earned a B.A. in 1983.

Six

The Eighties

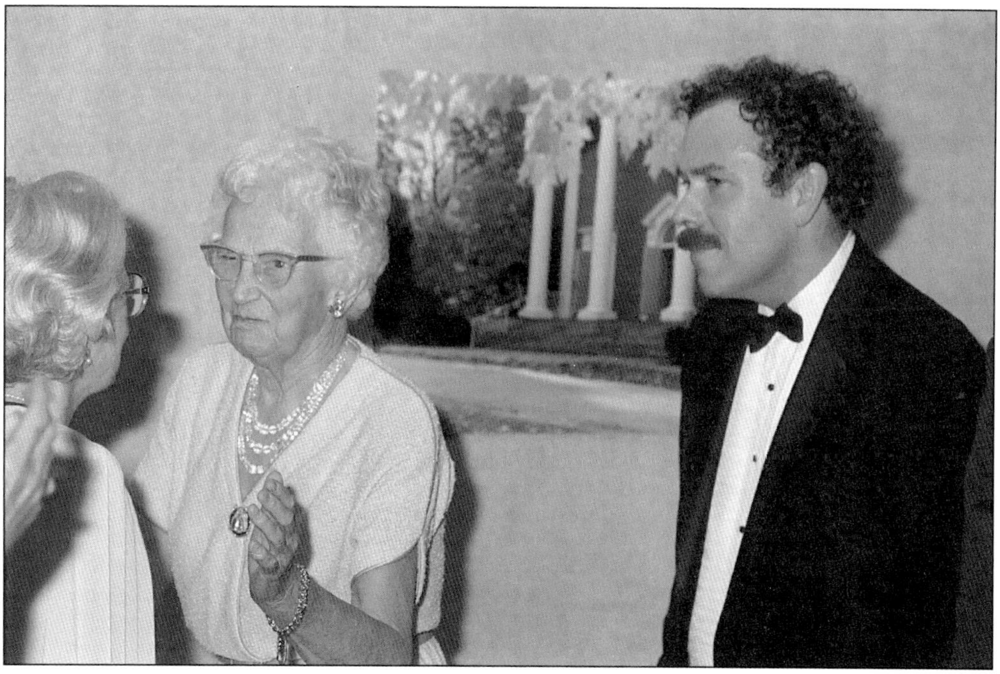

Bradford's Past and Present. Bradford's second president, Dorothy Bell, returned to the campus for what would be her last visit in 1984. (She died in 1988.) The occasion was the kickoff dinner for a $5 million fund drive. Her host was sixth president Dr. Arthur Levine, right. Levine was selected to head the college in 1982. Like President Armstrong, Levine and his wife Linda Fentiman brought a young family into the President's House. Like President Bell, he brought Bradford to national attention with his curricular innovations and mastery of public relations.

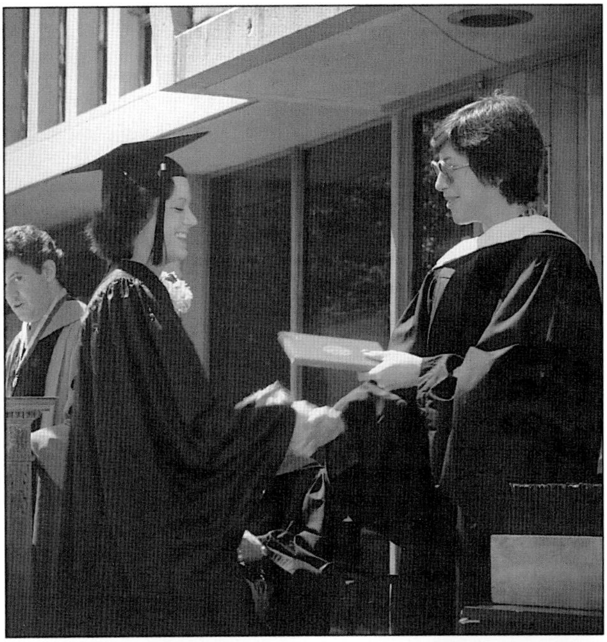

President Inge Heckel. Dr. Jack Armstrong left Bradford early in 1979. The trustees appointed one of their members, Inge Heckel, A.A., '59, right, to replace him as Bradford's fifth president. Heckel is shown at the 1980 commencement awarding Rosemarie Santoro a bachelor's degree. On the left is Dr. David Harnett, Ph.D. from Harvard, who served as dean of the college from 1979 to 1980.

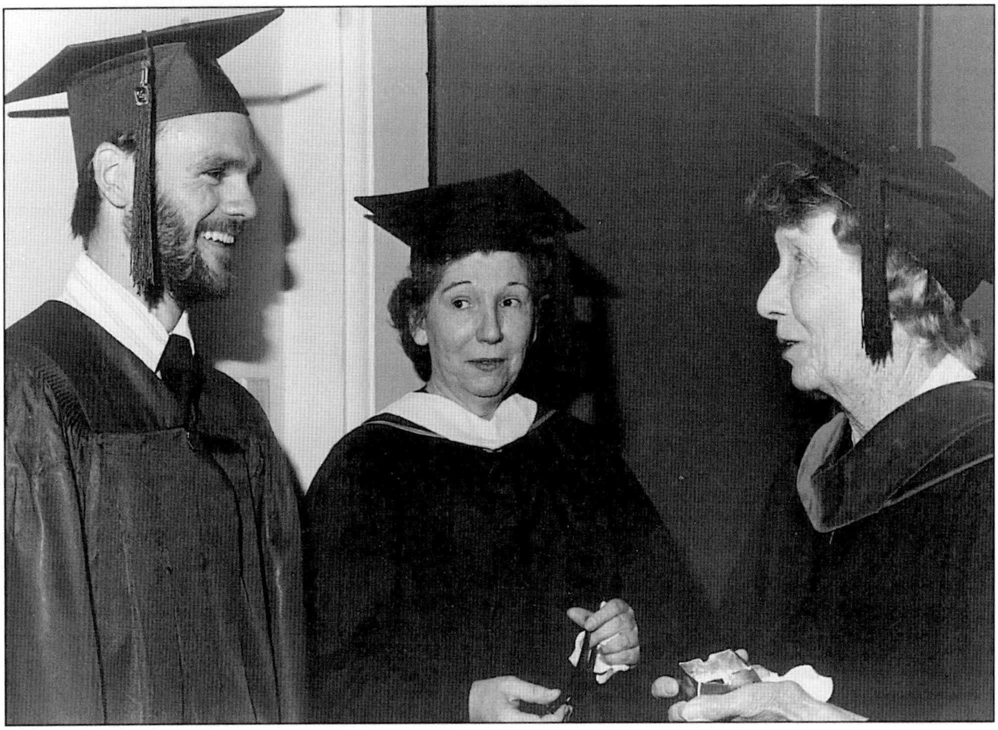

Elizabeth Knapp, Registrar. Miss—never "Ms."—Knapp, center, served as registrar from 1978 to 1989. She brought an air of southern propriety and decorum to the campus and will long be remembered for the bourbon balls she gave out to faculty as a reward for their timely delivery of final semester grades. She is shown with Thomas "Tommy" Thompson, A.A., '79 and B.A. '80, left, and Udell Redmond White '26, right, president of the Alumni Association. Elizabeth Knapp was awarded the Bell Medallion at the 1989 commencement.

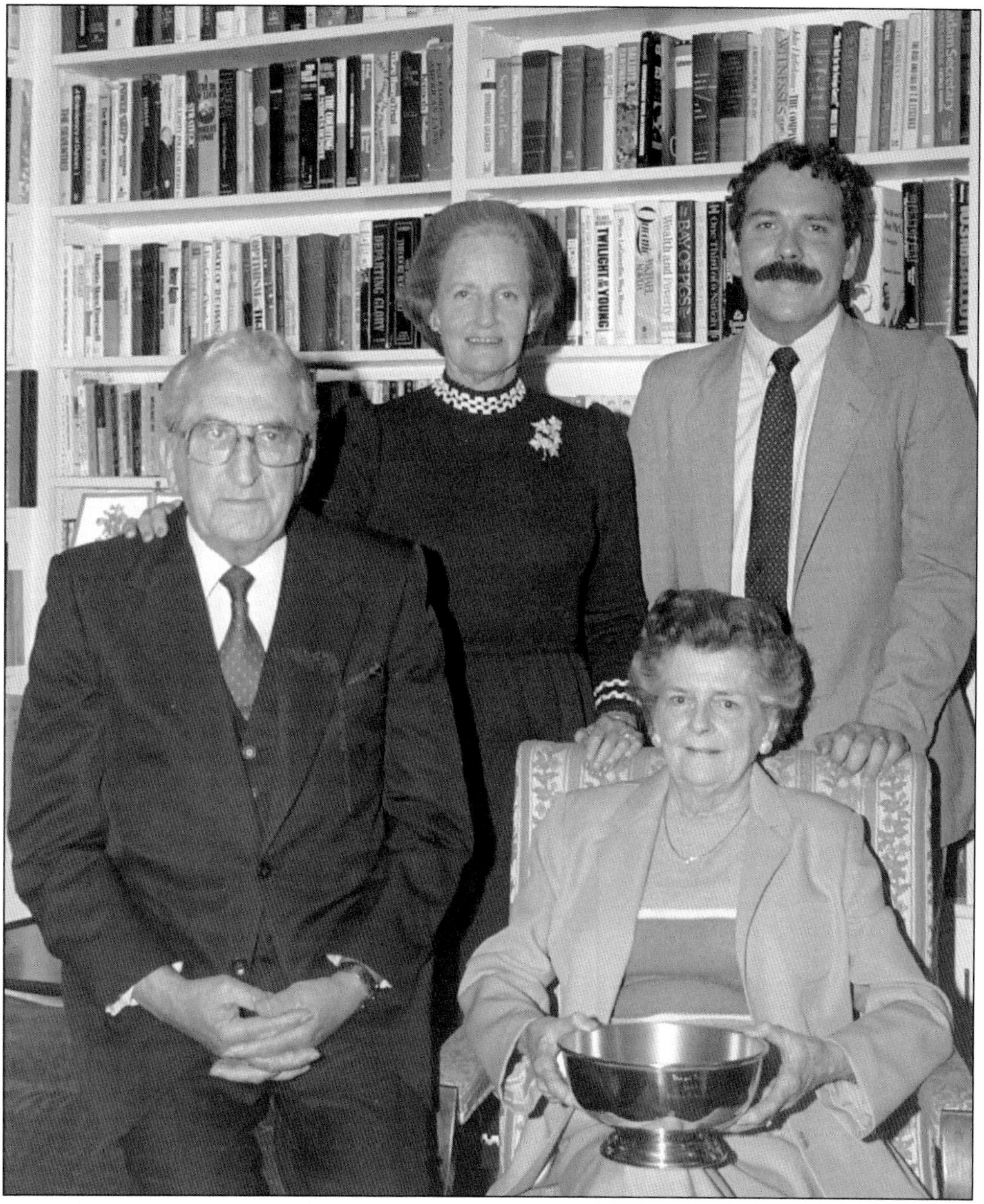

Dr. Arthur Levine. President Levine, right, came to Bradford in 1982 with an idea. For Bradford to compete and survive, it would need to revise its curriculum with a set of interrelated courses and a focus on the practicality of the liberal arts. Thus was born the Bradford Plan for a Practical Liberal Arts Education. The college was revitalized and gave a new emphasis to its four-year program. With Levine in the library of the President's House in 1986 are two women who were very important to Bradford. M. Elaine Willett, front right, served as secretary to five presidents and to the Board of Trustees for over 20 years. She received the Bell Medallion from the college in 1982 and the Paul Revere Bowl, which she holds, from the trustees at her retirement in 1986. Next to her is her husband, Franklin Willett. Abby Milton O'Neill '48, back left, served two terms as a trustee (1956–1973 and 1974–1991) and was honored with the college's first doctor of humane letters.

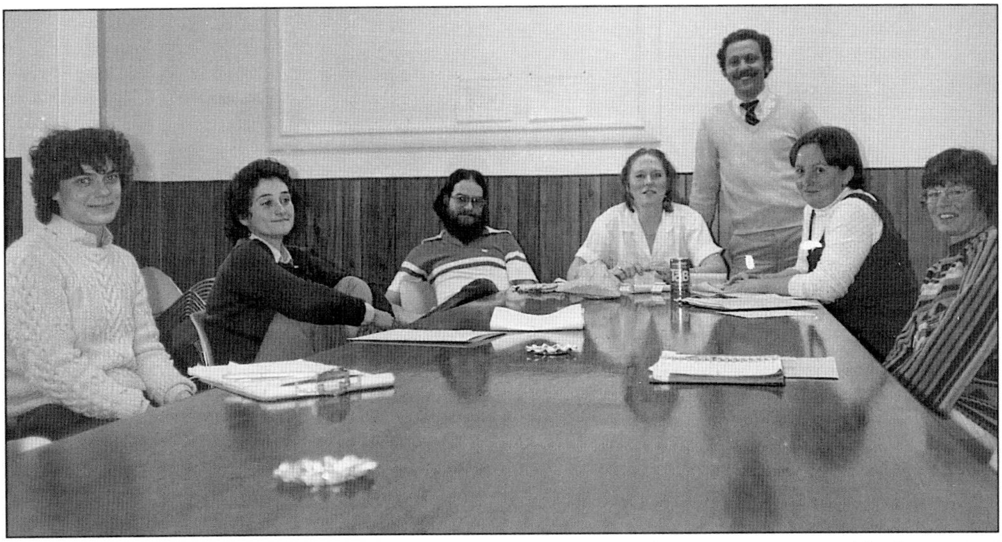

The Student Services Staff, 1981. Joseph Forgiano, standing, came to Bradford in 1975 as a one-year replacement in the drama program. He was asked to stay on as associate dean for student services. Shown with him are some of his staff, from left to right, Dr. Frances Bigda-Peyton, Dr. Theo Capaldo, Jim Kreider, Kate Fahey, Mary Paulson, and Beverly Hoering, R.N. Forgiano and his wife, Martha Forgiano, also served as residence directors for Tupelo East, and she was on the College Learning Program staff. The couple left Bradford in 1982 so that he could complete his doctorate.

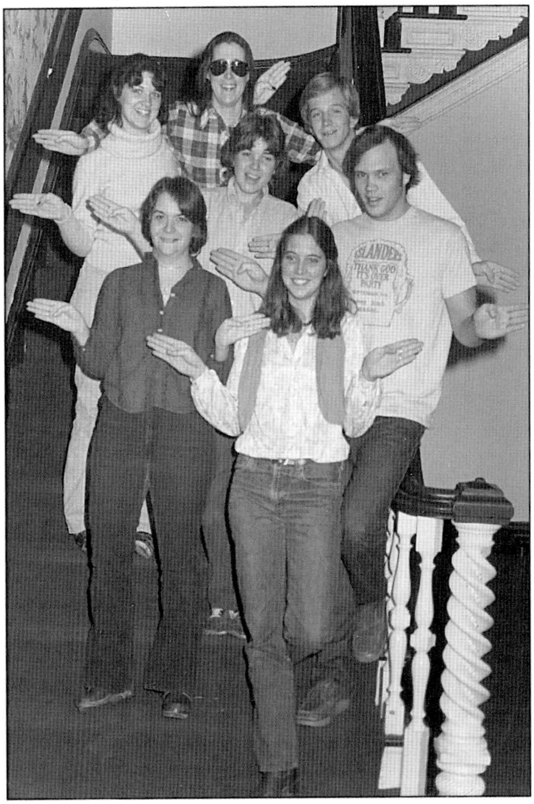

Resident Assistants. Students took over greater responsibility by the late 1970s, serving as resident assistants in the dormitories. These seven students were in charge of Academy Hall in 1981-82. Seen here, from left to right, are the following: (front row) Wendy Petit and Debbie Brown; (middle row) Michelle Rocheford, Susan Blatchford, and Scott Leonard; (back row) Sarah Galvin and Colin McCarty.

Dean of Students. Donald McClain became dean of students in 1982. He came to Bradford from Holy Cross College. A kind and gentle man, he was unflappable under the most stressful conditions. He served as dean until 1987 and then was appointed vice president for student development and dean of freshmen, in which position he served until 1991.

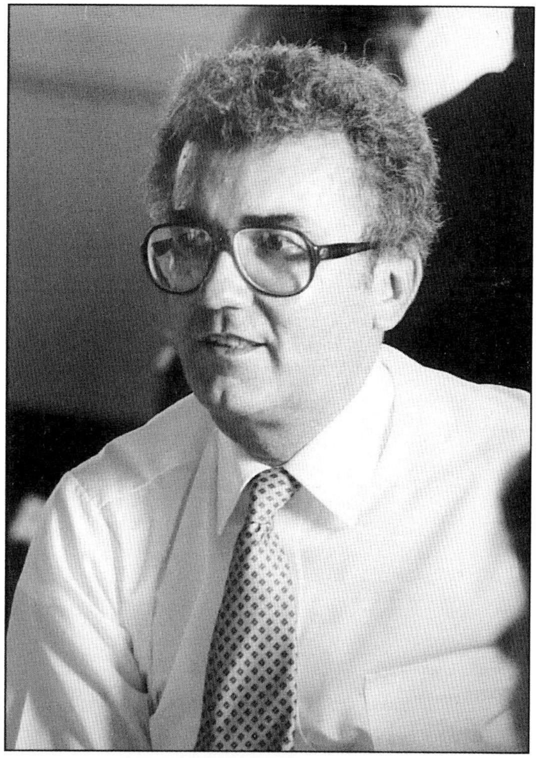

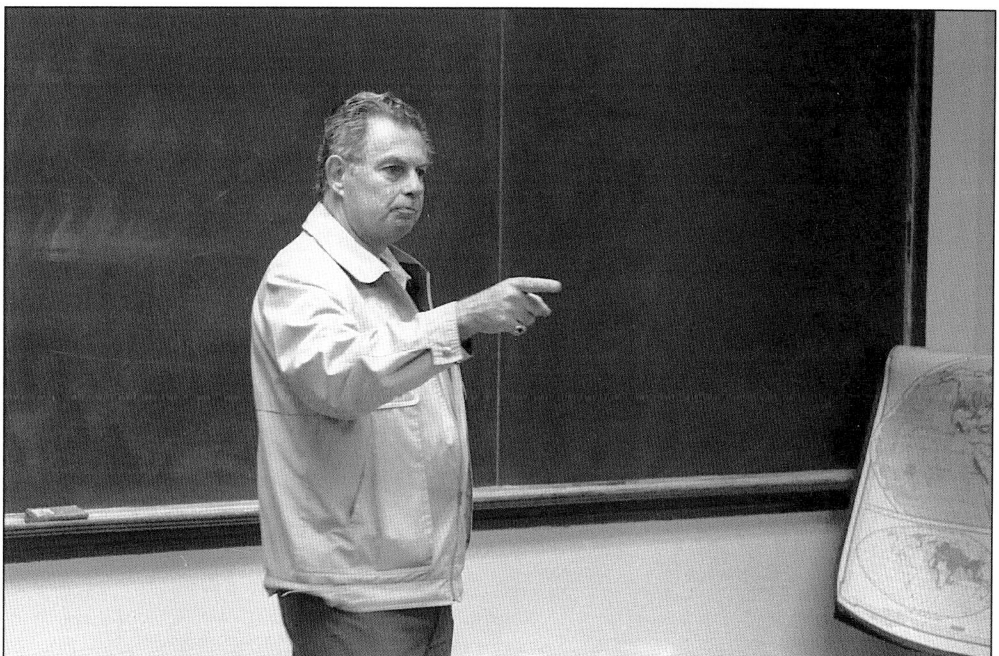

Dr. Miller Graf, Management. A retired U.S. Air Force officer with 24 years of service, Miller Graf came to Bradford in 1980. He had a doctorate in public administration from Nova University. He was the first chairman of the Administration and Management Division and taught a variety of economics and management courses.

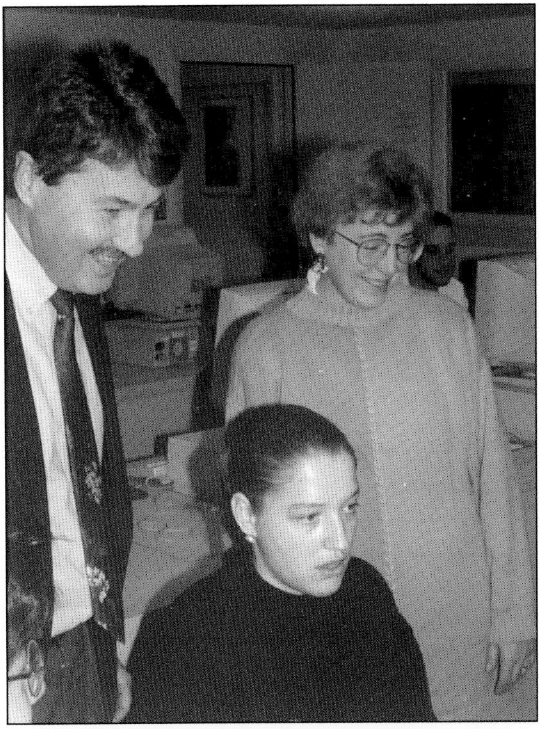

The English Language Institute. Bradford inaugurated a new program in 1979 to boost its enrollment and add more diversity to the campus. This was the English Language Institute, which provided an intensive program of English language study for foreign students. Paul Abraham, left, succeeded the first director, Dennis Weyant, in 1982. Standing beside Abraham is Linda Miller, an instructor in the program from its beginning, who also taught courses in the freshman writing program.

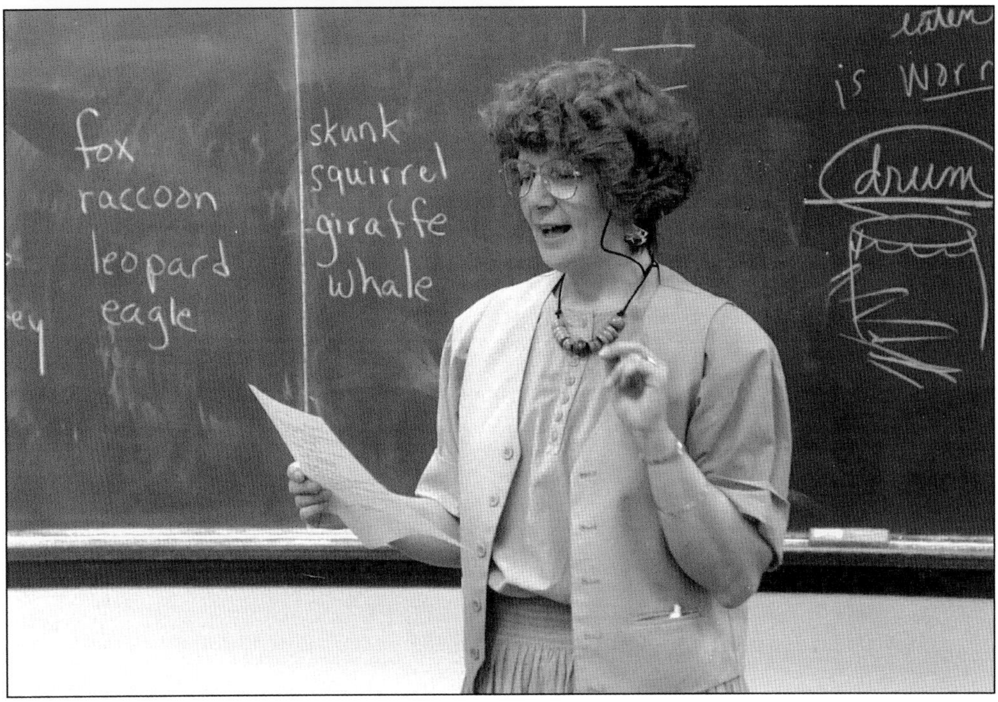

Carol Allen, English Language Institute. Professor Allen joined the faculty of the English Language Institute program in 1980, its second year. In addition to the language courses, she tutored foreign students in the world history course Human Heritage and taught speech communication for the Humanities Division.

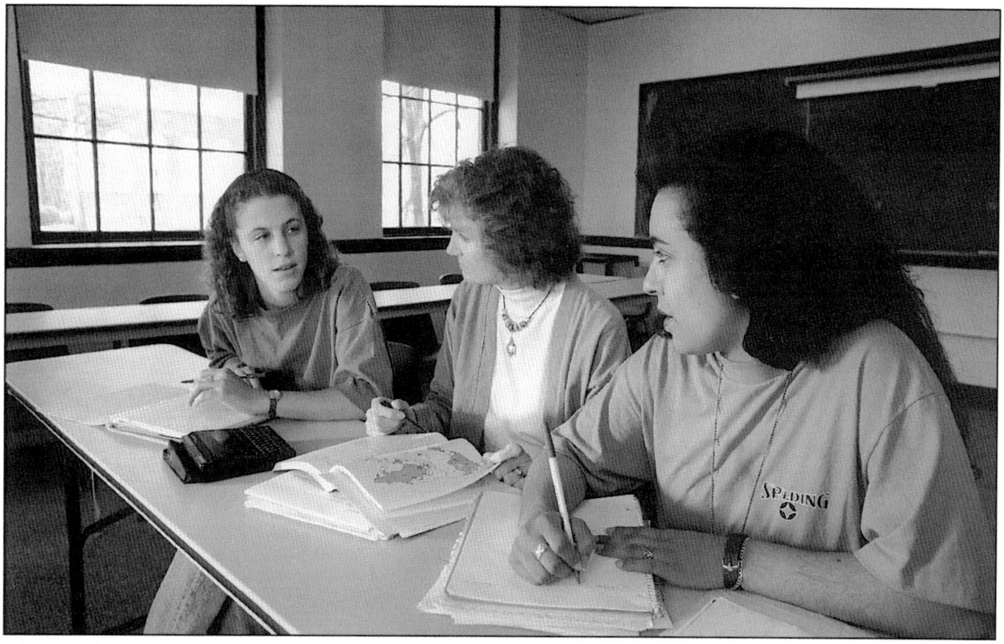

The College Learning Program. A second new program, added to the college in 1980, was the College Learning Program. It was designed to meet the needs of students with moderate learning disabilities. Through a combination of tutorial sessions, alternative testing procedures, and special workshops, enrolled students were taught to help themselves attain their fullest potential. Diane Waldron, center, served as director of the program in the 1980s.

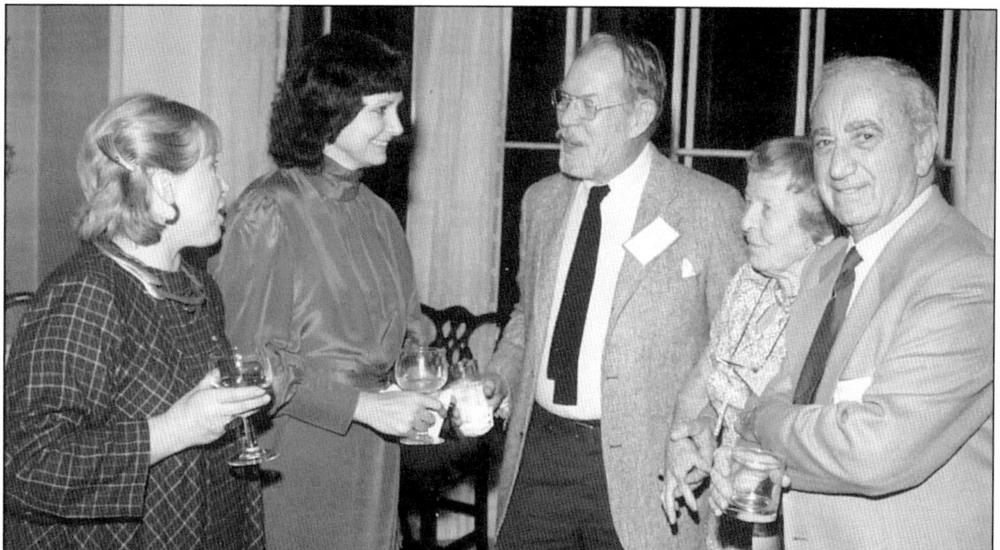

Special Friends of Bradford. Ann Armstrong Powell, director of college relations during Arthur Levine's presidency, shares a moment at the President's House with some special supporters of Bradford. Seen here, from left to right, are Rita (Mrs. Samuel) Robert, Ann Powell, Clark Gowen, Rosamond Ingalls Gowen '19, and Samuel Robert. Samuel Robert served two terms on the Board of Trustees. The Samuel K. Robert Computer Center in Hasseltine Hall was donated in his honor by his family.

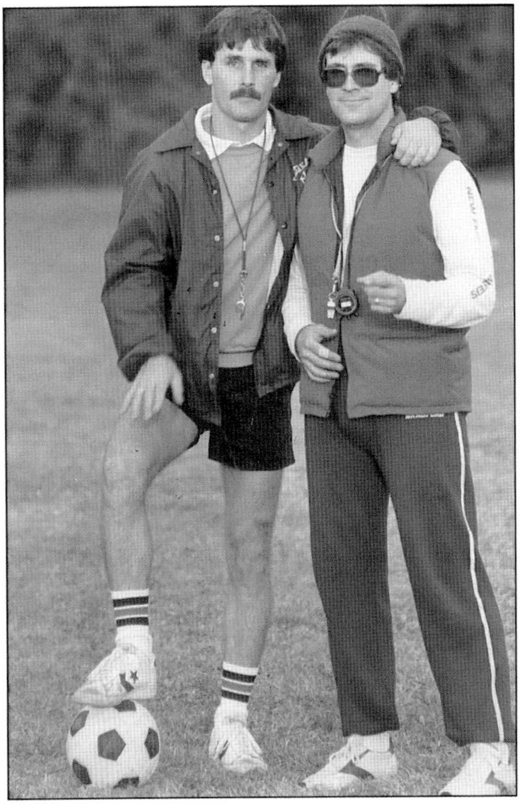

Physical Education Staff. David Paling, left, came to Bradford in 1981 with a master's from the University of New Hampshire. He and his wife, Sue Paling, served as dormitory directors, in addition to his work in the physical education program until he left in 1986. His colleague Rick LaRue, right, arrived in 1982, took a year off in 1983 to work on his doctorate at Springfield College, and returned to teach from 1984—when this photograph was taken—to 1990.

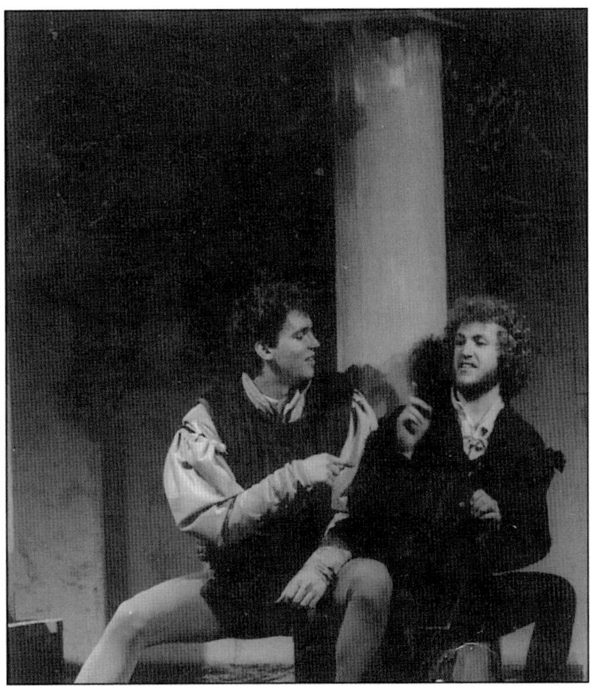

Drama in the 1980s. Bradford's theater program in the first half of the 1980s was under the direction of Kim Mancuso, who had a M.F.A. from Yale. Her 1984 production *Romeo and Juliet* starred graduate Stephen Haley '83 and Prof. Peggy Rambach. The supporting cast included Terry O'Malley '85, left, as Benvolio and Kevin McGee '85, right, as Mercutio.

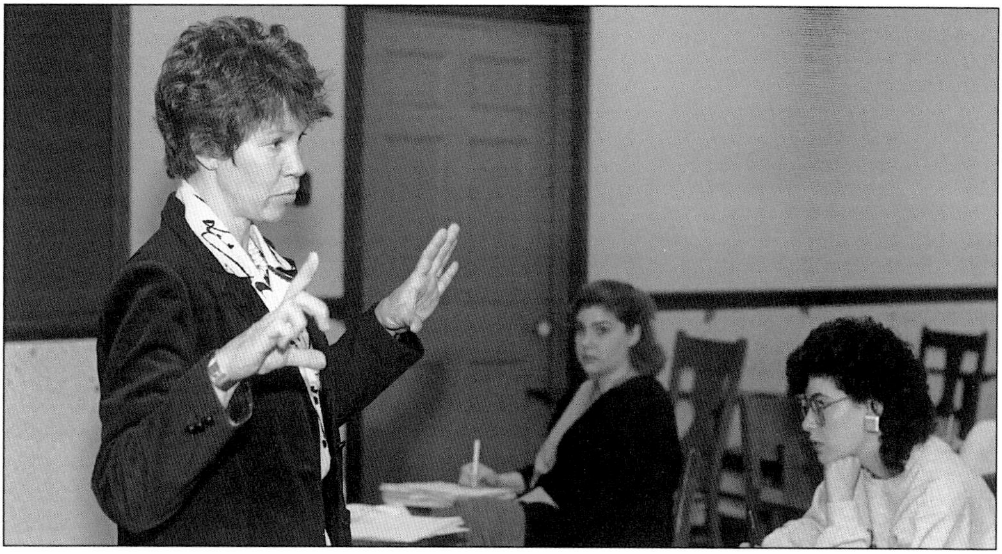

Dr. Patricia Cronin, Psychology. Pat Cronin joined the Bradford faculty in 1981 with a doctorate from Kansas State University. She served as chairman of the Division of Human Studies and was promoted to professor in 1996. She was much honored for her teaching and community service. She was appointed to the Abby O'Neill Chair for Distinguished Teaching in 1990. In 1992, she was named Woman of the Year in Greater Haverhill and in 1997, she was proclaimed Bradford's Professor of the Year. The student on the right is Vanessa Newman '90, daughter of Profs. Dick and Rochelle Newman.

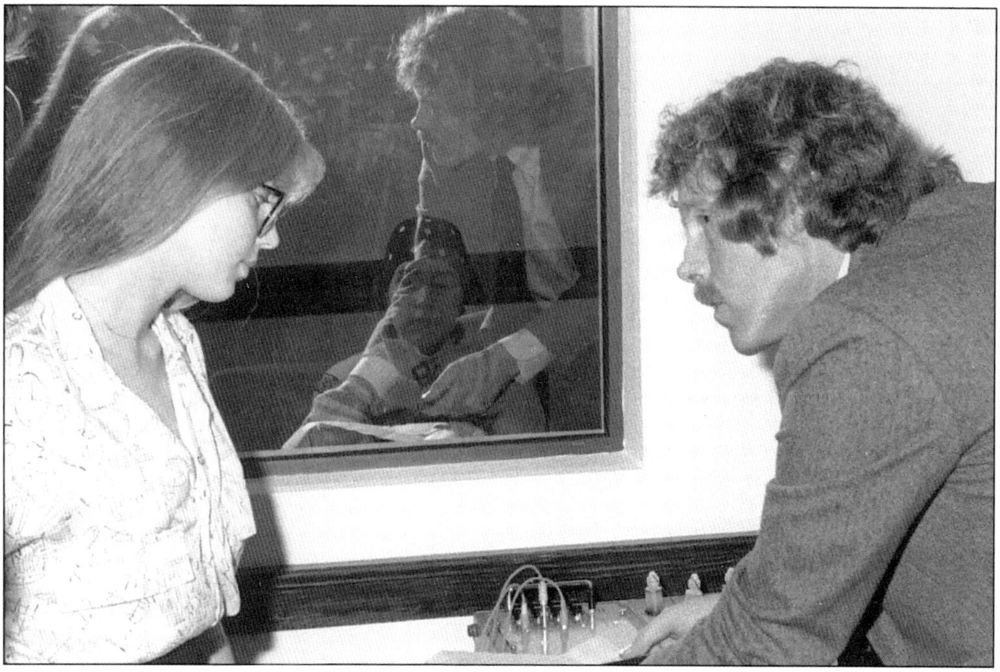

Dr. Jonathan B. Earle, Psychology. Jon Earle earned a Ph.D. from Tufts University and came to Bradford in 1982. He was instrumental in having a psychology laboratory created on the third floor of Hasseltine, where he is shown. Christine Moritz '89, left, was in the first group of science majors to graduate. Earle left Bradford in 1997 and died of a heart attack in 1998.

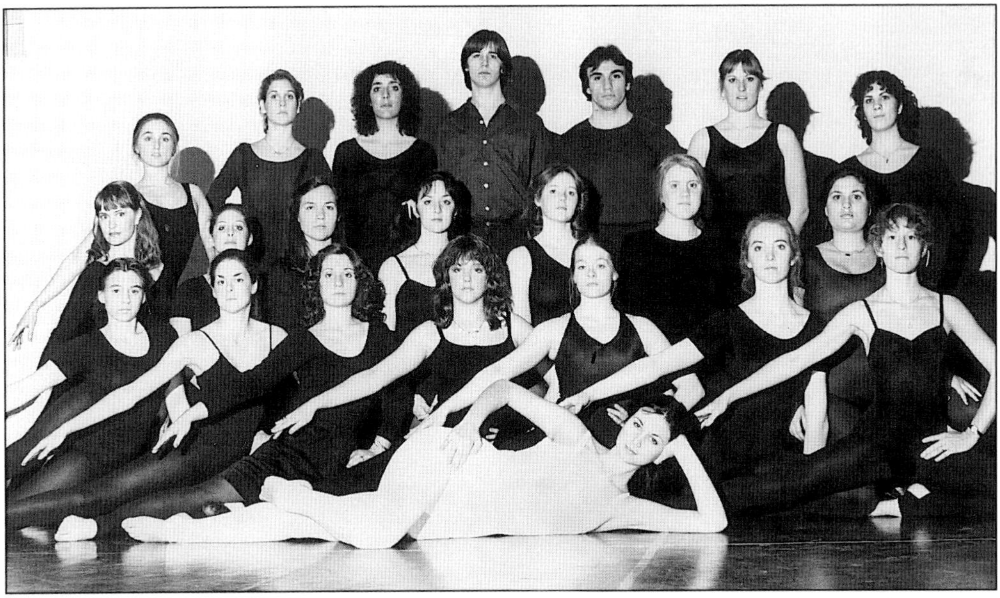

Bradford Dancers. Dance had been a part of the Bradford curriculum for decades. It was included in the Physical Education Department until the 1980s, when it was placed in the Creative Arts Division. Dance became a concentration within the creative arts major. These are the Bradford College dancers in Spring 1980, shown with their teacher Prof. Ann Marie Borkowski, second row on the left.

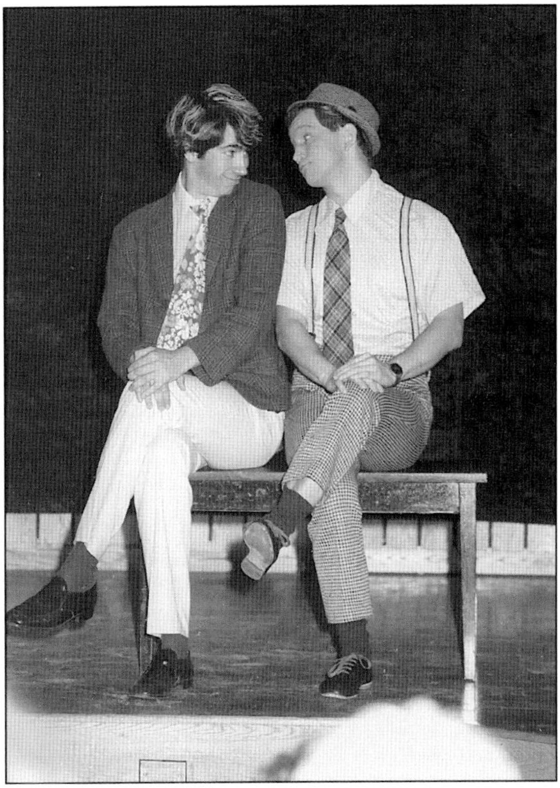

Cabaret Performers. Prof. Charles Ludington began a very successful Music Theater workshop program. Each fall semester, during Alumni Weekend, the students in the workshop put on a cabaret performance. Each spring they appeared in a full-scale musical. In 1983, Ludington invited a group of alumni to return and perform during Alumni Weekend. Ian McNeil, A.A., '82 and Colin McCarty, B.A., '82 perform *Never Say No* from *The Fantasticks*.

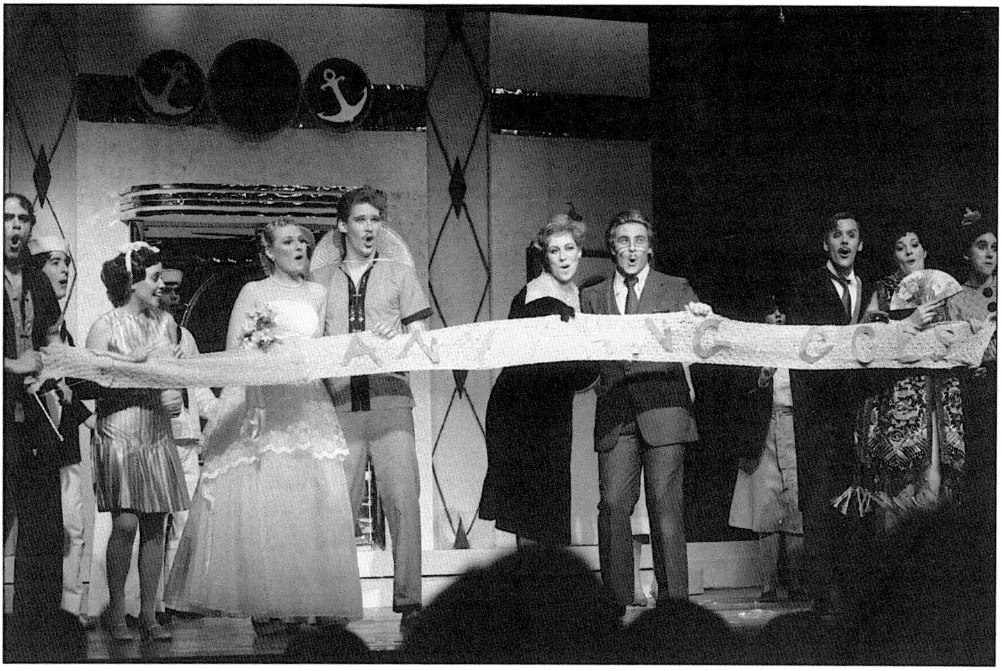

Anything Goes. This 1983 musical production was Cole Porter's *Anything Goes*. Cast members included, from left to right, Russell Cohen '85, Laura Batchelder '85, Leslie Mooers-Benvenuti '84, Terrence O'Malley '85, Holly Margeson '83, Jordan Kaplan '86, Douglas Chamberlain '85, and Michelle Rocheford '83.

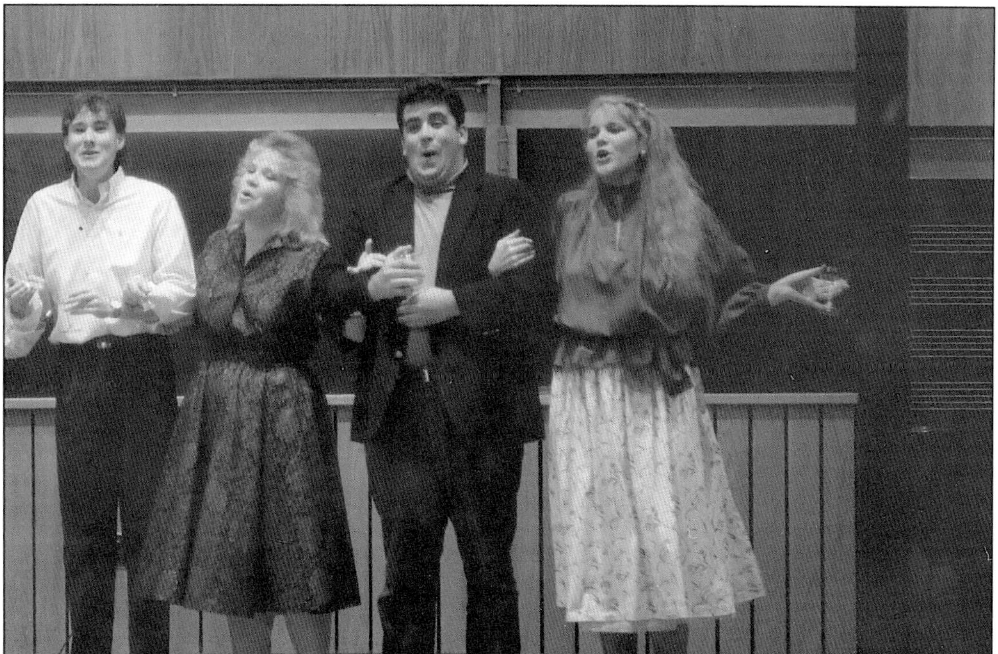

Cabaret, Too! Arm-in-arm-in-arm-in arm, these four singers entertain in a cabaret show from the mid-1980s. Seen here, from left to right, are Edmund Byrne '88, Laura Preston '87, Christopher Wolfe '87, and Barbara Norris '87.

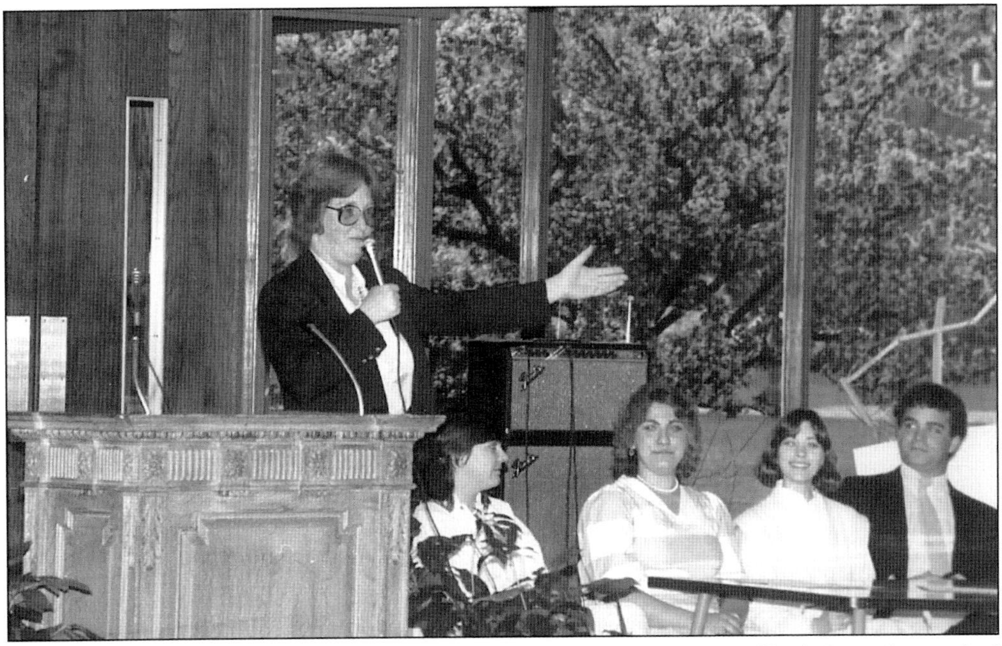

Intellectual Celebration, 1985. A new tradition was begun with the Bradford Plan—the week of Intellectual Celebration. It included senior project presentations, guest speakers, performances, the awarding of academic honors, and a Dean's Dinner for those who had made the dean's list in the past year. As part of the Dean's Dinner "entertainment" in 1985, Dr. Pat O'Malley, left, put four of her students through a rapid-fire demonstration of the Socratic teaching method. The students, from left to right, are Lisa Donovan '86, Deanna Yameen '85, Elisabeth Bossi '85, and Todd Hamilton '86.

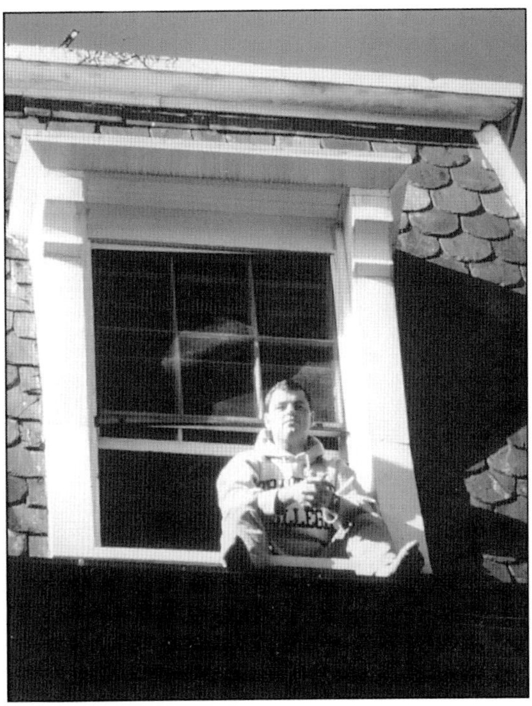

Above It All. Thomas Fishel '86 contemplates the world from his perch on the fourth floor of Academy Hall. Earlier classes would have had access to the rooftop but, with that area closed off, the best that Fishel could do was to sunbathe his bare feet outside his dorm room window.

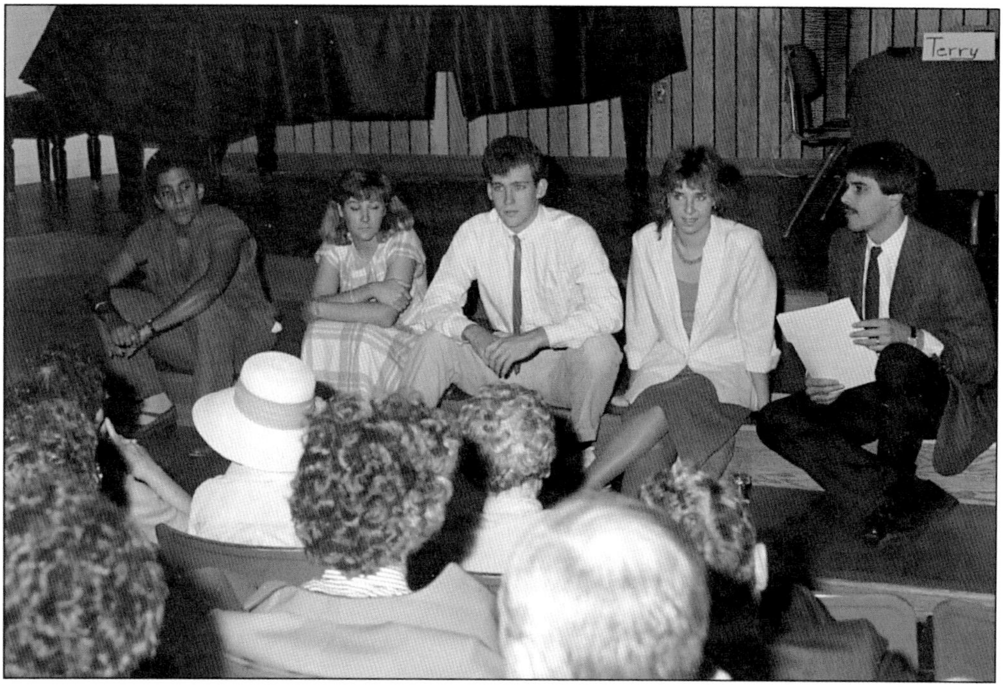

Addressing the Alumni. Four students faced an audience of alumni in 1984 to discuss their futures as liberal arts graduates. Seen here, from left to right, are John Ward '86, Barbara Lorenz '88, Terry O'Malley '85, and Doris Doonan '87. David Bell, right, career resources director, moderated the session.

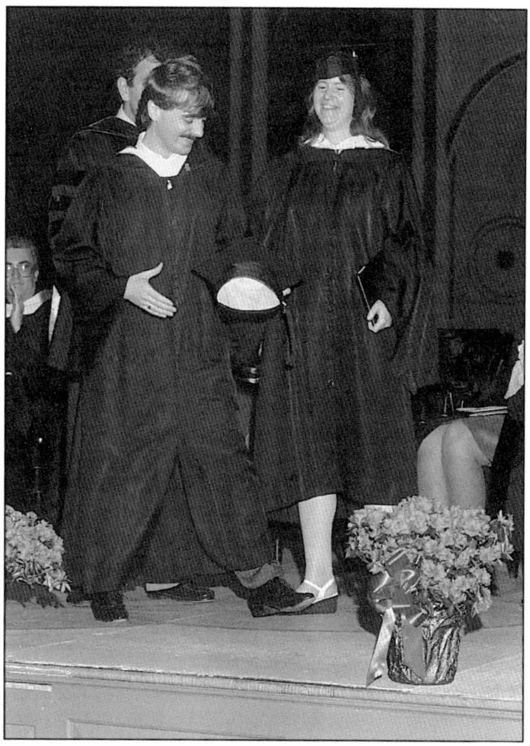

Mary C. Barrett Prize Winners. One of Bradford's highest awards at commencement is the Barrett Prize for the student "who has made the greatest contribution to the college community through character, effort, and influence." Peter A. Carey, left, and Kathy Ann Stewart shared the award in 1985. Both were active in the arts at Bradford and at the same graduation, Carey received the Dangerfield Dance Cup and the Special Award in Theater for best performance. Stewart, who was the student speaker, won the Theresa A. Mors Award.

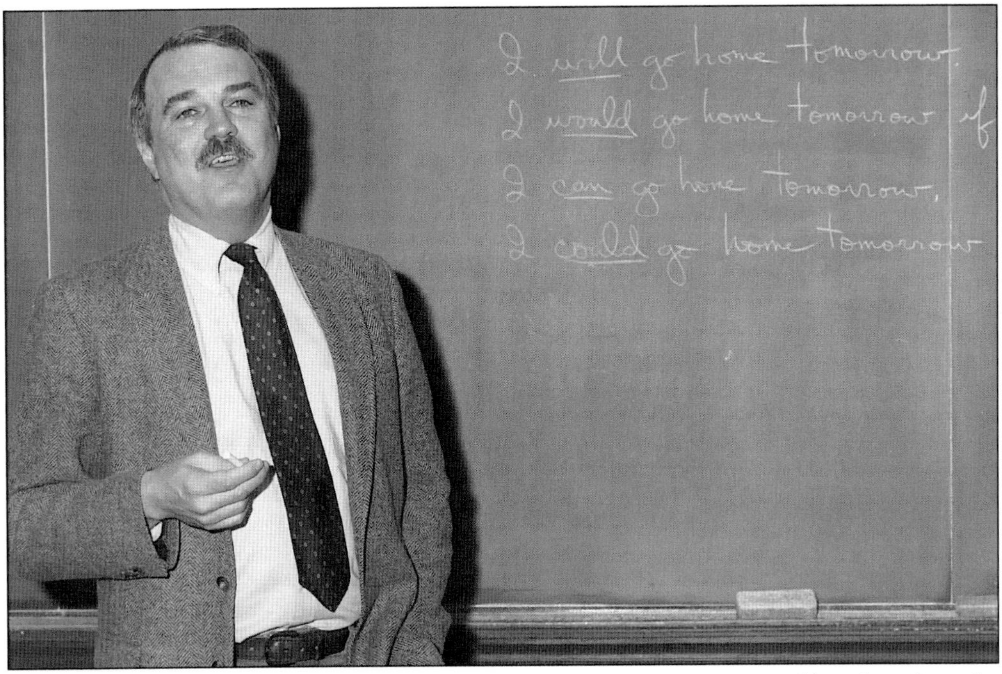

Dr. Francis L. Nye, Literature. Frank Nye, a native of South Carolina, earned his Ph.D. from the University of North Carolina, Chapel Hill. He joined the Bradford faculty in 1982 and specialized in British literature. He served as chairman of the Humanities Division and was promoted to professor in 1992.

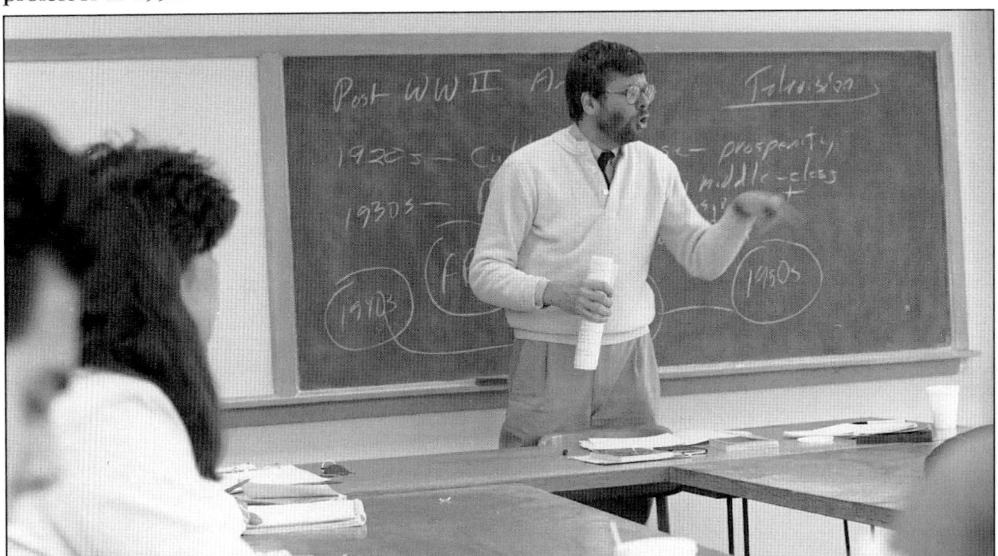

Dr. Mark K. Kosinski, American Culture. Mark Kosinski, who was at Bradford from 1984 to 1997, was hired to teach courses in American history and literature. He added to his repertoire numerous courses in American popular culture. Kosinski took an active part in the local community. He wrote a regular column for the newspaper and hosted an interview program on local cable television. He served as chairman of the Humanities Division from 1991 to 1997 and was promoted to professor in 1995.

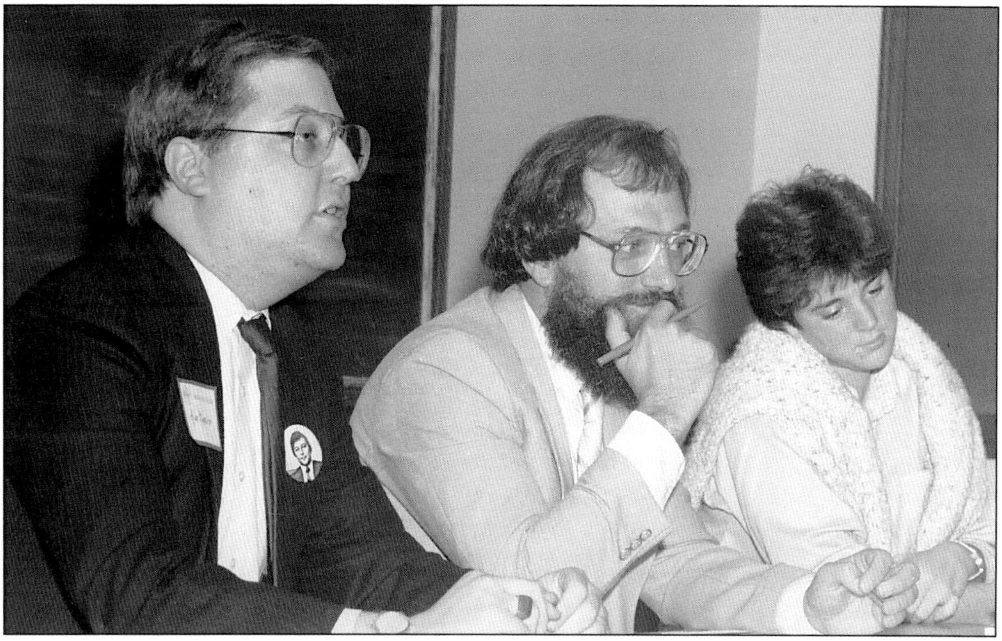

Dr. Robert A. Smart, Writing Program. Bob Smart, center, was invited to join the Bradford faculty in 1984 to coordinate the writing program and to teach what became a wide range of literature courses, from the classics to tales of vampires. He has been much honored. He was the first, and only, recipient of the Dorothy Bell Chair in Writing and was the first faculty member to be awarded the title Professor of the Year (1990). He has been chair of the Humanities Division and of the Faculty Senate. He was promoted to professor in 1993. With Smart at an alumni reunion discussion are Alan Mounty, B.A., '78, left, and Katina Lee Manko, B.A., '88.

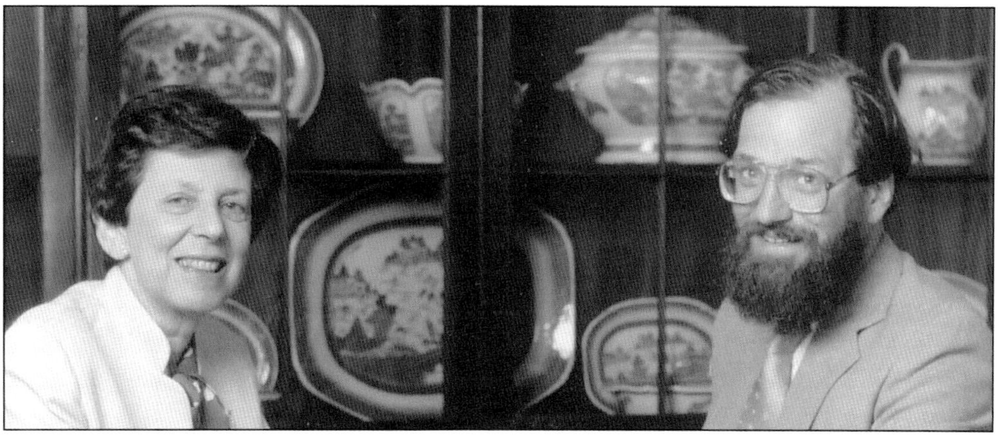

Dr. Janice Green, Dean. Janice Green, left, came to Bradford in 1981 and brought stability to the office of the academic dean. Four people had served as dean in the three years proceeding. She also brought professionalism to her post and was the first to carry the title of vice president and academic dean. It was her responsibility to turn the idea of the Bradford Plan into an organized curriculum. She also created the criteria for dividing the faculty into academic ranks, the procedures for promotion, and led the final transition from a two-year college with associate's degrees to a four-year college with bachelor's degrees. In the fall of 1987, while President Levine was on sabbatical, she served as acting president, while Dr. Robert Smart, right, filled the office of acting dean.

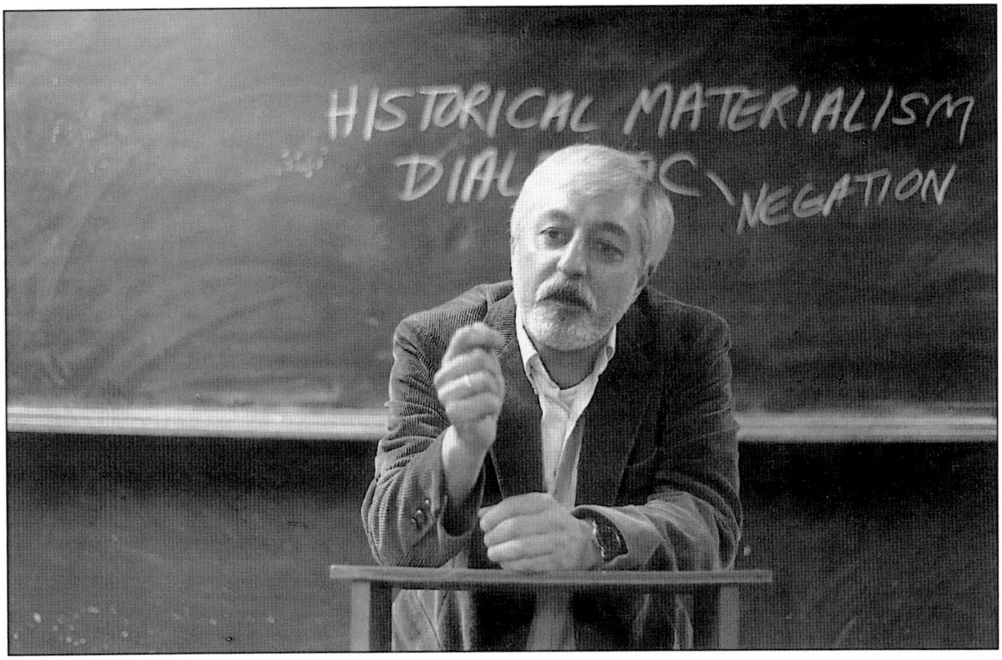

Dr. Robert Freysinger, Politics. Bob Freysinger earned a Ph.D. at the University of Massachusetts. He was appointed to the Bradford faculty in 1984 to teach courses in political science and international relations, including a special course on international terrorism. He was promoted to professor in 1996 and in the same year was appointed the O'Neill Distinguished College Professor. He became the chairman of the Human Studies Division in 1991.

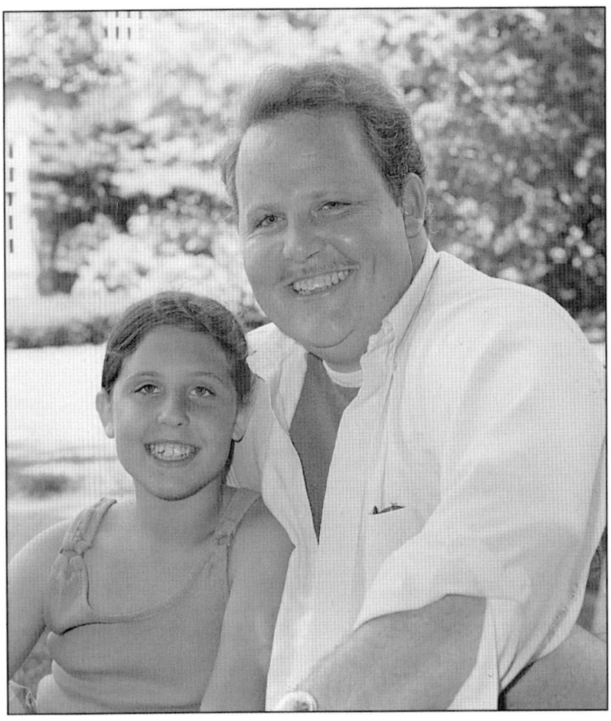

Prof. Perry Glasser, English. Glasser was invited to join the Bradford faculty in 1985 to take over the creative writing program begun by André Dubus. Glasser, an essayist and short story writer, earned a master of fine arts at the University of Arizona. He was promoted to professor in 1995. He left Bradford in 1996 and was succeeded by his former pupil David Crouse '90. With Glasser is his daughter Jessica.

Prof. Richard Murphy, English. Rich Murphy, right, was hired to run the writing laboratory and to supervise the student tutors who assisted students in the composition classes. A published poet, Murphy added courses in the writing of poetry and in the study of poetry as literature to the composition and literature courses that he taught. He holds an M.A. from Boston University.

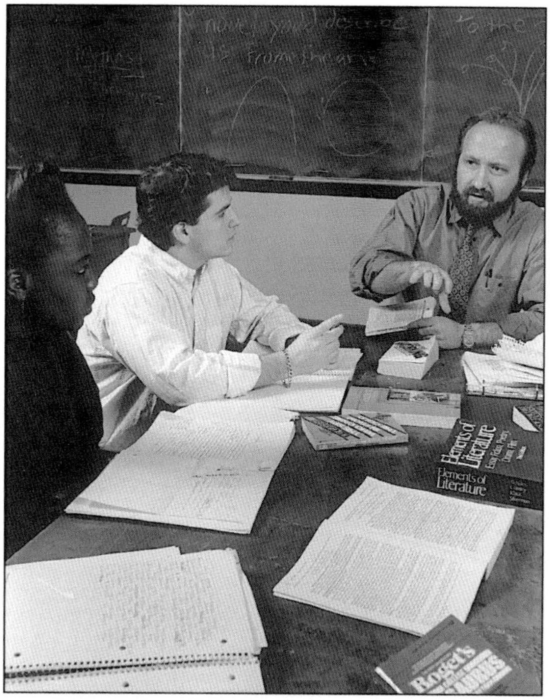

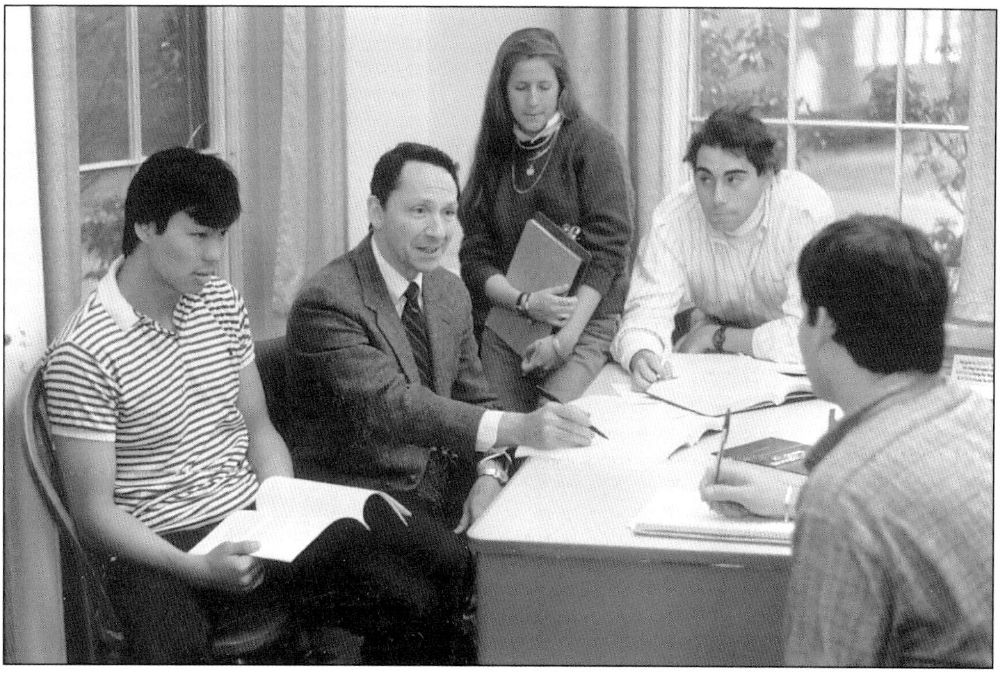

Dr. Howard Brown, Management. Howard Brown, second from left, came to Bradford in 1986 to be chairman of the Management Division. In that same year, he became the first, and only, recipient of the Ann Hemingway Symington Chair in Administration and Management. Brown, who earned an Ed.D. from Boston University, was promoted to professor in 1991. He was named Professor of the Year in 1995. With him, from left to right, are Tang Tang, Sally McInnes '88, Andres Maduro '87, and Bill Flanagan '88.

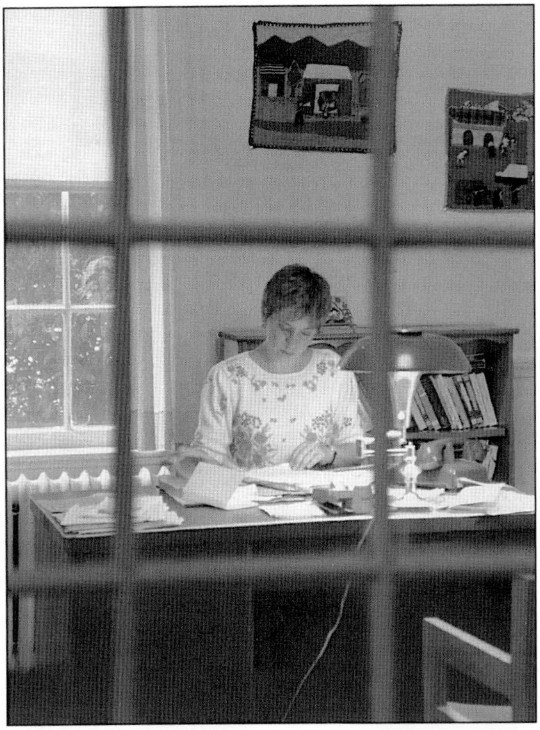

Dr. Joanne Megna-Wallace, French. Though foreign language had long ceased to be a requirement, French and Spanish courses continued to have their disciples. Joanne Megna-Wallace brought her many talents to Bradford in 1985. She had a Ph.D. from the University of North Carolina, Chapel Hill. In addition to courses in the French language and literature, she also taught courses on the Images of Women in Literature and Ethnic American Women's Literature. She was promoted to professor in 1997.

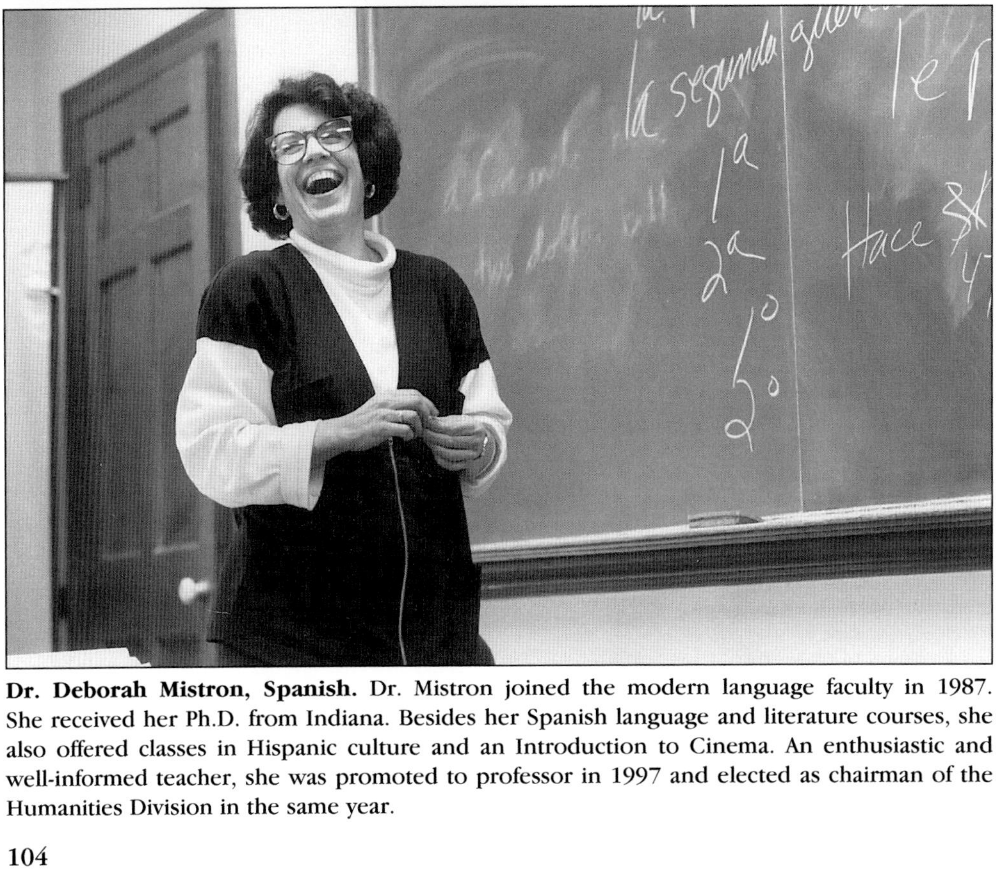

Dr. Deborah Mistron, Spanish. Dr. Mistron joined the modern language faculty in 1987. She received her Ph.D. from Indiana. Besides her Spanish language and literature courses, she also offered classes in Hispanic culture and an Introduction to Cinema. An enthusiastic and well-informed teacher, she was promoted to professor in 1997 and elected as chairman of the Humanities Division in the same year.

Prof. Peter Waldron, Theater. Peter Waldron, left, was a 1986 addition to the Bradford faculty. He was the director of the Kemper Theater in Denworth Hall, a set designer, and a teacher of technical courses in theater. A recipient of an M.F.A. from New York University, Waldron was honored to be chosen Bradford's third Professor of the Year (1994) and was promoted to professor in 1996. He chaired the Creative Arts Division and was very active in Haverhill cultural and charitable causes. He became the manager of the Rogers Theater at Merrimack College in 1999. He is shown in this 1997 photograph with his former student and protégé, set designer Sean Reese '89.

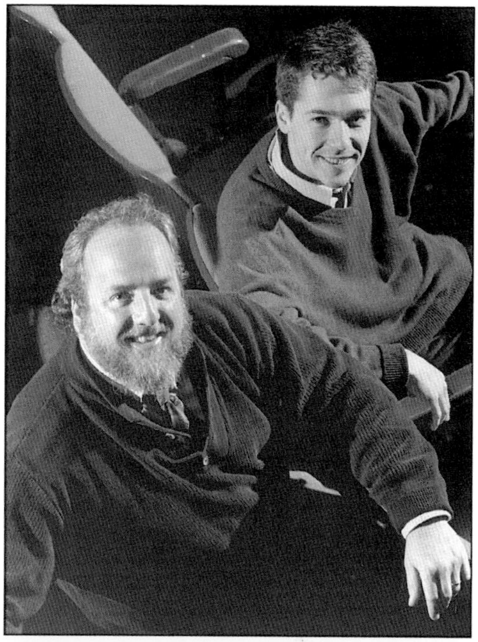

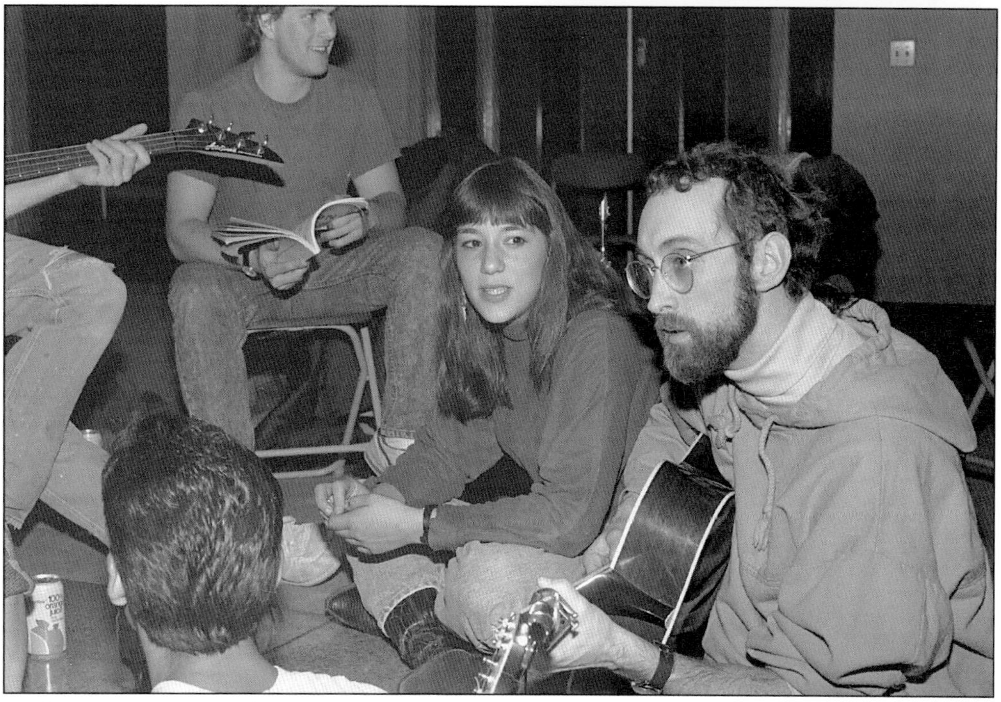

Prof. R. Scott Stroot, Theater. The other half of Bradford's theater tandem since 1986 was Scott Stroot, right. Stroot, who had originally trained as a nurse, earned an M.F.A. from Minnesota. At Bradford, he taught acting and directing classes, directed a major production each semester, and supervised student productions. He was also an accomplished actor and musician and active in the local community New Moon Coffeehouse. He was promoted to professor in 1997, served as acting associate dean from 1998 to 1999, and became chairman of the Creative Arts Division in 1999.

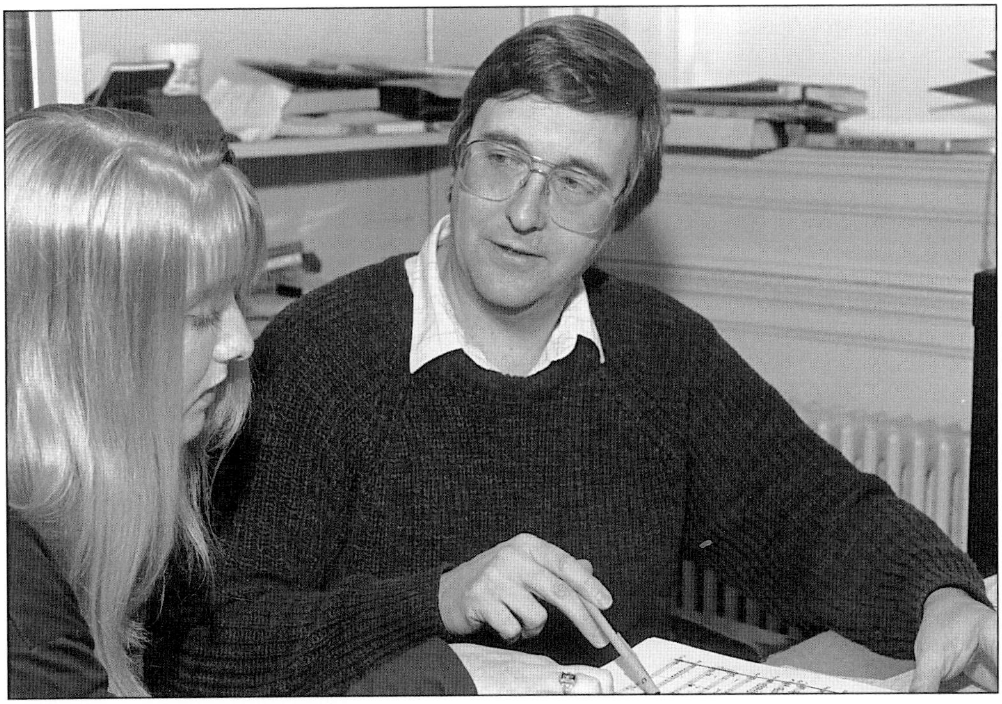

Dr. Frederik Schuetze, Music. Charles Ludington's successor in the Music Department in 1986 was Frederik Schuetze, right, who continued the level of excellence long expected of that program. Schuetze received a doctorate in music from the University of Missouri Conservatory of Music. He taught voice lessons, music theory courses, and continued the very successful Music Theater workshops, with the annual cabaret and musical productions. Schuetze was promoted to professor in 1997. He and his wife, Joy Schuetze, also formed the Merrimack Valley String Orchestra

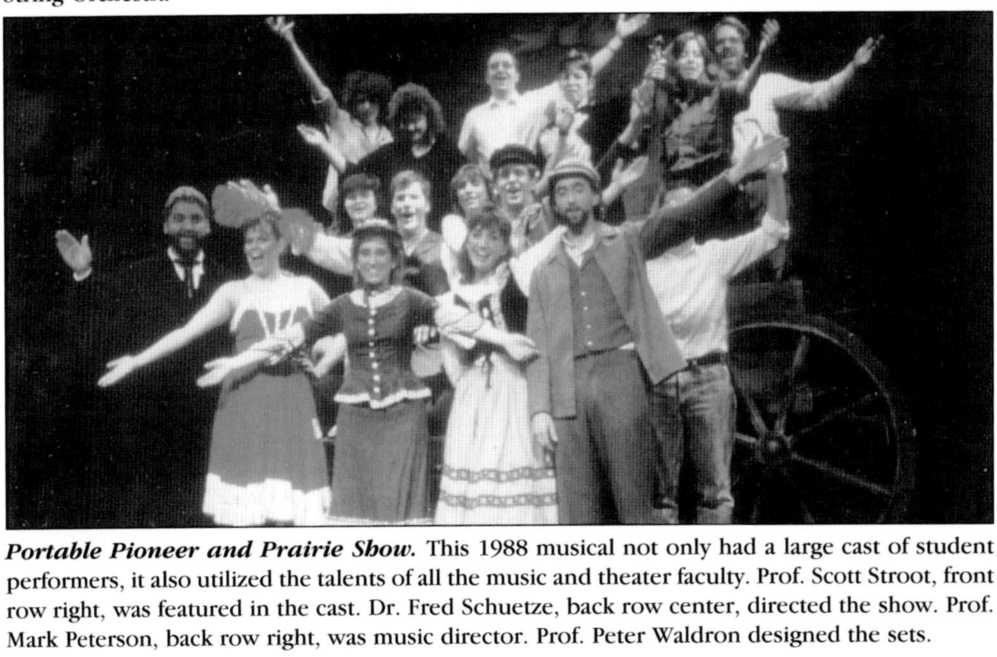

Portable Pioneer and Prairie Show. This 1988 musical not only had a large cast of student performers, it also utilized the talents of all the music and theater faculty. Prof. Scott Stroot, front row right, was featured in the cast. Dr. Fred Schuetze, back row center, directed the show. Prof. Mark Peterson, back row right, was music director. Prof. Peter Waldron designed the sets.

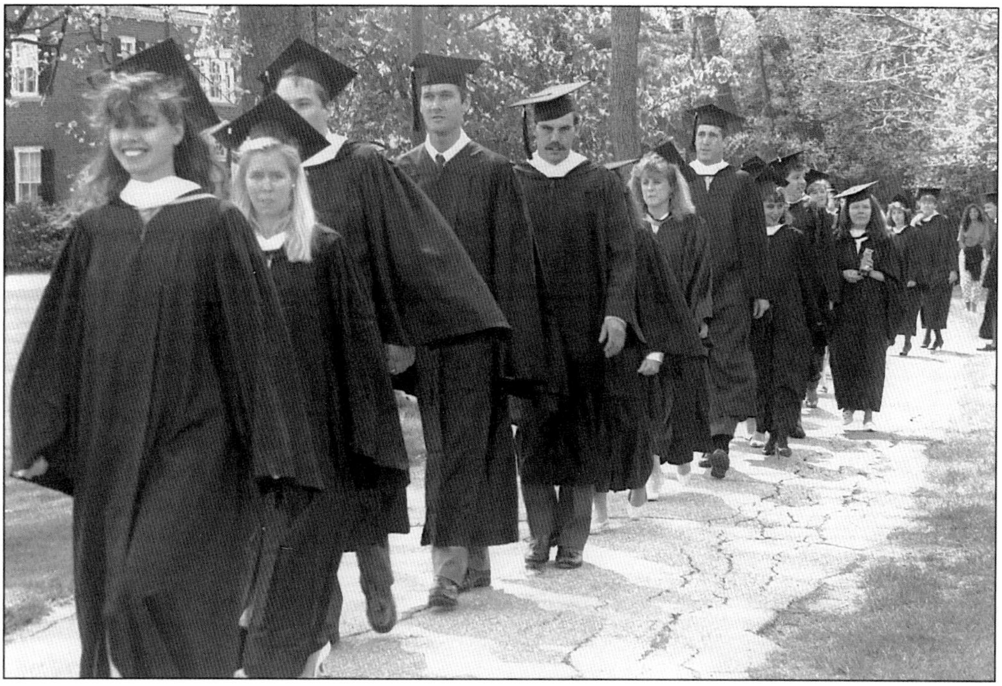

The Class of 1988. The students who entered Bradford in 1984 were a specially recruited group, for they were to be the first to experience the Bradford Plan in its totality. Theirs was the first graduation for B.A. candidates only, the associate's degree having been eliminated. Shown, from left to right, as they processed to their graduation ceremonies are, Stephanie Gutierrez, Augusta Henley, Philip Hever, Joseph Homans, Joel Hustis, Martha Karoutas, William Katzenbach, Kristy Lamb, Howard Lederman, and Maria Lehan.

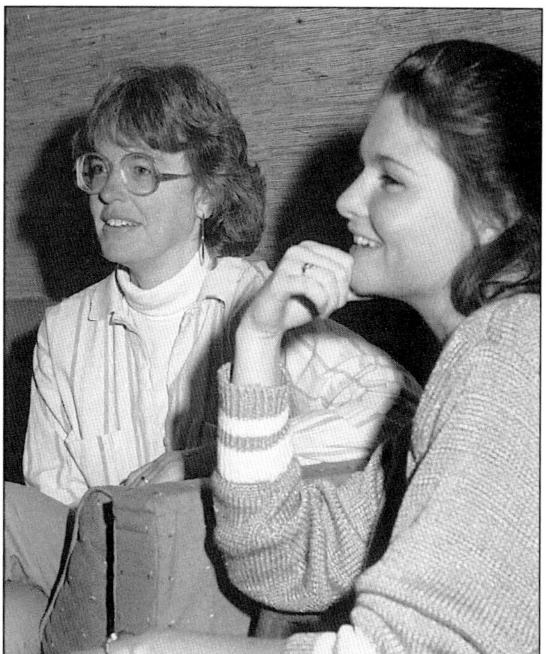

Denise Moynihan, 1988 Graduate. Denise Moynihan, right, demonstrated the wide-ranging possibilities that Bradford offered to its students. A liberal studies graduate with a concentration in history, she graduated magna cum laude in 1988. She was also very active in the theater while at Bradford, for which she was awarded the Theresa Mors Prize. For her required senior independent project, she produced a video based on the letters of an Irish-born Civil War soldier from Haverhill. Like many of her classmates, she went on to graduate school. She became an attorney. Pictured with her is Dr. Peggy Walsh.

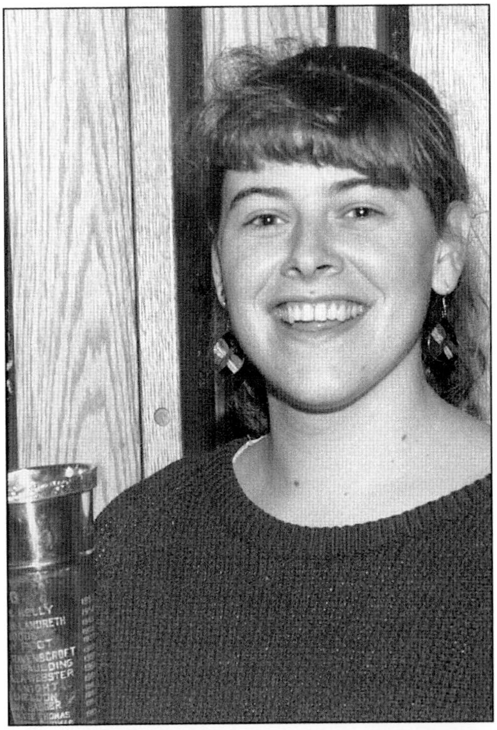

Kelley Donovan, Dancer. Kelley Donovan, a member of the Class of 1989, is shown holding the Florence Eisenhardt Dangerfield Dance Cup, awarded each year to an outstanding dancer. She won the award in 1988 and again in 1989. A choreographer, as well as an actress and singer, she has lived up to her award by becoming an acclaimed dancer and choreographer in the Boston area.

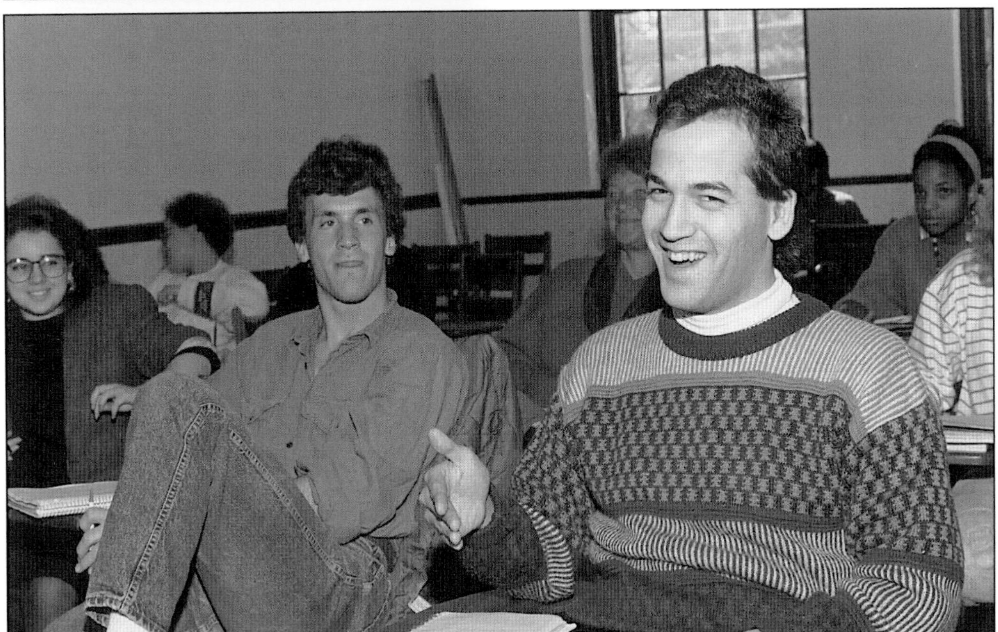

Classroom Scene, 1989. A typical upper-level class at Bradford by the 1980s included a mix of students from different years and backgrounds. This group in Hasseltine 206 includes Patricia Garcia-Dergay, left, and Larry Kunz, who began as freshmen at Bradford and graduated in 1991; Nancy Goldman, back row, a nontraditional student who earned her degree in 1990 and went on to Harvard for an M.Ed.; and Tom Ellis, right, who transferred from the local community college and graduated from Bradford in 1989.

Seven

The Nineties

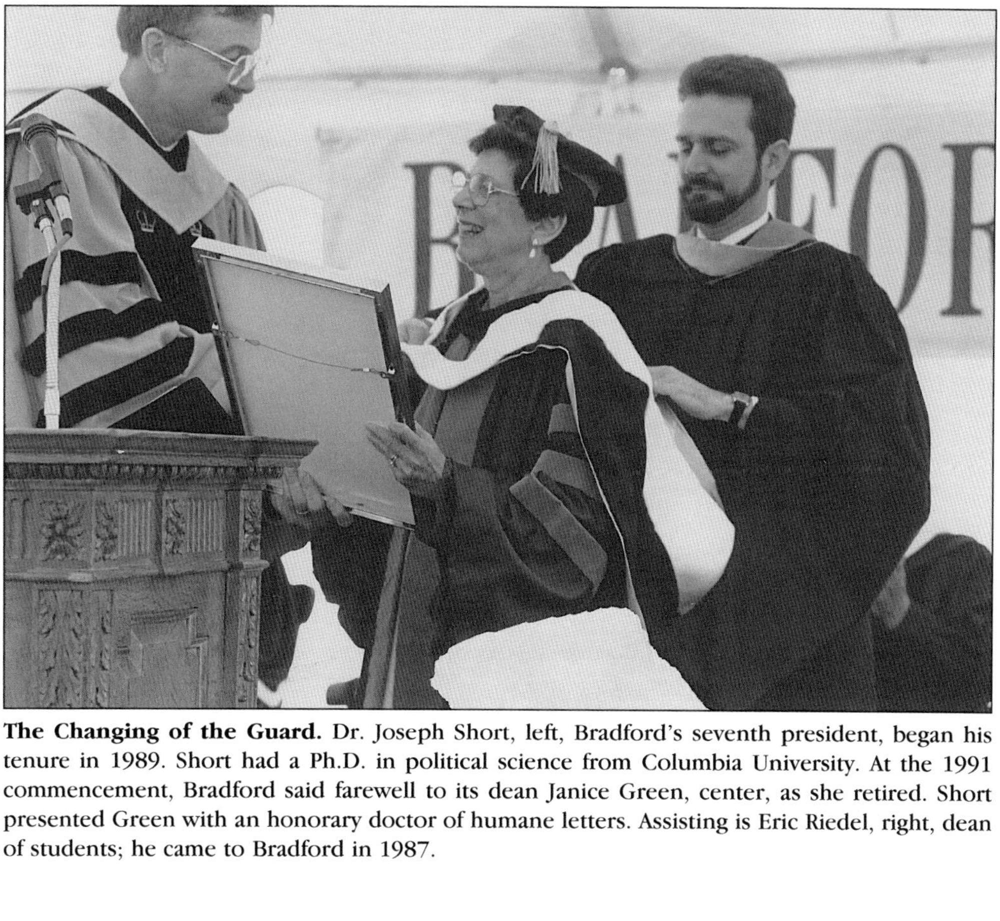

The Changing of the Guard. Dr. Joseph Short, left, Bradford's seventh president, began his tenure in 1989. Short had a Ph.D. in political science from Columbia University. At the 1991 commencement, Bradford said farewell to its dean Janice Green, center, as she retired. Short presented Green with an honorary doctor of humane letters. Assisting is Eric Riedel, right, dean of students; he came to Bradford in 1987.

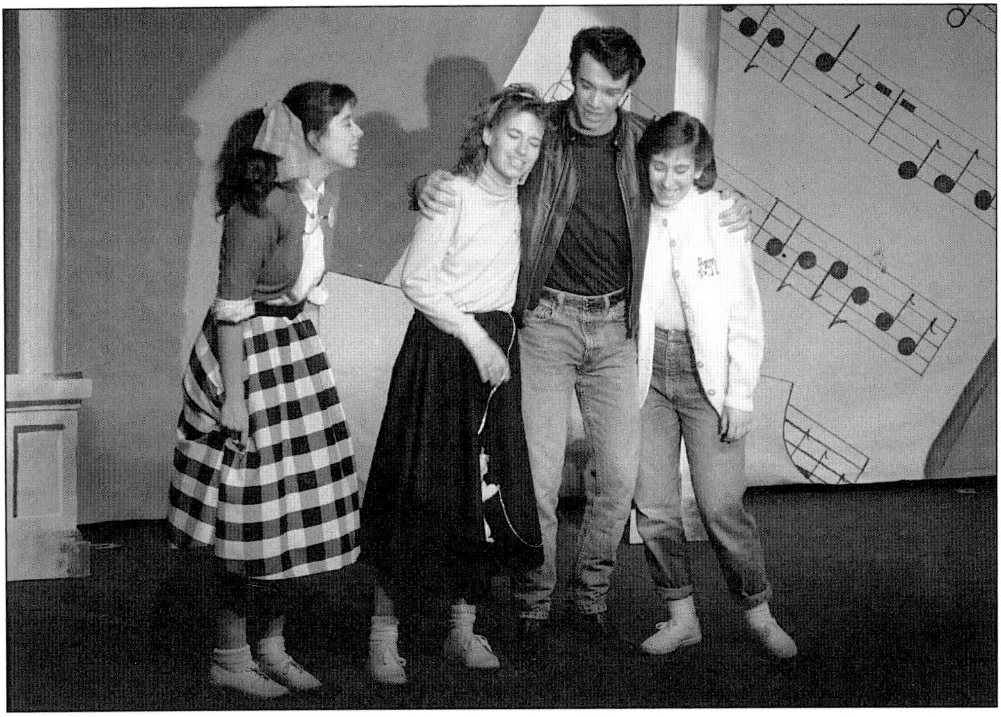

Bye, Bye Birdie! Versatile Eric Riedel, dean of students from 1987 to 1992, was also an accomplished performer. He shared the lead role in the 1989 production of *Bye, Bye Birdie!* with Donna-Marie Sullivan '89. Also in the cast were, from left to right, Lynda Blair '91, Carol Boris '90, Nathan Robbins '90, and Cindy Willey '91. Nathan Robbins wrote the lyrics, with music by Prof. Mark Peterson, of the "new" alma mater *Old Bradford*.

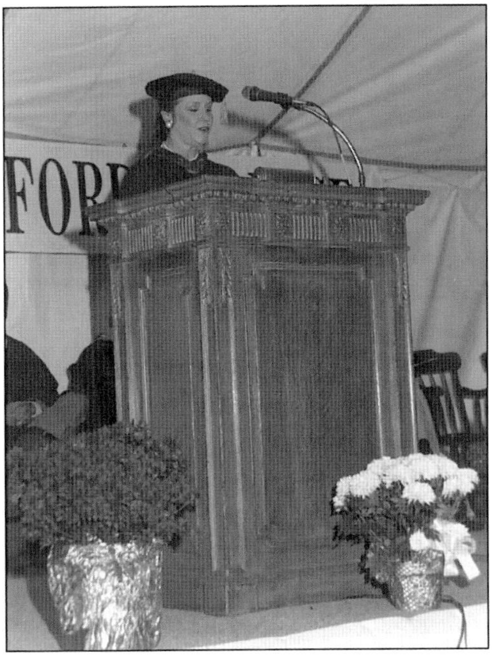

Dr. Peggy Maki, Academic Dean. Dr. Maki succeeded Dr. Green as vice president and academic dean in 1991. Her doctorate was in history from the University of Delaware. Maki introduced the concept of individual assessment through the portfolio process and the requirement of community service. She was at Bradford until 1997.

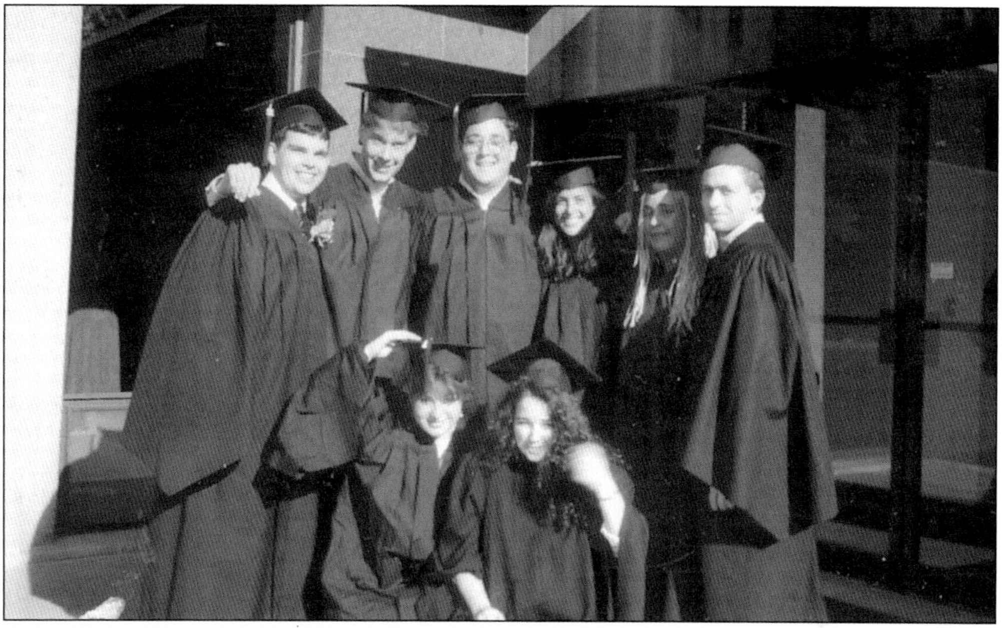

The Class of 1991. Gathered outside of the Bell Center after their baccalaureate service are the following members of the Class of 1991, from left to right: (front row) Pamela "P.J." Corrigan and Patricia Garcia-Dergay; (back row) Scott Prince, Mark Hayes, Charles Dominguez, Melissa Goldberg, Donnamarie Catalfo, and Marc Mirabella.

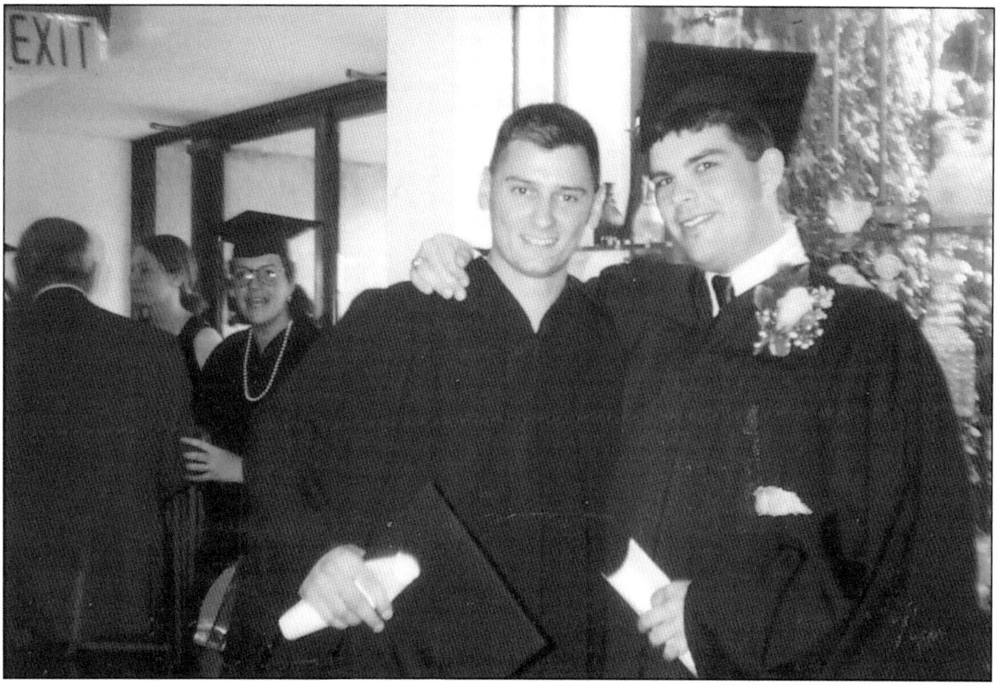

Friends Good and True. Classmates Gene Henley, left, and Scott Prince of the Class of 1991 share a moment of celebration. Henley was the class president and the student speaker at commencement. Prince served his alma mater as a member of the Alumni Board and joined the Board of Trustees in 1999.

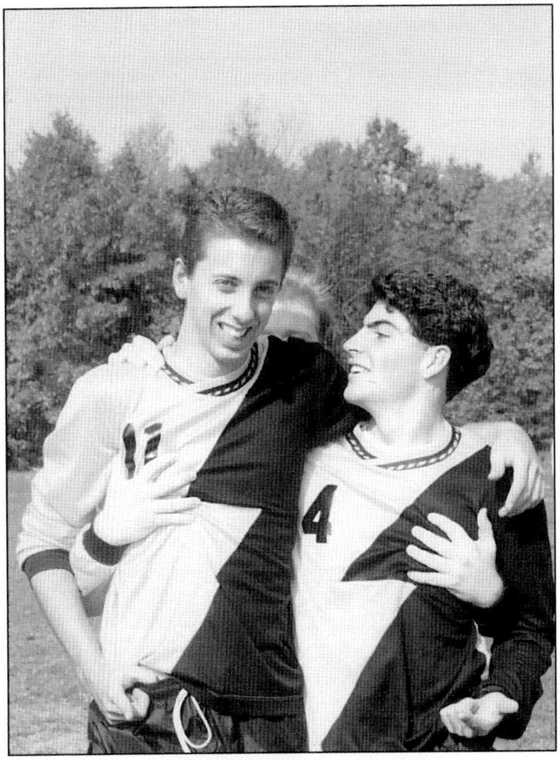

Soccer Champions. During the late 1980s and early 1990s, Bradford dominated the New England small college soccer league. In 1991, it won the New England championship. The leader of the team, and its high scorer, was Edward "Ted" Cotton '93, left, shown being congratulated by teammate Jeremy Cornfeldt '93 and an unidentified pair of hands!

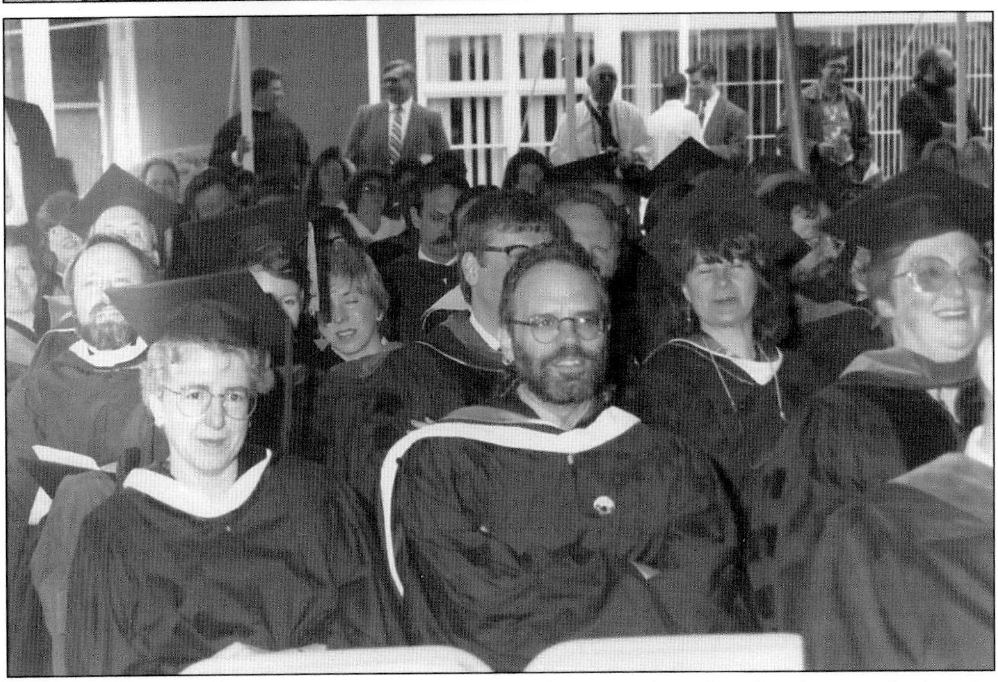

Commencement 1991. Familiar faces among the faculty gathered under the tent during the graduation ceremonies include those of Dr. Barbara Ann McCahill, Prof. Rich Murphy, Prof. Linda Miller, Dr. Pat Cronin, Dr. Joanne Megna-Wallace, Prof. Marvin Sweet, Dr. Mark Kosinski, Prof. Marc Mannheimer, Prof. Carol Allen, Dr. Bob Smart, and Dr. Pat O'Malley.

Dr. Allan Rachlin, Sociology. Dr. Rachlin came to Bradford in 1987. He had earned a Ph.D. from State University of New York, Buffalo. He was a member of the Human Studies Division. He is shown in 1996 during a symposium at the President's House, where he addressed the faculty and staff about his sabbatical in South Africa. He served as coordinator for planning and transition from 1997 to 1999.

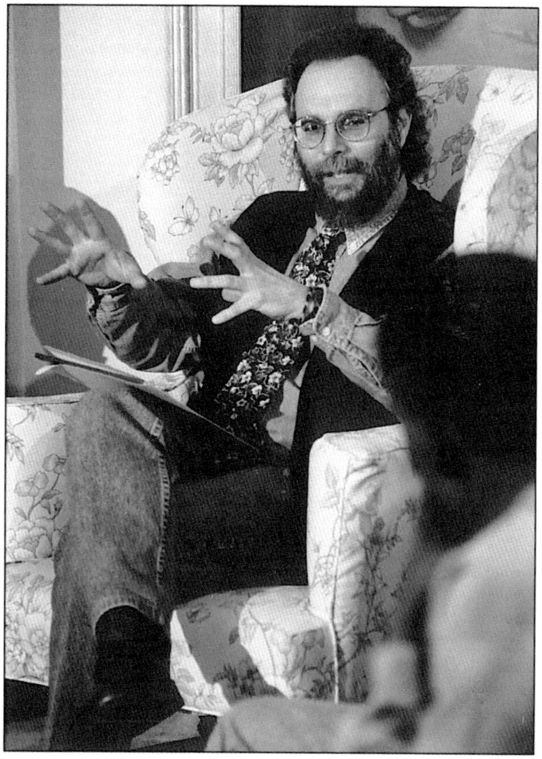

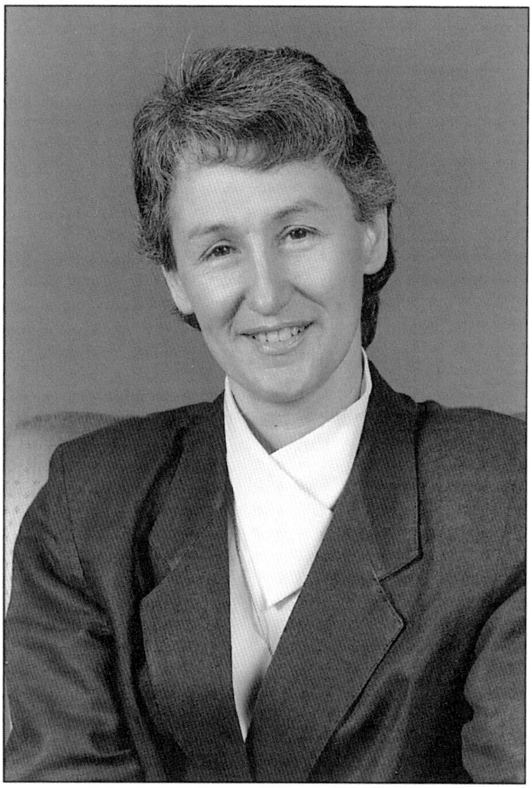

Dr. Paula Sable, Education. Education courses were added to the curriculum in the late 1980s. A student could earn a minor, but not a major, in the field and be eligible for certification to teach elementary grades or high school English or social studies. Paula Sable joined the faculty in 1989 to run the education program. She took a hiatus to complete her Ed.D. degree at Harvard and returned to Bradford in 1994.

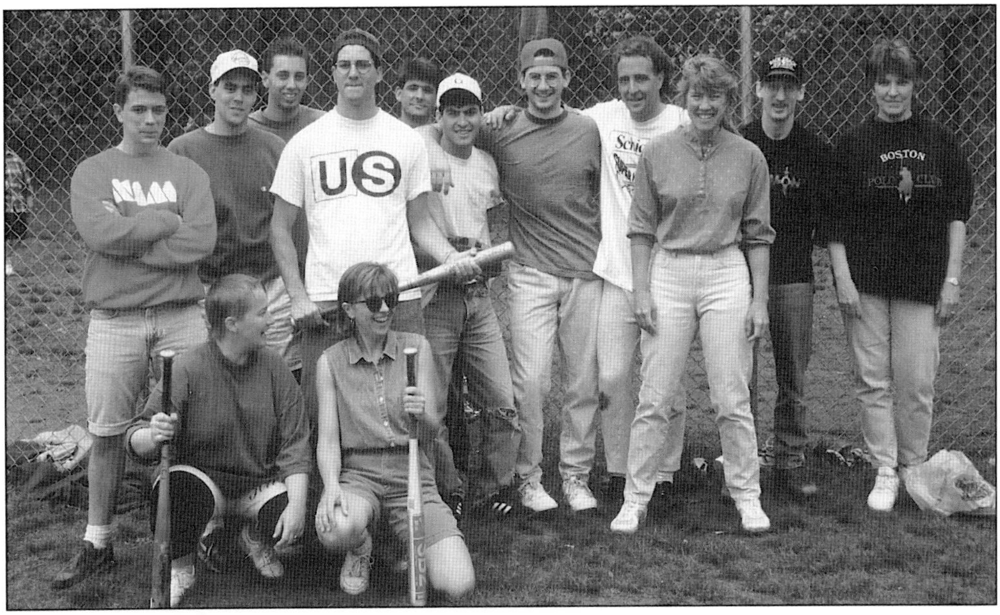

The Seniors' Softball Team. One of the most anticipated events of Senior Week was the annual faculty-senior softball game. Invariably, the faculty with its greater seniority, skill, and sobriety, won the match. But the Class of 1993 had a quartet of nontraditional-aged coeds who led their team to victory. Seen here, from left to right, are the following: (front row) Linda Maddox and Leslie Costello; (back row) Tayde Sullivan, Dan Messina, Ted Cotton, Ken Dara, Scott Fitzgerald, Jeremy Cornfeldt, Sean Marr, Steve Burns, Jeanne "Jon" Colgate, Harry "Scooter" Hardin, and Dorothy Currier.

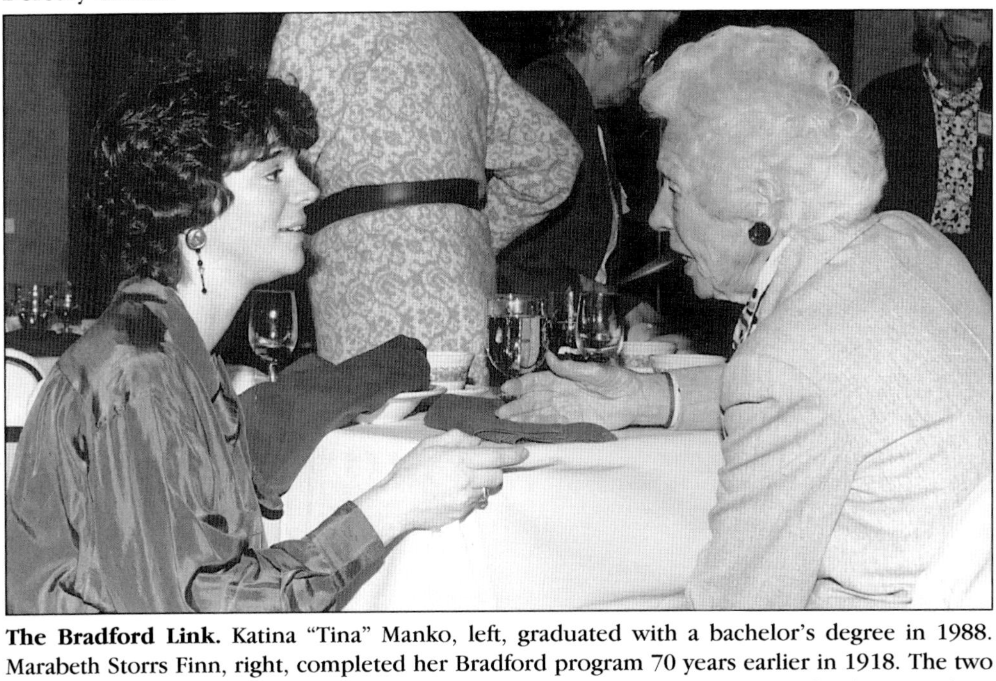

The Bradford Link. Katina "Tina" Manko, left, graduated with a bachelor's degree in 1988. Marabeth Storrs Finn, right, completed her Bradford program 70 years earlier in 1918. The two met at the 1993 alumni reunion. Manko was a Hagley Fellow at the University of Delaware, where she earned her Ph.D. in history.

Commencement 1993. Prof. Marvin Sweet had been teaching the fine art of ceramics at Bradford as an adjunct professor since 1987 when he was selected Bradford's Professor of the Year in 1993. Because of that honor, he joined the platform party at commencement and had the pleasure of announcing each graduate. Pictured are, from left to right, Ariel Dorfman, commencement speaker; Leslie Ferlazzo, trustees chair; Professor Sweet; and Sheila Murphy, dean of students from 1992 to 1994. Sweet was appointed visiting assistant professor in creative arts in 1997.

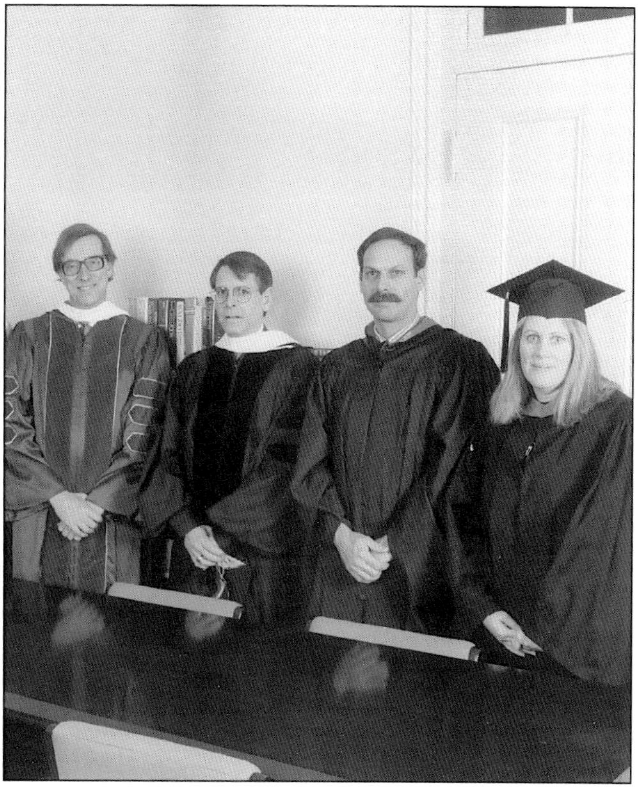

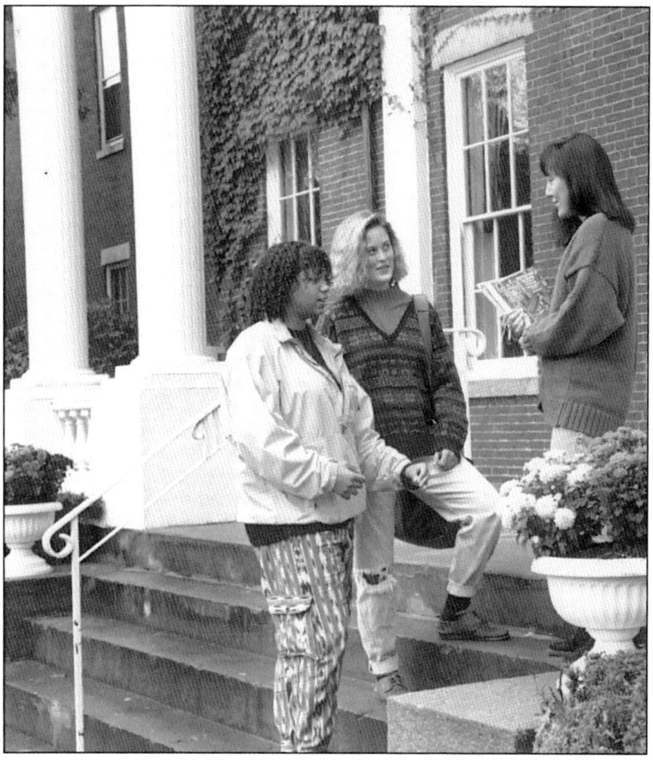

A Class Break. For generations, the steps of Academy Hall have been a favorite gathering place for students. These three coeds take a break between classes, from left to right, Clare Wilson '94, Stephanie Seale '94, and Sonya Rivard '94. Seale won both the Harris Athlete Scholar Award and the Division of Management Prize in 1993.

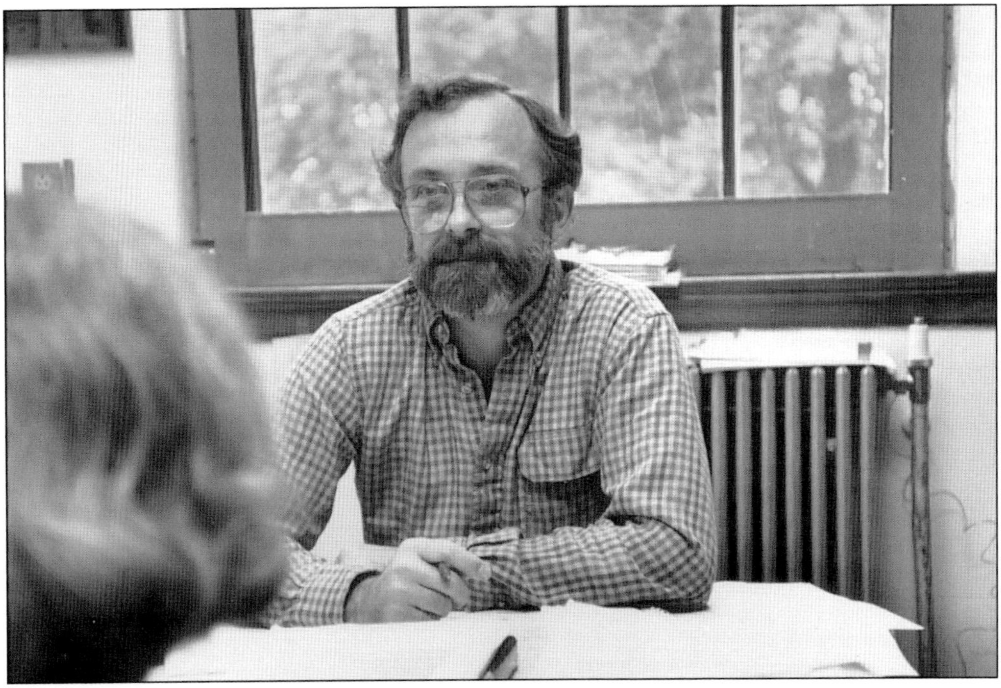

Dr. Thomas Reitz, Chemistry. Science laboratories in Hasseltine Hall were renovated and upgraded in 1985 and rechristened in 1987 in memory of Peter S. Freedman, vice president for administration (1981–1986) A new Division of Natural Science and Mathematics was created, and the first students to receive bachelor's degrees with a concentration in science graduated in 1989. That same year, Dr. Tom Reitz joined the faculty to teach chemistry. He had a Ph.D. from Michigan State. Reitz became chairman of the Science Division in 1993.

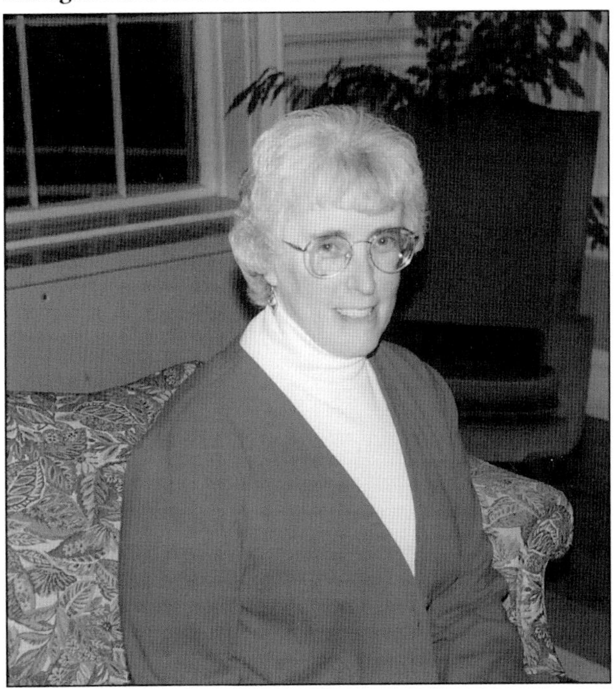

Dr. Ruth A. Young, Biology. Professor Young came to Bradford to join the Division of Natural Science and Mathematics in 1994. She earned a Ph.D. from the University of Vermont. She taught a wide range of courses in plant and animal biology and also served as secretary to the Faculty Senate.

Prof. James Steele. Jim Steele has worn many hats since he arrived at Bradford in 1988. He was hired originally as a lecturer in English. He had a M.F.A. from Indiana University. But he also added history courses to his teaching load as he pursued a doctorate in that subject at the University of Massachusetts. When computers became an integral part of teaching, he was named coordinator of faculty technology training.

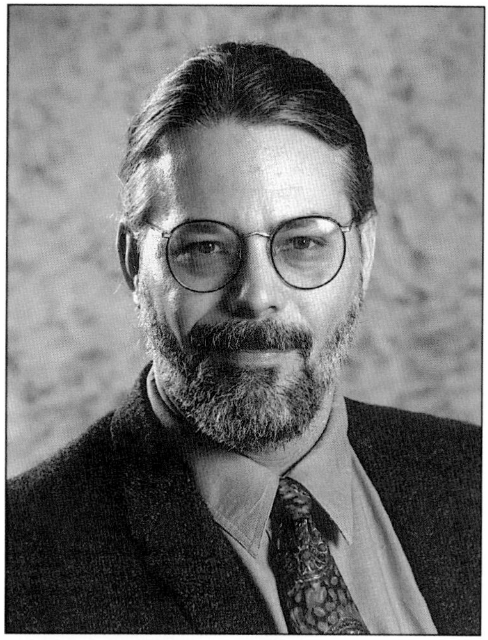

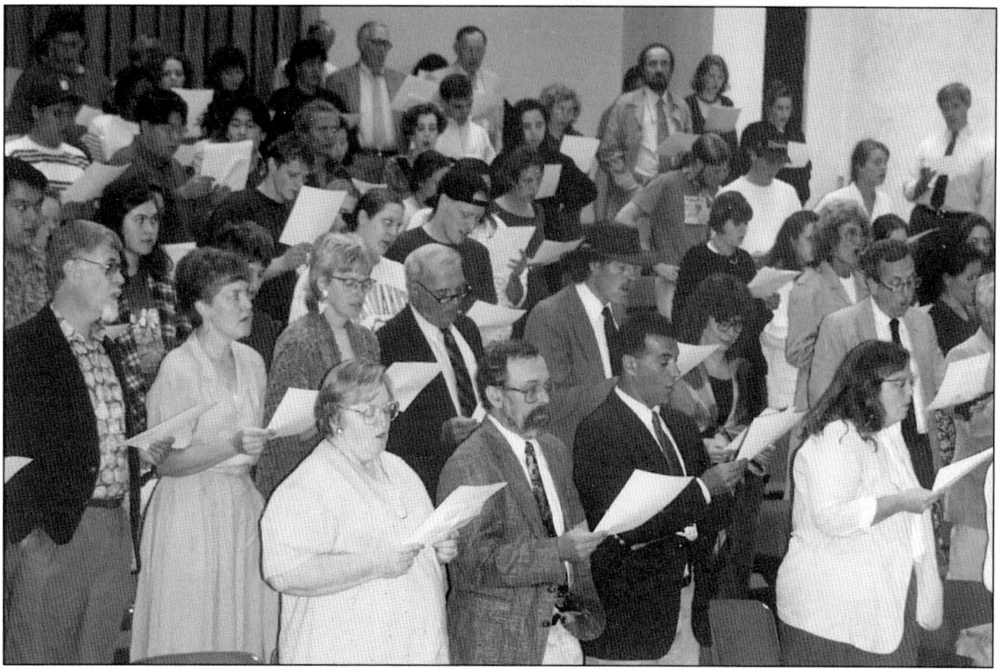

Honors Convocation. The highlight of the week of Intellectual Celebration at the end of the spring semester has been the Honors Convocation, when academic prizes are announced. Faculty members at the 1994 convocation included this group, from left to right, as follows: (front row) Prof. Marcia Pelletier, who joined the faculty to teach accounting in 1989; Dr. Tom Reitz; Dr. Harry Davakos, physical education (1990–1996); and Dr. Helen Meldrim, communications (1990–1994); (back row) Prof. Dick Newman; Prof. Martha Boles; Dr. Peg Walsh; Dr. Frank Nye; Dr. Jon Earle; Dr. Diana Reynolds, politics (1989–1995); and Dr. Tom Gallagher, history (1987–1995).

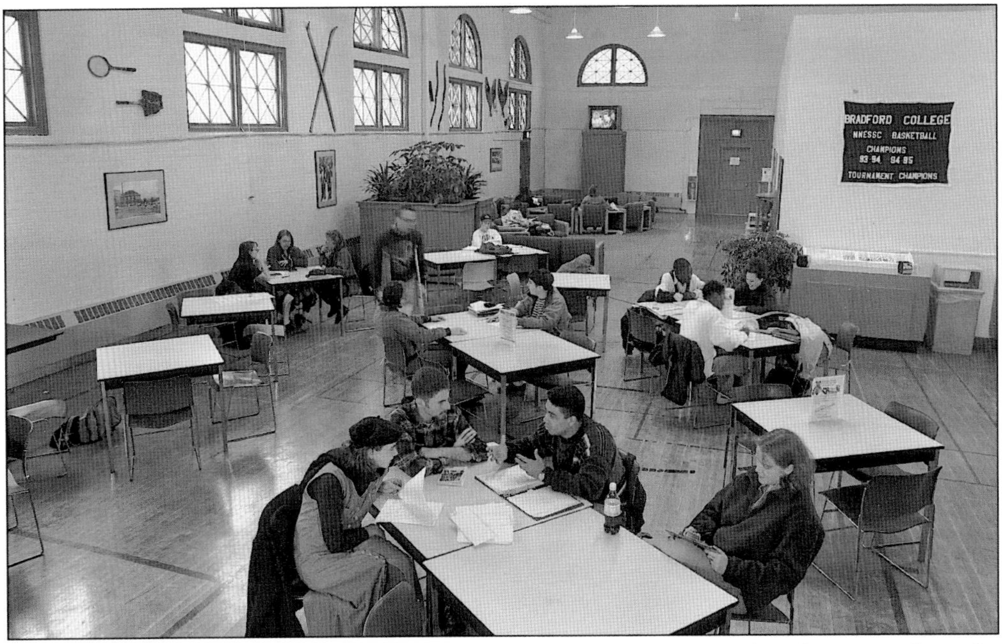

The New Campus Center. By the mid-1990s, enrollment had increased to the point where the allocation and use of space had to be significantly adjusted. A series of interrelated moves were made. The gymnasium became redundant after the college worked out an arrangement with a local fitness center. So, the gym was reborn as the Campus Center, with a limited cafeteria. In turn, the former Snack Bar was converted into a new book store and a commuter center. The book store's former location in Conover Hall became offices and teaching space for the music faculty.

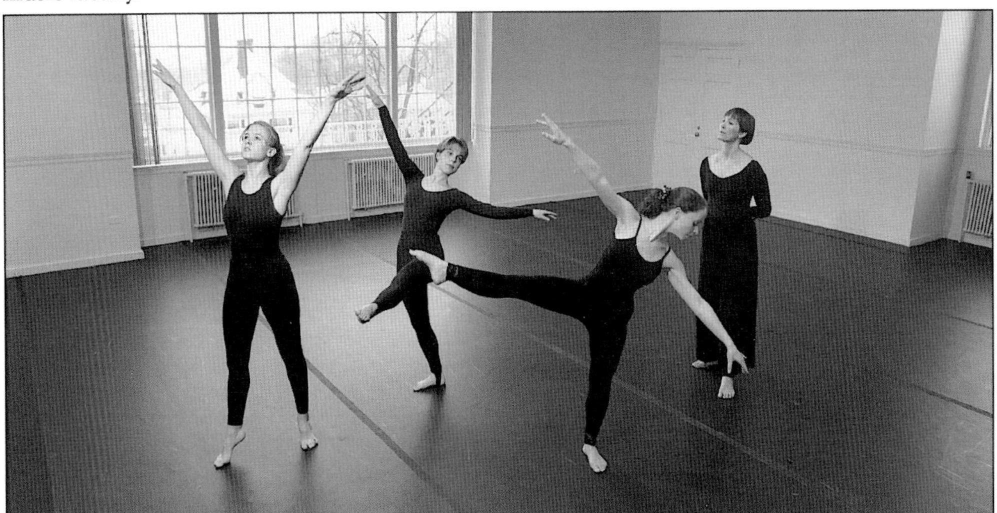

Prof. Mary Lee Karlins and the Dance Studio. With the music faculty moved to Conover Hall, the vacated third-floor space of Denworth was converted to the dance studio in 1995. This was the same space that was first used as an art studio. Prof. Mary Lee Karlins, right, who earned an M.F.A. at Smith, took over the dance program in 1986. She was promoted to professor and to the Johnson Chair in Ethics and Values in 1997. Her dancers are, from left to right, Wendy Hamel, Jenna Milton-McMahon, and Kelly Mischetti.

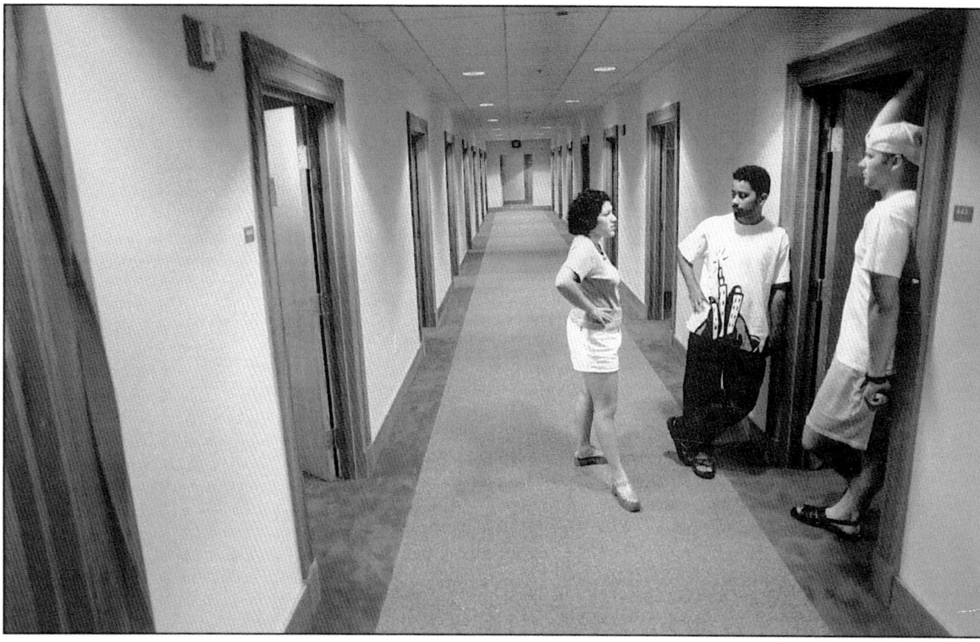

New Dorm Rooms. The old dance studio reappeared in 1995 as two floors of dormitory rooms. Over the decades of Academy Hall's existence, this space had served as a study hall, an auditorium, a library, and a dance studio. Now, in its fifth and final appearance at Bradford, it became, in the students' words, "the Bradford Marriott."

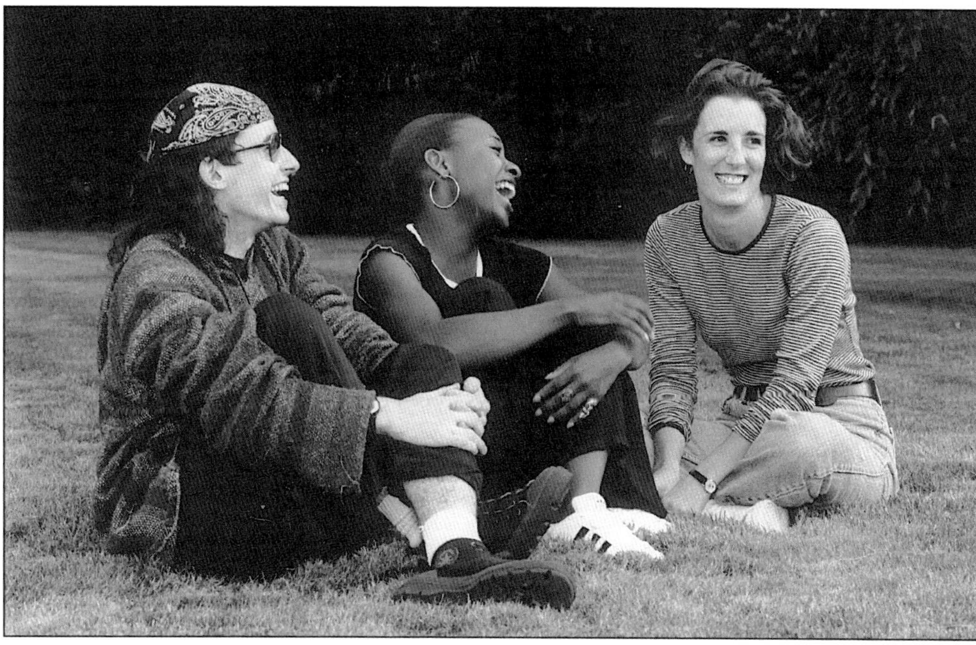

Creative Artists. These three students from the late 1990s excelled in the arts at Bradford. Brian Moakley, left, a filmmaker, was also the student commencement speaker in 1997. Michelle Patrick, center, was a talented actress and won the Dangerfield Dance Cup in 1998. She shared the 1994 Special Theater Program Award for outstanding performance with Synge Maher, right, a superb actress, who won the Special Theater Program Award in 1995 and 1997.

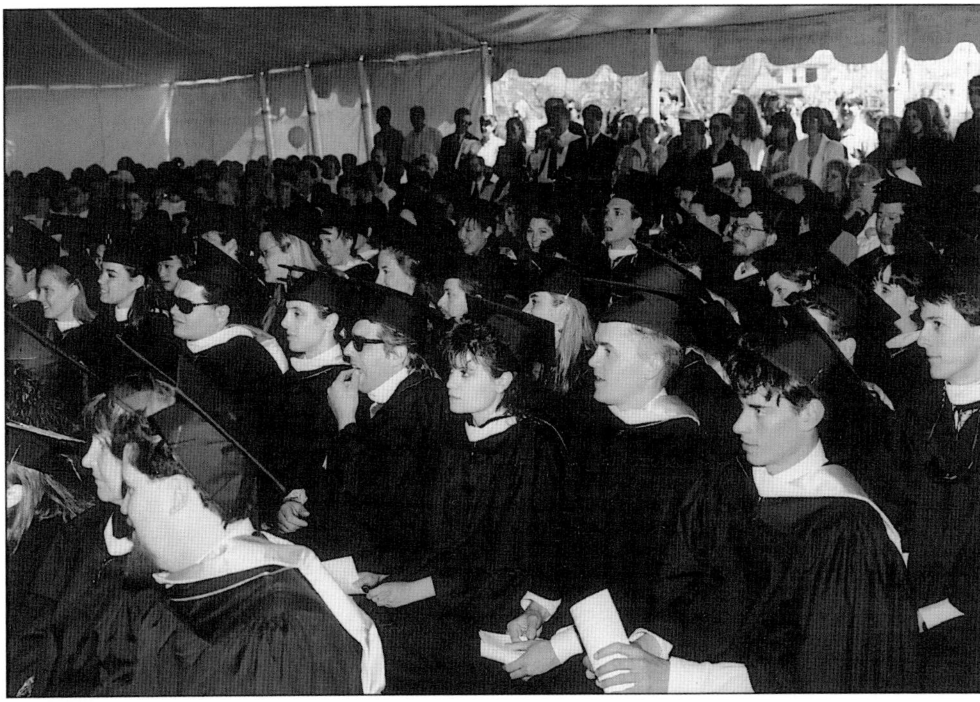

The Class of 1994. The total number of B.A. graduates had grown very slowly through the 1970s and early 1980s. But by the late 1980s, the numbers began to average between 80 and 100. Pictured are some of the 86 students to graduate in 1994, from left to right, as follows: (first row) Dorothy Currier and Seth Cooper; (second row) Kerry Herlihy, Melissa Hamm, Richard Hamilton, Geoff Hough, Bart Hackett, Lisa Grillo-Andrew, Brian Greenlaw, and David Glidden.

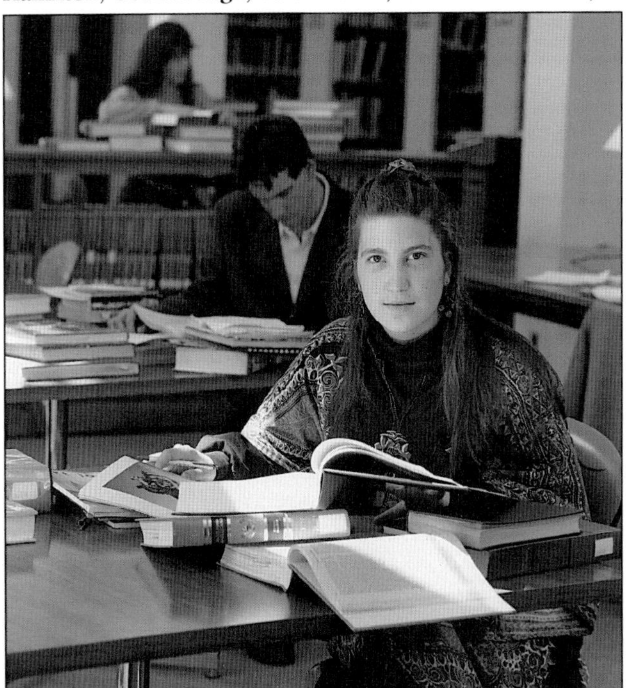

Wendy Ormiston '95. Bradford students in the 1990s had access to a wide variety of programs that allowed them to study abroad or to develop the practical aspects of their education as a tutor on campus or in an internship off campus. Wendy Ormiston '95 came from California and used her time at Bradford well. She spent a semester abroad in Tibet and was the first recipient of the Arthur Levine Fellowship as head tutor of the Writing Center. Wendy graduated magna cum laude and won the Plummer Award in Humanities and the Barrett Essay Prize.

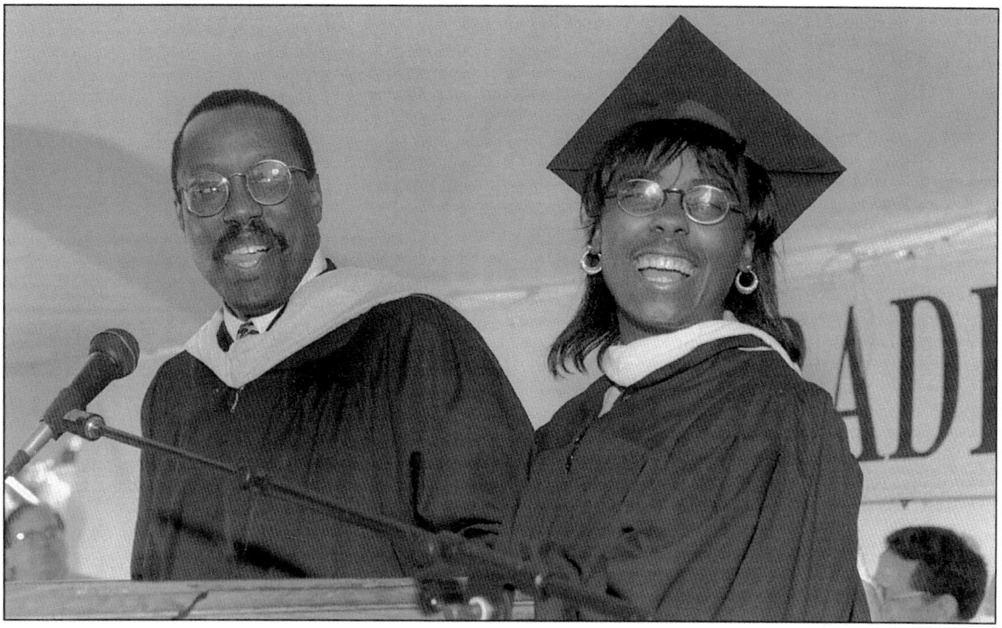

Trey Williams, Dean of Students. Trey Williams, left, was chosen to be vice president and dean of students in 1994. He had a master's in student personnel administration from Colorado State. His office had responsibility for residence life, campus activities, health and counseling services, athletic activities, and community service. With him at the 1995 commencement is graduate Kalise Jacobs, who delivered the senior address and won the Student Leader Award. She was actively involved in all aspects of community life at Bradford and went on to the University of Vermont to pursue a graduate degree in higher education administration.

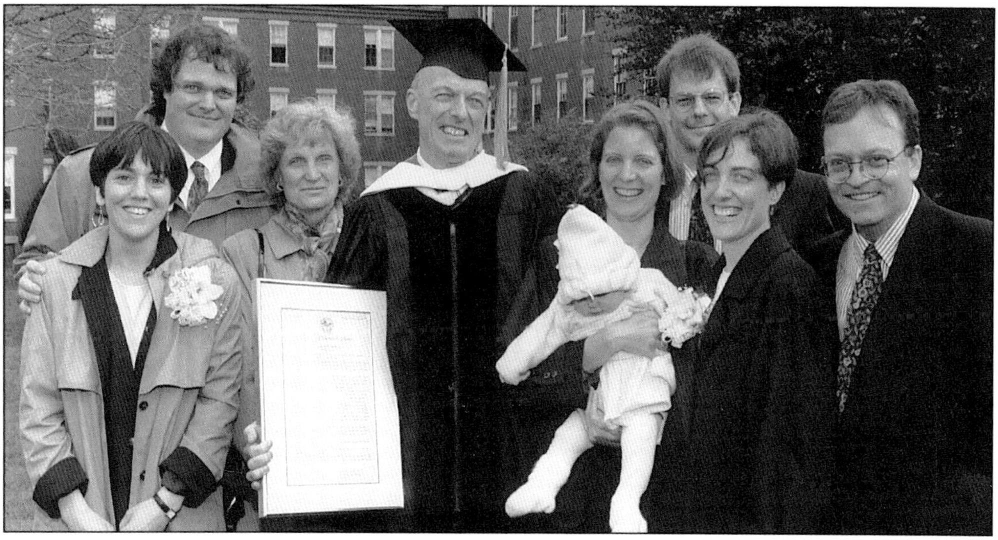

The Freeman Family. When Jefferson Freeman, center, married Landa Montagu '58, he got more than a Bradford bride. He also found a place on the Bradford Board of Trustees. He served two terms (1971–1985 and 1986–1995), including a stint as chairman. He was rewarded for his services with an honorary doctor of humane letters in 1995. With him, from left to right, are Sharon (Sherar) Freeman '90, Peter Freeman '89, Landa Montagu Freeman '58, baby Louise, Willoughby (Freeman)Lévesque, Marc Lévesque, Allison (Freeman) Hinton, and Tim Hinton.

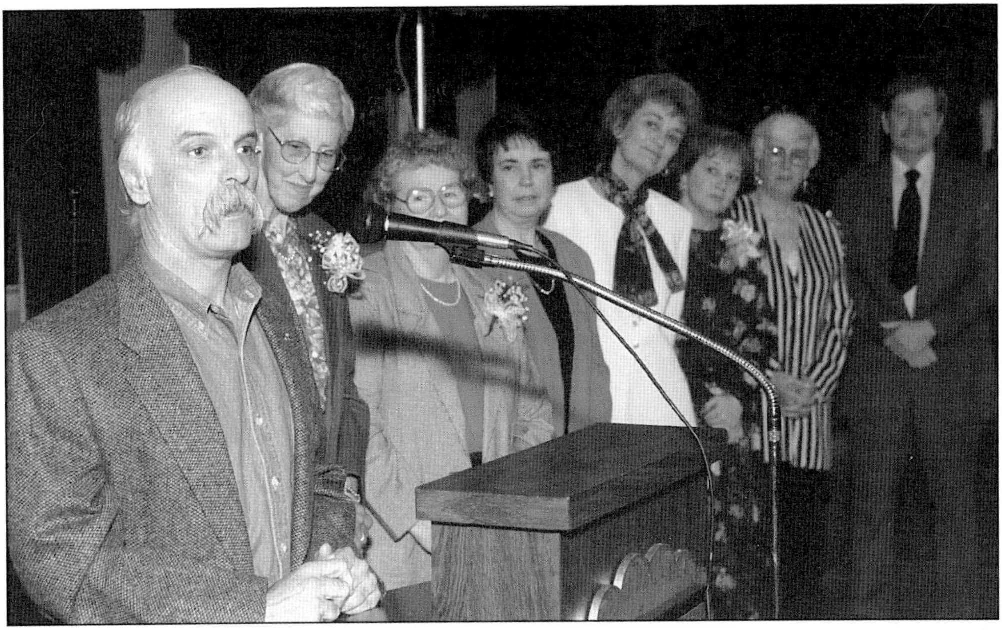

Bradshaw Award Winners. Bernard Bradshaw, who had been a chef at Bradford for 40 years, died in 1986. The college honored his memory by establishing an annual award for staff members. In 1996, Jim Flood, left, director of network operations, was honored. Seven previous Bradshaw Award winners were on hand to congratulate him, from left to right, Gretna Abbott, Eileen Welch, Betty Malbon, Judy Bologna, Sandy Anderson, Jean Flaherty, and George Lally.

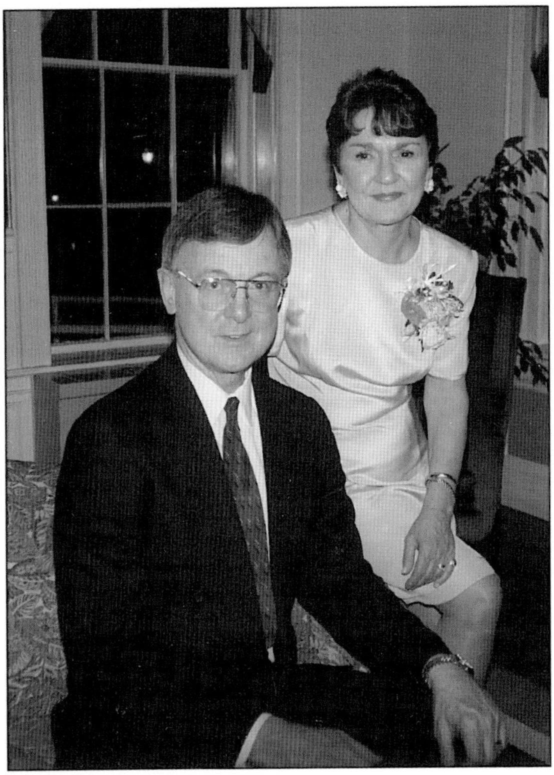

Claire Wilson, Bradshaw Award. Claire Wilson, right, began to work at Bradford in the 1970s. She served as the alumni secretary and as a secretary to the vice president for administration. The college honored her service with the Bradshaw Award in 1998. With her is President Joseph Short.

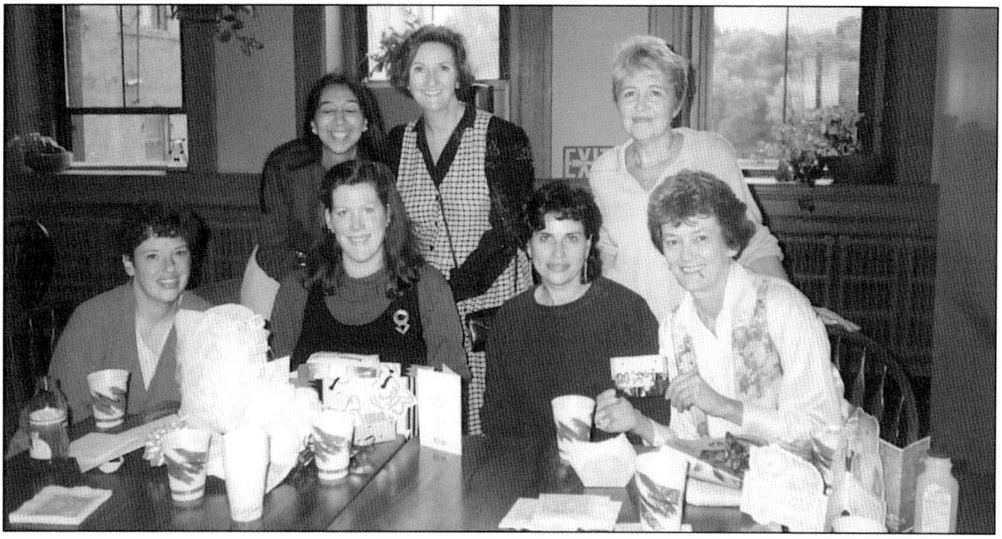

Bradford Staff in the 1990s. Past and present Bradford staff gathered for a baby shower in 1996. Pictured, from left to right, are the following: (front row) Jennifer Jones, director of Community Service Learning; Sandra Swain Bromwell '83, former alumni director; Barbara Canyes, director of the Career and Internship Center; and Judy Bologna, academic support adviser; (back row) Robin Thomas, secretary in the alumni office; Ann Shaw, assistant director of the Career and Internship Center; and Kathleen Bresnahan '88, transfer coordinator in the admissions office.

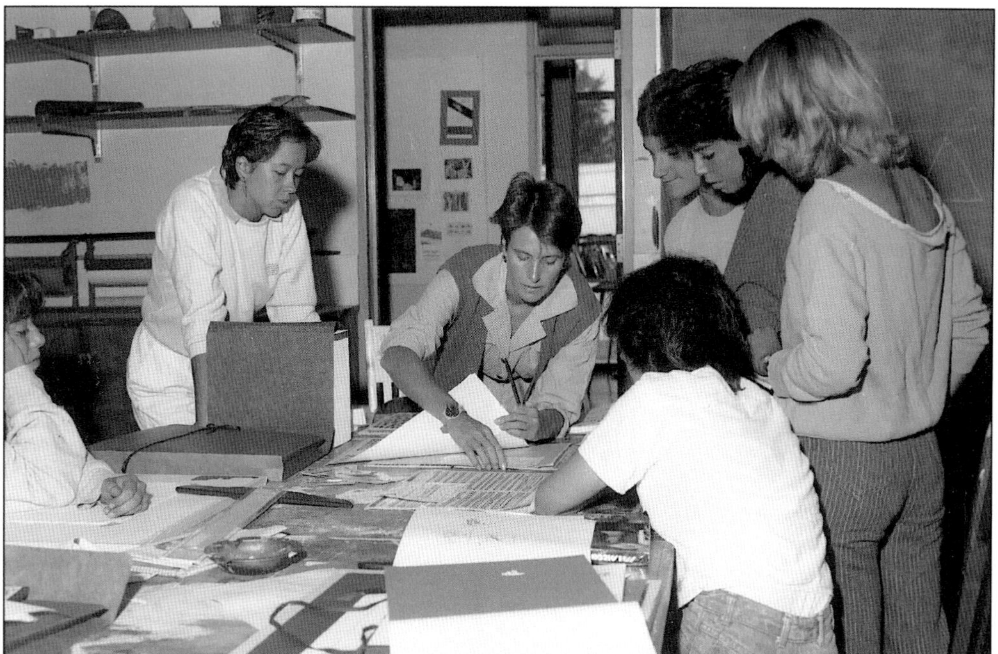

Prof. Sally Fine, Creative Arts. Sally Fine first taught at Bradford in the early 1980s as an adjunct professor teaching ceramics. Over the next years, she taught occasional courses in the arts while pursuing her own professional career. In 1996, she was appointed assistant professor to teach in the new graphic arts program. She earned an M.F.A. at Boston University.

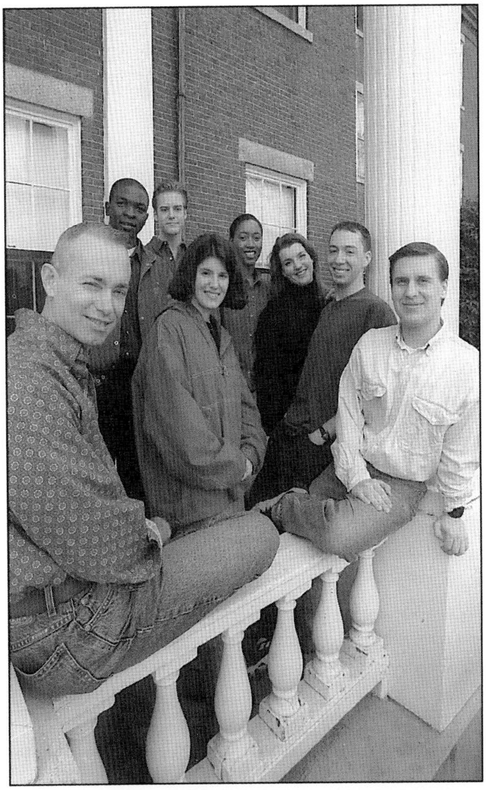

Dr. Michael Budd, History. Dr. Budd, left, came to Bradford in 1995. He took Bradford students to the international Model United Nations for college students three times. The first group went to Budapest, Hungary, in 1997 and included the following, from left to right: (front row) Tami Brunelle and Russel Bigleman; (back row) William Munyoro, Andrew Majewski, Karla Haynes, Melissa Byrd, and Ryan Bolin. Budd, who earned a Ph.D. from Rutgers, also took students to Brussels, Belgium, in 1998 and to New York City in 1999.

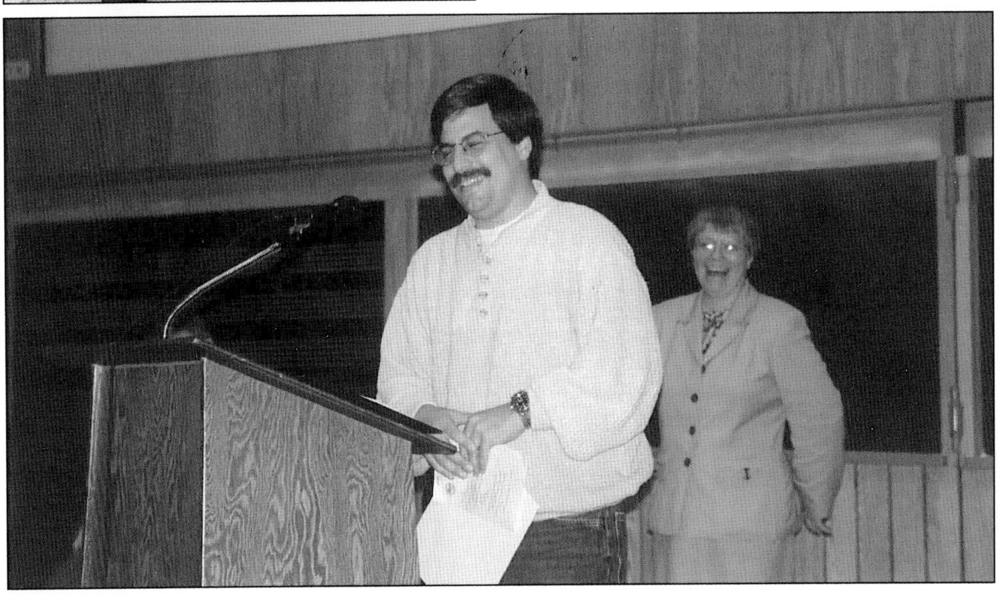

1998 Professor of the Year. Dr. John Cigliano, left, joined the natural science faculty in 1996. His Ph.D. was from Boston University. His fieldwork in environmental biology and his study trips for students to exotic locales, such as the Amazon River, earned him the accolade of Professor of the Year in 1998. He is shown after receiving his award from Dr. Janet Schulte, right. Schulte came to Bradford in 1994 as associate dean for academic affairs. She served as acting dean from 1997 to 1998, before moving on to become provost at Lesley College.

Into the Woods. The Music Theater production in April 1997 was Stephen Sondheim's *Into the Woods*. It had a large cast of very talented students, including Jason Prokowiew, left, as Cinderella's prince and Heather Darrow '98, right, as Cinderella. Darrow won the Jack Fisher Award in Music Theater in 1995 and the Special Theater Award in 1998. Dr. Fred Schuetze directed the production, and Mark Peterson was music director.

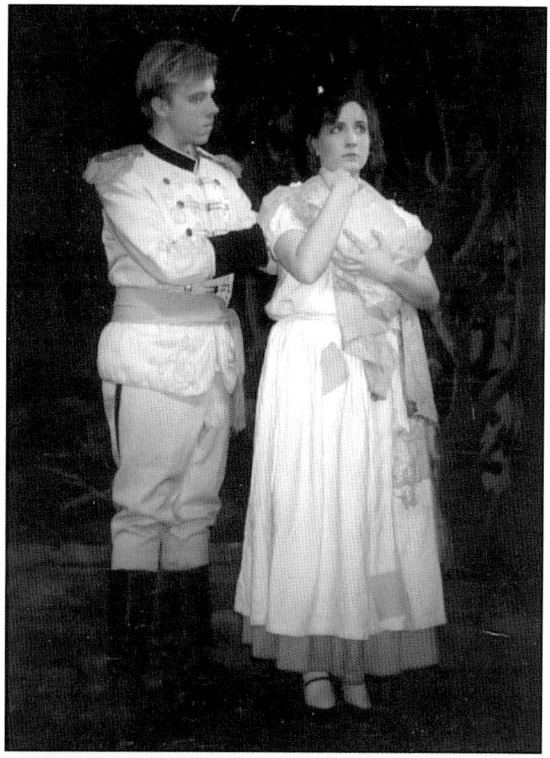

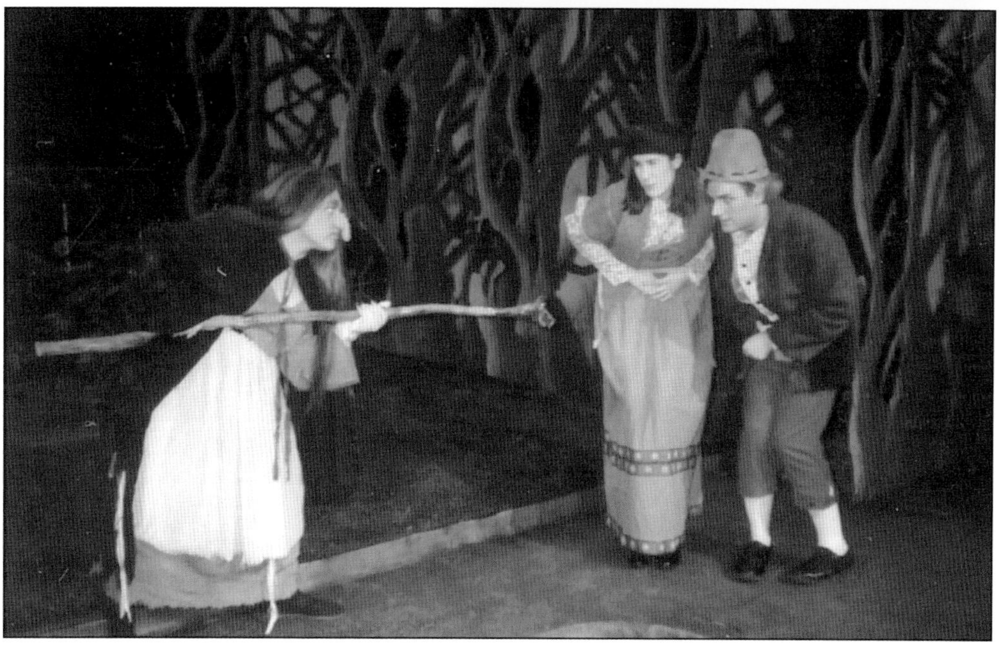

***Into the Woods*, Part II.** Cristina Zaccheo '99, left, played the protagonist, the wicked witch. Robyn Blanchard '99, center, as the baker's wife, and Jason Ricardo '99, right, as the baker, were the primary targets of her vengeful tricks in this 1997 musical. Zaccheo received the Jack Fisher Award in 1997 and the Special Theater Award in 1999. Ricardo won both the Jack Fisher and the Theresa Mors theater awards in 1999.

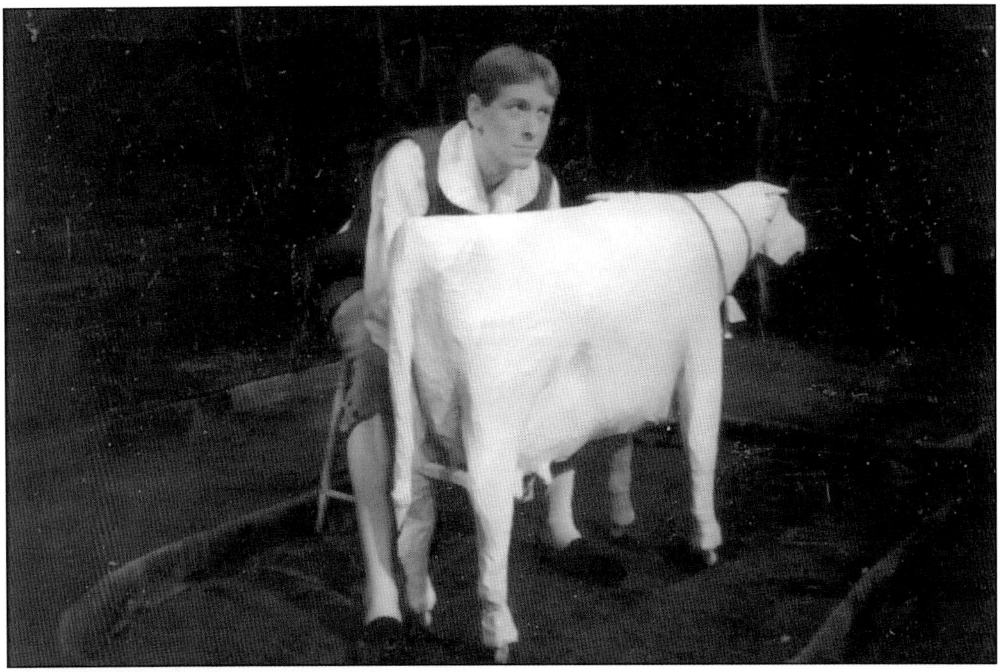

***Into the Woods*, Part III.** Paul Vandeman '98 took on many lead roles in his four years at Bradford, but only in *Into the Woods* was he upstaged by this pet cow Milky White, who put on a "wooden" performance. Vandeman had the role of Jack, of Beanstalk fame. He won the Jack Fisher Award in 1996 and the Theresa Mors prize in 1998.

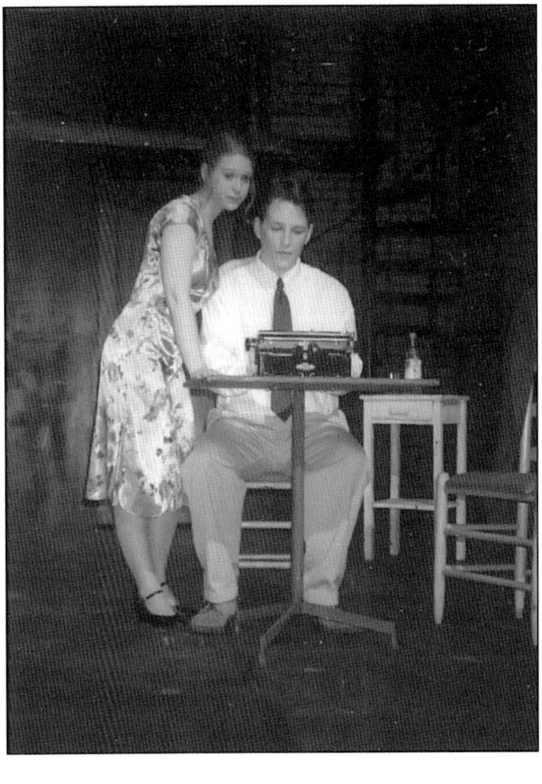

Cabaret. Amanda Damstra '00, left, first burst onto Bradford's musical stage as Little Red Riding Hood in *Into the Woods*. Two years later, she played a far different role as Sally Bowles in the Kander and Ebb musical *Cabaret*. Her costar, in the part of Clifford Bradshaw, was Kevin Traver '00, right.

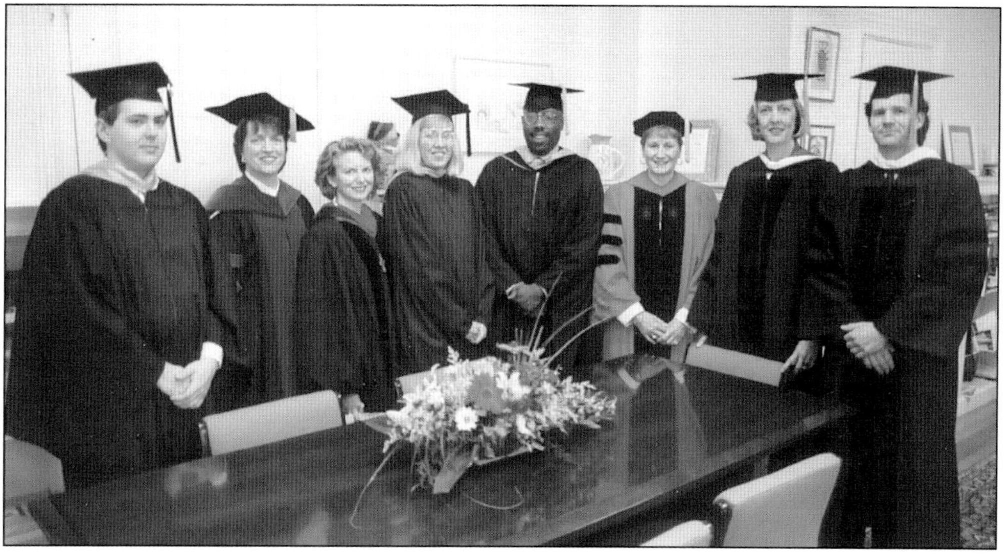

Commencement 1999. Dr. Jean Scott, third from the right, became Bradford's eighth president in 1998. She arrived with a Ph.D. in history from Harvard and experience in enrollment management. She was joined on the platform at her first Bradford commencement in May 1999 by the following, from left to right: Christopher Clark '99, student speaker; Dr. Lynn Champion, interim vice president and dean of faculty; Rev. Marlayna Schmidt; Mary Jane Lavoie, registrar; Trey Williams, dean; Karen Sughrue '70, trustee chairman; and André Dubus III '79, commencement speaker.

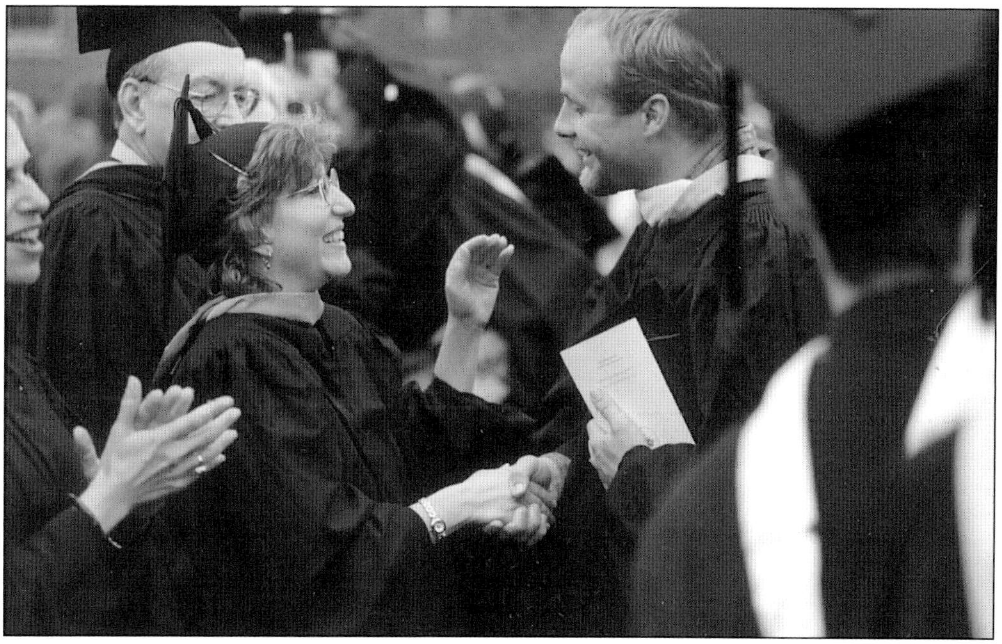

Major Award Winner. Jason Shiers '99, right, walked off with most of the major awards at the 1999 commencement. He graduated summa cum laude and received the Plummer Award in Humanities, the Davis Award in History, the Barrett Prize as top scholar, and the Delafield Award as student leader. He is congratulated by Rae Trachtman Perry, associate dean of students and director of residence life. Shiers went on to Columbia Teachers College for a graduate degree.

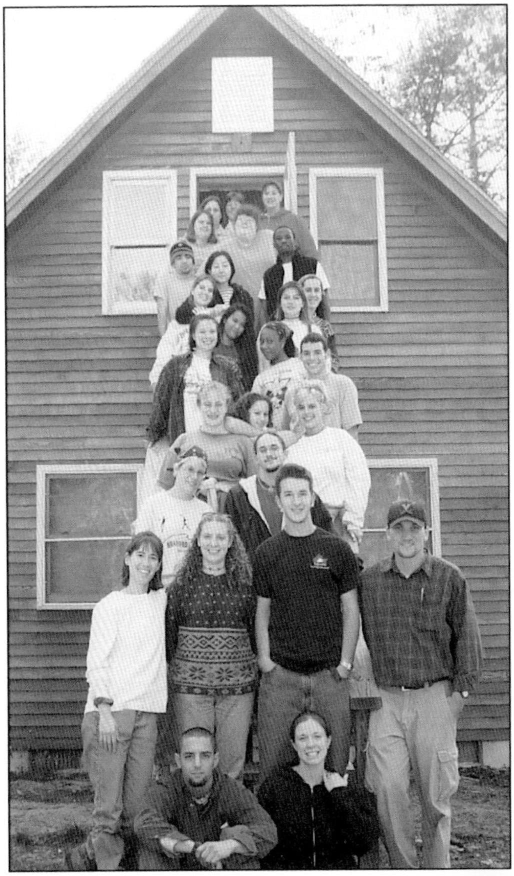

Student Leaders, 1999–2000. Bradford's student leaders, including senior class officers, members of the Senate, heads of clubs and other organizations on campus, gathered at a leadership retreat at Lake Ossipee, New Hampshire, at the beginning of Bradford's final academic year. Roger Benson, second row right, has the dubious distinction of being Bradford's ultimate senior class president.

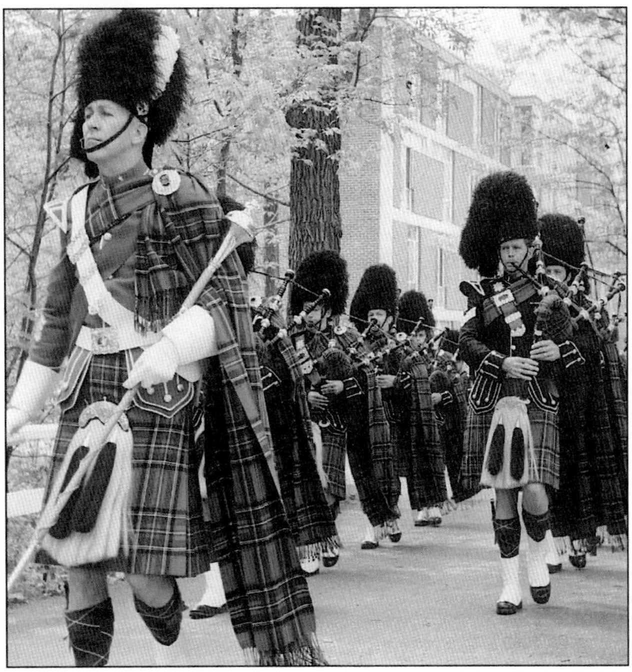

Clan MacPherson Bagpipe Band. Commencement 2000 marked the pipers' 28th year in association with the college. The band has led commencements, performed at inaugurations, and provided the single piper who awakened students on Spring Day—the annual ritual day off for fun and games. For many years, the band was led by Ed Morrissey, left, an imposing figure well over 6 feet tall, and made more impressive by the bearskin headpiece. Morrissey and the band received the Dorothy Bell Medallion in 1990 for their contributions to Bradford. On Saturday, May 20, 2000, the band made its final contribution at Bradford's last commencement.